The Genius Figure
in Antiquity
and the Middle Ages

The Genius Figure
in Antiquity
and the Middle Ages

By

Jane Chance Nitzsche

COLUMBIA UNIVERSITY PRESS
NEW YORK AND LONDON 1975

The Andrew W. Mellon Foundation, through a special
grant, has assisted the Press in publishing this volume.

Library of Congress Cataloging in Publication Data

Nitzsche, Jane Chance, 1945–
    The genius figure in antiquity and the Middle Ages.

    Bibliography: p. 171
    1. Genius (Companion spirit)   I. Title.
BL477.N57   292'.2'11   74-17206
ISBN 0-231-03852-6

For Tracy

Contents

Preface

Genius, a puzzling allegorical figure, appears in several major Latin and vernacular works of the later Middle Ages. Originally a spirit or god that survived in Roman religion for at least seven centuries, its history and significance—religious, philosophical, and literary—have not previously been examined in detail. The recent resurgence of interest in the twelfth century, in allegorical and mythical figures derived from the classical period, and in medieval poetic theory provides both a backdrop and an impetus for this study of Genius.

Unlike Natura, Fortuna, Orpheus, and other figures, Genius does not denote a single central concept or meaning, nor is it included in a familiar mythical framework upon which subsequent moralization is based. Instead, its forms and associations constitute a bewilderingly diverse array. Originally a begetting spirit, *genius* was later defined as *animus* (life, energy), personality or temperament, a personal god, the rational soul, the *daemon,* good and evil impulses, an angel, a demon, the star or horoscope, reason, and concupiscence; it was affiliated with the family, its paterfamilias, the individual, the Emperor, the city, the State, Jupiter, other gods, the World Soul, the stars and planets, demons in hell, the allegorical goddesses Natura and Venus, and the Bon Pasteur, Christ. A clear understanding of Genius and of the relationships between its many forms and contexts, therefore, requires familiarity with the figure's history and development.

In setting the boundaries for this investigation, at the beginning I have ignored Egyptian, Etruscan, and Greek analogues of the Roman *genius* unless they directly influence its development at any point or are identified with the figure (as in the case of the Greek *daemon*). Nor, at the end, does the sixteenth-century treatment of Genius receive much stress:

the major depictions occur in Spenser's *Faerie Queene,* and, as E. C. Knowlton and C. S. Lewis have observed, are drawn directly from earlier Greek and Neo-Latin literary models and from Renaissance mythography. It is upon the Roman types of *genius,* discussed in late classical and early medieval patristic and philosophic commentaries, and the medieval literary Genius derived from these and earlier sources but transformed into a unique allegorical figure, that this study focuses.

The limitations of the analysis will be apparent. First, not every instance of Genius in classical and medieval works has been mentioned. Rather, I have tried to demonstrate representative types and forms by citing examples from such works. Second, to comprehend the full meaning of the medieval Genius requires some knowledge of classical religion, art, and history, astrology, and Stoic, Hermetic, and Neo-Platonic philosophy. Material drawn from these areas is presented primarily to illuminate aspects of the figure's development. Third, the study's narrow focus, necessitated by the complexity of the figure, precludes close attention to other allegorical personifications, themes, motives, and conventions used in the literary works in which Genius plays a major role. Fourth and finally, the Genius figures of Jean de Meun and John Gower, and their specific prototypes, receive only cursory attention in the last chapter, partly because the study is cumulative, and partly because their significance depends upon a general awareness of earlier conceptions implicit in their allegorical functions but not explicitly demonstrated in the texts.

While this work was in progress, many friends, colleagues, and former professors offered much appreciated help, encouragement, and support. In particular, thanks are due to Professor Richard H. Green, who directed my attention to the problem of Genius in Gower's *Confessio Amantis,* and who guided and inspired the dissertation upon which this investigation is based. I am also grateful to Professor George D. Economou: as reader for the Press, he offered valuable suggestions concerning its revision into a book. Very special thanks are extended to my good friend, Professor Kristine Gilmartin, from whose careful reading of the manuscript, criticism of the text, and correction of translations this study has greatly benefited.

In addition, several institutions have generously contributed aid in bringing this work to completion: the University of Illinois subsidized the initial research and writing with a Dissertation Fellowship; Rice University granted funds for its final typing and graduate assistance for the checking of transcriptions and references. To both I am indebted.

The Genius Figure
in Antiquity
and the Middle Ages

Introduction

In the fourteenth-century *Confessio Amantis* of John Gower, a curious figure named Genius, identified only as a clerk and priest of Venus, shrives a lover named Amans, and instructs him in the seven deadly sins by relating classical stories of distraught lovers. Gower neither describes the clerk nor elucidates his significance, although there is much that is puzzling about the figure. First, it is not clear why he has selected "Genius" as a name, a word the modern reader equates with great mental ability, inventive powers. Second, Gower sees no contradiction in employing Venus' agent in a sacerdotal or clerical role. Finally, the priest illustrates the seven deadly sins by reciting various classical tales. The inference drawn from these unexplained anomalies is that Gower must have assumed his readers' familiarity with the figure and its meaning.

Accordingly, scholars have attempted to explain Gower's Genius by returning to his sources. Thus, "Genius is borrowed from the *Roman de la Rose,* and the idea of using the form of a Confession might easily be suggested by any of the poems where Venus's temple figures prominently." [1] The medieval view of courtly love as a religion does help to clarify the appearance of Genius as priest of Venus in the *Confessio.* However, in the *Roman,* he is a priest of Nature, not of Venus: he advocates unremitting devotion to sexual reproduction and condemns chastity—but also exhorts men to live virtuously. The figure's anathema toward the seven deadly sins links him with Gower's Genius, yet the difference between the two is more striking than the similarity. Gower substitutes Venus for Nature, changing Genius from a generation force stressing procreation to a priest of courtly love. Even more confusing, the paradoxical roles of Jean's Genius—generation force and priest of virtue—seem clearly unrelated.

Investigating the sources used by Jean de Meun, C. S. Lewis discovers there is a Genius in the twelfth-century *De Mundi Universitate* of Bernardus Silvestris which ". . . sufficiently explains the Genius in the *De Planctu Naturae* [of Alanus de Insulis], who is the enemy of unnatural vice because he is the patron of generation and therefore of heterosexuality. From him the Genius of Jean de Meun and of Gower directly descends." [2] His assertion not only affirms the mimetic nature of medieval literary representations of the Genius, but also illuminates the meaning of the figure. The "patron of generation," who adheres to natural law, discourages both physical and spiritual infractions of it.

Unfortunately, C. S. Lewis does not reveal that there is more than one Genius in the *De Mundi Universitate,* and that there is an important difference between the generative figures depicted by Bernardus and Alanus. In the first work, the Genius mentioned by Lewis is a ruler of the sphere of the fixed stars who ascribes differences of form to all things. In other passages, *genius* is described as a planetary ruler, an aerial sprite who sends man warnings of future danger through dreams and omens, a natural power which makes flowers bloom and plants grow at the approach of the figure Natura, and a double who controls human breeding. Nowhere does a Genius per se promote virtue and denigrate vice. Yet in the *De Planctu,* this *is* Genius' primary function: he censures homosexuality, that unnatural vice, but he also censures the seven deadly sins, and excommunicates from the realm of nature all who have succumbed to such sin.

The contrast between the generative fixer of forms in *De Mundi* and the moralistic Genius hostile to unnatural vice in *De Planctu* suggests there may be earlier, possibly divergent, sources used by both authors. In fact, C. S. Lewis proclaims that "the two-edged use of the name Genius, in general, is explicable by his history." [3] E. C. Knowlton agrees: both begin their brief studies with reference to his early Roman inception. Lewis notes his appearance as a "spiritual double," representing the continuity and reproductive power of the family; Knowlton identifies him as the animating and protective spirit of a place. [4] Their research on the original classical Genius is derived from classical scholars who have thoroughly described its various manifestations. However, there is little consensus among these scholars concerning the precise meaning of the spirit: some perceive it as a spiritual double, [5] some, as the reproductive power and luck of the family,[6] and others, as a spiritual double embodying this reproductive power.[7] In addition, it appeared in so many forms that these interpretations do not entirely account for all of them: it was associated with things (cities, walls, taxes, places), with the gods, with the State, with aerial messengers, with the souls of the dead. An explanation is again provided by its history: belief in a Genius lasted at least seven centuries, from the earliest literary references by Plautus in the third century B.C. to its condemnation in the *Codex Theodosianus* of A.D. 392. And the earlier Italian worship of the figure, recorded in burial art and shrines, extends backward by several centuries, in addition. Clearly its form and meaning must have changed over this long span of time.

Tracing the development of these changes will elucidate the meaning of the god Genius in the classical period and its appearance as an allegorical personification in the medieval period. The primary purpose of this study is to organize and unify the many different meanings, and to show there is a common denominator between the earliest classical Genius and the later medieval literary figure, but without neglecting the differences that inevitably arise. Beginning from the brief summaries of the figure's history offered by C. S. Lewis and E. C. Knowlton, it will probe more deeply and extensively into sources and meanings, including a reappraisal of the earliest classical meanings. Unlike classical studies of the god, it will emphasize the later philosophical conceptions appearing in the first five centuries A.D., which made religious beliefs in the god more accessible to medieval moralization. This study will then demonstrate the twelfth-century awareness and use of these classical meanings, after which the two literary roles of Genius—generative force and priest—will become clearer. These roles are fully developed in the works of Bernardus and Alanus, the focal points of the study, from which later medieval representations were drawn.

The key to the relationship between the classical and medieval Genius is its Horatian definition—a god of human nature, born with each man and living until his death. The definition was explicitly acknowledged by Bernardus and his contemporary, Guillaume de Conches, in the twelfth century. However, like other false pagan gods, Genius was regarded as a demonic inhabitant of hell. Thus, he was identified with Euridice, natural concupiscence born with each man, who descended into the underworld of temporal good when she succumbed to its delights. The god of human

nature was affiliated with other similar descents into an underworld,
which exemplified the central experiences of human life possible for each
man. At birth, man's soul naturally descends from the heavens into the
underworld of the sublunar region or of the human body. During his life,
he may, like Euridice, descend viciously, or, like her husband Orpheus,
virtuously into the underworld of temporal good in order to familiarize
himself with it and thereby protect himself from its temptations. Finally,
he may descend into hell, not only literally at death, but artificially
through magic art, when he consults its demons about future life. This
pattern of descents unifies and moralizes the classical meanings of Genius, and makes the pagan god palatable to the Christian Middle Ages. It
also explains the frequently discordant meanings or roles of the personification in medieval literature.

Beginning with these classical meanings, Chapter One examines the
early popular religious beliefs in Genius, the begetting spirit of the family
embodied in the paterfamilias. In time it came to be associated with the
husband, and then any man, married or unmarried; accompanying each
man from birth, it signified not only virility, but also life, energy, and
even temperament or personality. Its early paternalistic affiliations encouraged its transfer to other "fathers": the founding father of the city
and institution, then the gods, the Emperor, and finally the State. Eventually deified as the personal god of each man, this external double
safeguarded his life and fortune and was worshipped on his birthday.

In Chapter Two, later classical philosophical and cosmological conceptions of the figure extend its significance. The birth god, under the aus-
pices of astrology, represented the birth star or horoscope of the individual. Its early begetting power was similarly cosmologized into the "seed
power" (generative reason) of the "Father" of the gods, Jupiter, the
Stoic World Soul. Eventually *genii* were ascribed to the planets and
luminaries of the universe, which aided the World Soul in its generative
and fatal tasks. The regions in between the gods and men were also
believed to be inhabited—by cosmic messengers or *daemones,* Greek
spirits who were related to the souls of the dead (Di Manes) and to the rational souls of men (*daemones*). Eventually the Greek concept of the
daemon influenced the Roman *genius,* so that each man was said to
possess a "soul" (*genius* or *daemon*) born with him, or a good and evil
nature (good and evil *daemon, genius, manes*). The messenger *daemon,*

under the influence of Christianity, became an evil demon or renegade angel connected with astrology, dreams, and the black arts, and was itself replaced by the good angel.

In Chapter Three, these classical concepts are discernible in the twelfth-century pattern of descents which emphasize Genius as a god of human nature. The natural descent of the soul into the body at birth, achieved in part with the help of the cosmic generative *genii* of the World Soul, endows the individual with concupiscence (or *genius*). The vicious descent of Euridice (concupiscence or *genius*) into the underworld of temporal good, contrasted with the virtuous descent of Orpheus (*nous, rational soul, daemon*) into the temporal world in order to apprise himself of its nature and thereby rescue his concupiscence from it, dramatizes the two basic moral choices available to man during his life. The artificial descent, or the consultation of demons from hell by means of magic art to discover the future, stresses the late classical relationship between messenger *genii* and *daemones* (later, evil demons) with fortune and astrology, magic art. This artificial descent also corresponds to twelfth-century theories of poetic artifice, whose integumental *figurae,* gods, and personifications partly resemble the false demonic inhabitants of hell, and partly the *aenigmata* of dreams originally conveyed by *daemones*.

Chapter Four outlines the process of the natural descent described in the second book of *De Mundi Universitate.* Every sphere of Bernardus' Calcidian universe is ruled by its own *genius,* all of whom participate in this archetypal descent. The regions in between the spheres are also inhabited by various spirits—Seraphim, early Christian *angeli,* late classical *genii,* and the fallen angels or demons, among others—who function primarily as cosmic messengers between God and man.

In Chapter Five, discussion of the Genius figure in Alanus' *De Planctu* reveals the work's dependence on all four descents, although its allegory stresses the vicious and virtuous descents. Genius as the "other self" of Natura personifies a generation force, particularly for human nature; as her priest, he duplicates the descent of Orpheus, or the generalized rational soul of mankind, into the temporal world, to excommunicate concupiscent and fallen men. He also personifies the "genius" of human creativity and art, especially poetry.

Chapter Six investigates the alteration, reinterpretation, and elaboration of the descents by Jean de Meun and John Gower. Jean's good Genius

abhors vice and artifice, but praises natural reproduction and virtuous behavior. Gower's Genius, in contrast, serves an artificial function: this *artifex* regenerates Amans, divided by demonic love fantasies into an unnatural (inhuman) and artificial creature, with the aid of the artifice of
classical myths, the confession of sin, and the promotion of virtue, wisdom, and *caritas* (heavenly Venus, whose restorative powers here are essentially psychological).

This is not, then, merely the history of the moralization of a pagan
god: the Genius and its Greek and Christian analogues influenced the medieval period in other ways. They were used to express the complexities
of human nature, particularly in regard to moral or psychological conflicts troubling men. They provided the Middle Ages with various symbols—sexual, natural, moral—which dominated the literature for centuries. Finally, their influence also fostered the development of a theory
of poetic art, most notably manifested in the dream vision genre. Even in
the Middle Ages, "genius" was linked with "inventive powers," "mental ability." Its earliest religious function—generation and creation—bore
the seeds for a later artistic flowering on many levels. Thus it is with the
earliest function that this study begins.

CHAPTER ONE

The Early Classical Genius:
Popular Religious Beliefs

THE BEGETTING SPIRIT OF THE PATERFAMILIAS

The earliest concept of the *genius* is rooted in ancient Italian animism and worship of household spirits.[1] This religious phenomenon, which flourished from the earliest times until the third century B.C., is important in understanding the later philosophical developments of the *genius,* for cosmological systems involving *genii* are predicated upon the early function of the *genius* as a begetting spirit.

The Latin *"genius"* is derived from *gignere,* "to engender"; this word can be traced back to IE **gen* found in words suggesting begetting and engendering, primarily "specializations of 'get, obtain' or derivatives of words meaning 'child, offspring.' " [2] The *genius* worshipped by the first Italian farmers retains this generative meaning.

The *familia* encountered great difficulty in cultivating the land. The farmer's dependence upon and fear of the forces of nature gradually evolved into a belief in animism or pandemonism, in which every object, process, and place was invested with a protecting spirit or demon.[3] The *genius loci* was such a spirit; it represented the continuity or unifying principle of a place.[4] The house itself was inhabited by spirits: Vesta guarded the hearth and its ever-burning fire, signifying the continuity of family life; the Penates protected the stores of the family; the Lar Familiaris ensured its safety and luck; the Di Manes, which apparently had access to the house, were the collective and unindividualized ancestral dead of the family. The Genius of the house, a more specialized *genius loci,* represented ". . . the life of the family. . . . the idea implicit is that of the procreative force which makes it possible for the family to exist or continue.'' [5]

The Genius of the family acted as "a simile for the male seed," which was transmitted from one generation to another by father to son,[6] and which embodied the primitive equivalent of the genetic code. Artistic depictions of the figure usually included a cornucopia, symbolizing the seed, frequently containing *phalli,* and held in the left hand.[7] The paintings and shrines preserved at Pompeii also picture the Genius as a serpent or snake, a totem suggestive of its phallic nature: in one family shrine, the Genius appears as a bearded snake; in paintings, we find a serpent curled around an altar, with an offering of fruit nearby.[8] It has been suggested that Etruscan phallus worship was responsible for such symbols of the Italian Genius: the Etruscans regarded their deity, Mutinus Titinus, as a god with a phallic form, and this phallus frequently adorned grave monuments.[9]

Later literary and historical references to the Genius mention both the cornucopia and the serpent. According to Ammianus Marcellinus in the late fourth century, the Genius of the State ("speciem illam Genii publici") appeared one night before Julian, whose imperial fortune was soon to decline, with both head and cornucopia veiled.[10] And legends of the conception of famous figures—Alexander, Augustus, Scipio Africanus— describe the Genius as a snake, which functioned symbolically as a surrogate for the father. Livy in the first century B.C. speaks of the begetting of Alexander by an immense Genius-serpent observed frequenting his mother's chambers.[11] Suetonius (c. A.D. 75–160) read in the *Theologumena* of Asclepias of Mendes about the discovery of a snake in Atia's bedroom; a serpent-shaped mark subsequently appeared on her body, and ten months later Augustus was born.[12] Aulus Gellius (fl. A.D. 169) recounts the legend of Scipio Africanus' conception: after Publius Scipio and his wife had given up hope of offspring, a huge serpent, the Genius, was seen lying by her side one night while she slept; when observers cried out in fright, it slithered away and could not be found. Several days later she felt the sensations of conception.[13]

The snake, totem of the Genius, is an archetypal symbol associated with begetting and fecundity and has been worshipped in many cultures, both past and present.[14] In early Italian religion, the snake represented the *genius loci,* the Genius of the house or the spirit of the father. It was

entirely possible to confuse the snake of a place with the snake of a father; witness Aeneas' confusion over the snake crawling from Anchises'
tomb: he did not know whether it was "geniumne loci famulumne paren-
tis." [15] All three manifestations are linked: the Genius of the household,
a special *genius loci,* was incarnated in the father of the family, and artistic evidence suggests the Genius was also portrayed in the form and likeness of the paterfamilias. [16] The creative spirit protected a particular
place; the paterfamilias, responsible for begetting new members, guaran-
teed the perpetuation of the family stock, the clan. This spiritual embodi-
ment in the father underscored his already dominant position in the family, for he became its priest, conducting rituals, slaying victims for
lustratio, uttering prayers; other members of the household swore by his
Genius, and the oath attested to his sacred importance. [17].

Thus the nuptial bed, its function primarily procreative, came to be
called *genialis lectus* (the term, used widely in the classical period, was
transmitted through the Middle Ages as late as the thirteenth century).
Catullus (c. 84–54 B.C.), for example, speaks of a cushioned bed designed for a goddess as "pulvinar . . . divae geniale." [18] And to com-
mit adultery, in the words of Juvenal (c. A.D. 55–140), is "sacri genium
contemnere fulcri"—to affront the Genius of the sacred couch (the *ful-
crum* or the head of the couch was frequently adorned with the bronze
figure of the Genius). [19] Servius (fl. A.D. 389) lists *genealis* (or *natalis,*
"pertaining to birth") as a synonym for *genialis,* and explains that the
genial couch was covered with a veil or cloak and used for the begetting
of children. [20]

The Genius of the head of the household was complemented by the
Juno of the mother: the father begot the child, but the mother bore it, and
this feminine spirit protected the wife's fertility and capacity for bearing
children. [21] The word *"iuno,"* derived from the stem *iun-,* meant "man-
bearing wife," "young woman"; [22] the *iuno* was later identified with
Juno (or Hera), the great wife of Jupiter and the goddess of childbirth. [23]

The sexual nature of the early animistic Genius (and Juno) of the
household is unmistakable: the generation spirit embodied in the paterfamilias protected the future of the family. Its sacred place was the *lectus
genialis;* its totem, the snake; its symbol, the cornucopia. Vestiges of
these early beliefs were fossilized and transmitted in later literary and historical passages. Gradually the Genius of the head of the family came to

be associated with the husband, then with the individual. And the Genius accrued new meanings, as we shall see. But the earliest definitions did not entirely cease to exist: at the end of the third century A.D., we find Arnobius scoffing at bridegrooms who still cover their couches with togas and who invoke the Genii of husbands ("maritorum genios") when they enter wedlock.[24]

THE VIRILITY, ENERGY, "LIFE" OF THE INDIVIDUAL

The earliest literary allusions to the *genius* come from Plautus in the third century B.C. By this time, the generation spirit had undergone some changes. Each man, whether or not a father or even a husband, had a *genius*. It represented his virility, energy, liveliness, a concept related to the early *animus* of an individual.

The shift in meaning and emphasis occurred for a number of reasons. The paterfamilias as priest of the family performed sacrificial rites to propitiate a particular *numen* or spirit. In early household worship food was offered from the family meal, indicating the presence of the spirits of the house.[25] Because the paterfamilias embodied the Genius of the house, the celebration of this spirit took place on the day of his birth.[26] Each man possessed a potential Genius which would be fulfilled through marriage and procreation; other members of the family honored their Genius or Juno on their birthdays in private, joining the family for the more public celebration of the father's Genius. During this celebration, certain foods appropriate to his nature were offered to the Genius, and he was "indulged" (*indulgere genio*). It is perhaps to illustrate this ritual that one representation of a Genius, stretched out on a bed before a table, depicts a horn of plenty on the left and a cup on the right.[27]

By the third century B.C., each individual was also expected to indulge his *genius*. His virility or energy, his "life," depended upon a life-fluid or "sap" called the *sucus*, which circulated throughout the body, but which was particularly associated with the head and the knees.[28] This life-fluid, related to sexual power and the *genius*, increased with nourishment; the man who satisfied his *genius* was "genialis," the man who did not was "aridus," dry.[29] The young man or the man who "indulged" his *genius* was frequently juxtaposed with the old man or the miser who "defrauded" his *genius,* especially in the plays of Plautus and Terence.

According to Plautus, the man of robust appetite is well-acquainted with *genius.* In *Persa,* when Toxilus enthusiastically agrees to a helping of fish sauce, Saturio replies, "Sapis multum ad genium." [30] In *Stichus,* Epignomus conveys the very hungry Gelasimus to jail—a place, he comments, where the *genius* or comfort of his prisoner will not be enhanced ("Nam hic quidem genium meliorem tuom non facies," 622): incarcerated, he will not "indulge" his *genius.*

Often Plautus satirizes the concept of the parasite, a creature so dependent upon his patron that he has no *genius* of his own, by identifying the patron as his *genius:* in *Captivi,* the parasite Ergasilus addresses his patron, Hegio's son, as "genium meum" (879). And the hungry Curculio, a parasite in the play of the same name, begs to see "genium meum"— his patron Phaedromus—who will apparently provide him with food, hence comfort and well-being, and by extension, life itself (301).

To deny food or comfort to the *genius* is to defraud or cheat oneself— "defraudare genium." The miser obsessed with gold is guiltiest of this sin. In Plautus' *Aulularia,* after Euclio's carefully hoarded gold is stolen, he regrets depriving himself (more specifically, his soul and his *genius,* which appear to be related) in the past of comfort and pleasure ("egomet me defraudavi / animumque meum geniumque meum," 724–25). Terence (c. 185–159 B.C.) speaks sympathetically in *Phormio* of the poor friend who, with money saved and rationed at the expense of pleasure, must pay a debt, thereby "suom defrudans genium"; [31] money can provide the comforts of life and the satisfaction of the appetites. When Sagaristio in Plautus' *Persa* gives his master's money to his friend instead of buying oxen, he helps a friend and also benefits his own *genius* or well-being ("et genio meo multa bona faciam," 263). Misers who "war against their own *genii*" ("qui cum geniis suis belligerant parcipromi") [32] deny their own appetites, life itself.

The passages cited offer two choices to man in maintaining his *sucus* and his *genius;* later writers continued to define the *genius* as inclination or spirit, and to contrast the two attitudes toward it. Euclio coupled the *genius* with his *animus;* Martial, with the heart: Papylus, says Martial (fl. A.D. 40–104), eats cheaply but sends expensive gifts; he has neither heart nor *genius,* "habes nec cor, Papyle, nec genium." [33] Nonius Marcellus (fl. A.D. 373), in *De Compendiosa Doctrina,* distinguishes between the two ways of treating one's *genius* and the two types of personality designated by the treatment. After defining the relationship between parsimony and *genius* with an allusion to the Terentian miser who denies his appetites, he adds a line from Lucilius (180–103 B.C.) in *The Twelve Tables* (692–93) which describes the generosity of a parsimonious man: he may take care of a sick friend by paying for his expenses, but in turn he will neglect his own *genius* by refusing it proper nourishment (''curet aegrotum, sumtum homini praebeat, genium suum defrudet, ali parcat''). The genial man (''genialis''), in contrast, is a hospitable one (''hospitalis''): according to Santra's *De Antiquitate Verborum* (3), genial men were so designated by the ancients because they were always ready to invite guests for a bountiful dinner.[34]

The Stoics and Epicureans later utilized the two alternatives for advancing polemical arguments. From the Stoic stance, indulging the *genius* leads to hedonism, gluttony, excess, and is the recourse of the Epicurean. Conversely, excessive denial of the *genius* often develops into the antithetical evil, avarice. The most famous elaborations occur in Persius (A.D. 34–62) and Seneca (4 B.C.–A.D. 65). Persius' rich miser lacks self-knowledge: he is considered perverse (literally, ''on the left side'') both to the gods and to his *genius* (''hunc dis iratis genioque sinistro'').[35] But, Persius admits, the situation is complex: the man basking lazily in the sunshine is liable to be accused of vile practices. *Avaritia* prompts one to work and earn money; *Luxuria* finds this unpleasant, and exhorts man to ''seize the day'' by indulging himself and his *genius* in the pleasant things available in life (''indulge genio, carpamus dulcia, nostrum est / quod vivis, cinis et manes et fabula fies,'' 5.151–52). Seneca describes the same dilemma, but sides with one of the positions: continually indulging oneself and one's *genius* (''sibi hoc et genio suo praestet,'' as the gluttons say) is morally reprehensible.[36] He admits that an expensive inaugural dinner, sanctioned by custom and tradition, would be truly disgraceful if intended solely for the satisfaction of the appetite.

The choice, *indulgere genio* or *defraudare genium,* was again described in Servius' late fourth-century commentary on the *Georgics,* and associated with indulgence in, or denial of, sensual pleasure; the passage, repeated by Mythographus Tertius, fostered the medieval identification of the *genius* with the appetites and natural concupiscence.[37]

THE PROTECTIVE TUTELARY OF THE CITY, THE
INSTITUTION, THE GODS, THE EMPEROR, THE STATE

The introduction of Greek polymorphism into Italian culture, and the advent of Stoicism and other Greek philosophies in the second century B.C., influenced Roman religion [38] and helped, in particular, to broaden the scope of the *genius*. The original Italian deities were anthropomorphized; a system of gods permeated the universe. The *genius loci* grew specialized: it became a *genius urbis* and a tutelary spirit of legions, schools, colonies; it was attributed to the Senate, the plebs, granaries, storehouses, market places, treasuries, even to a particular tax.[39] The gods, especially Jove, were allotted *genii*.

In every case, however, it functioned as a generative spirit, as "life," or energy. The *genius* of the city was usually identified with that of its human founder, its "father"; [40] it protected the city from peril when properly propitiated. Livy (59 B.C.–A.D. 18) alludes to the Genius of Rome in his *Ab Urbe Condita:* the war in the winter of 218–217 B.C., with Hannibal wintering in north Italy, put the whole city of Rome into a religious panic. Sacrifices were made to Juno, Fortune, Hercules, and especially to the Genius of the city, for whom five victims were slain (21.62), in a gesture intended to bolster the "capacity of the State to increase its male population in the face of military peril." [41]

The *genii* of the legions, schools, and colonies functioned similarly to the spirits of cities: they were identified with their respective "fathers" or founders. The *genii* of granaries, storehouses, market places, and treasuries shared one trait: they were responsible for the stuff of life—grain, food, money. The "genius venalicius"—the protecting power of the tax placed on the sale of slaves—was honored by those collectors of the tax whose livelihood depended upon its continuance.[42]

A *genius* was ascribed to Jove and to other gods.[43] The *genius Iovis* was very likely influenced by early Etruscan beliefs in Mutinus Titinus, the god with the phallic form.[44] "Titinus" is a derivative of the Etruscan **titus,* which means "phallus." The concept of the *genius,* generative spirit, virility, energy, when applied to Jove, suggests a similar meaning.

The *genius* of an individual god was a final consequence of the anthropomorphization of the gods, and although it later represented the moral or psychic quality of the particular god,[45] it retained a generative sense in each application. For example, in the *Satyricon,* Petronius' Quartilla asks him how he can think of sleep, "when you know staying up all night is owed to the *genius* of Priapus" (" 'cum sciatis Priapi genio pervigilium deberi' ").[46]

Men often swore by the *genius* of a god or of Jove: Martial in his *Epigrams* (7.12.9–12) swears to his reader by the *genius* of Fame that his jests are harmless; as late as the third century A.D., Minucius Felix castigates men who think it safer to swear falsely by the *genius* of Jupiter than by the *genius* of the king.[47]

The early agricultural animism of the farmer has become urbanized; the *locus* of the *genius loci* has been shifted from the fields and the forests, and the house of the family, to the institutions of the city. The Genius of the family has been transferred to the city "family"; the "father" of the city family is its human founder. Animism has developed into polytheism; the family of the gods has been allotted *genii.* The father of the family, who protects its interests and future, has been supplanted by the parental deities who watch over the doings of man.

Concomitant with the urbanization of society (hence, the diminishing importance of the family), the introduction of polytheism and the anthropomorphization of the gods, and finally the influx of Greek philosophy stressing individuality in the second century B.C., the individual assumed greater importance in Roman religion. The Romans encountered foreign concepts of guardian spirits—the Greek *daemon,* the Persian *fravashi,* the Egyptian *ka;* this encounter revivified the notion of the individual *genius,* and influenced Augustus, in the last century B.C., to refurbish the old household worship for his own advantage through the establishment of a state religious cult.[48]

The Genius of Augustus became one of the State gods.[49] The Emperor erected shrines, containing his two Lares and his Genius (which was portrayed in his likeness), at the cross-roads in Rome. Ovid admitted there may have been a thousand such figures in the shrines intended for public worship of imperial divinity.[50] A decree ordered that a libation would be poured to the Genius of Augustus at every public and private banquet. Coins were minted bearing symbols of his Genius.[51] In 12 B.C. the invocation of the Emperor's divinity became part of an official oath form; Caligula would later punish men because they refused to swear by his Genius.[52] Victims were offered to his Genius during the public celebration on his birthday. A temple was built for the Emperor's divine ancestors and dedicated to his personal god; sacrifices were offered there and priests appeared in 2 B.C.[53] Municipal cults of the imperial deity sprang up in outlying areas.

Basically, the worship of the Genius of Augustus celebrated the procreative power of the Julian house which had endowed Rome with the Emperor and, secondly, it safeguarded the future of his house, of later generations of Augusti, and of the State.[54] The worship of the Emperor and of his Genius continued into the early centuries A.D. In the third century, Minucius Felix criticized such worship: although princes and kings may be great, they are not divine and should not be worshipped as gods. The practice of calling upon their deities for aid, making supplications to their images, invoking their Genii, and, in effect, elevating the king above Jove (by daring to swear falsely by the Genius of Jove, but not by the Genius of the king) he thought deplorable.[55] Nevertheless, Claudian (fl. A.D. 395–404), in his *Panegyricus de Sexto Consulatu Honorii Augusti,* rapturously describes the charisma of Honorius, which was apparently generated by the State's guardian Genius ("O quantum populo secreti numinis addit / imperii praesens genius!"): the noise of the adulation of his people, crowding the tiers of the circus, resounded through the air.[56] This imperial Genius gradually developed into a *genius populi* which was not necessarily embodied in the State "father." More important, its evolution fostered the private worship of the individual's *genius,* which, at the time of Augustus, had become a god.

THE FICKLE GOD OF BIRTH

The god Genius was born with each man, lived until his death, was celebrated upon his birthday, and controlled his personal fortune or destiny. Horace (65–68 B.C.), in a passage very popular in the Middle Ages, defines the Genius as an omniscient tutelary,

> . . . natale comes qui temperat astrum,
> naturae deus humanae, mortalis in unum
> quodque caput, voltu mutabilis, albus et ater.[57]

> . . . The companion which controls the natal star; the god of human nature, in that he is mortal for each person, with a changing expression, white or black.

This definition reappears in several twelfth-century commentaries; it also influenced many medieval concepts of Genius. Again and again the same idea is repeated with slightly different emphasis: the Genius is "quodam modo cum homine gignitur" ("begotten after a certain manner with man"), in the words of the second-century Apuleius.[58] Censorinus (c. A.D. 238) explains in *De Die Natali* that the god under whose protection each man lives when he is born is called "Genius" from the word "genendo"("begetting") for one of three reasons: either because he presides when we are born ("ut genamur curat"), because one is born with us ("una genitur nobiscum"), or because he takes up and protects us after we have been born ("nos genitos suscipit ac tutatur," 3.1) like the Roman father who acknowledges that a child is his by "taking him up" (*suscipit*). This faithful guardian never leaves us for a moment, but accompanies us from the time we leave the womb to the last day of our life (3.5). In the fourth century, Servius' commentary on the *Aeneid* (6.743) affirms the belief that *genii* are allotted to us along with life ("quos cum vita sortimur") when we are born. Martianus Capella describes the Genius, "most faithful tutelary and brother" ("hic tutelator fidissimusque germanus"), similarly in the fifth century: "he is called Genius, because when any man has been born, he is soon joined with him" ("dicitur Genius, quoniam cum quis hominum genitus fuerit, mox eidem copulatur"). [59] Commenting upon Martianus, the ninth-century scholars Remigius and Joannes Scotus gloss Genius as that which is born with each man; [60] in the twelfth century, Guillaume de Conches and Bernardus Silvestris reiterate the Horatian notion that a Genius is born with each man and dies.[61]

Despite this faithful transmission of the idea, there were many differences, contingent upon the context in which the "companion of birth" appears, between the classical Genius and the later medieval Genius. One such difference is simple but important: Horace does not explain that the Genius belongs only to the male; the female has her own birth goddess, the Juno. For example, Seneca (4 B.C.–A.D. 65) needles the Stoics, who believe, like his ancestors, that a Genius or Juno is assigned to each individual ("singulis enim et Genium et Iunonem dederunt," *Epistle* 110.1).

Pliny (c. A.D. 65) also disparages this belief, which, if true, implies that more celestial beings exist (including individual Genii and Junones) than human beings.[62]

The Genius or Juno, "natales comes," was often invoked by the name of "Natalis" or "Natales" when each member of the family celebrated and propitiated his personal god on his birthday in order to ensure his continued prosperity and life.[63] These celebrations and sacrifices mirror the nature and function of the deity. We know from the edict of Theodosius that such celebrations were still current in the year A.D. 392, and that the sacrifice of wine to Genius was an act punishable by death.[64] (The natal festival, however, did not cease: it is with us today in the form of the birthday party.)

Sacrifices to the deity were offered at an altar while a fire burned and incense perfumed the air. Ovid awaits his birthday god in a white robe, having already requested a smoking altar with chaplets, incense, fire, cake, and wine.[65] Tibullus' extravagant instructions for the festivity specify dancing and sports, the pouring of libations of wine, the application of ointment to his hair and the hanging of garlands around his neck, and, most important, the offering of incense and cakes sweetened with honey.[66]

The cake and honey, also offered to other deities, represented the energy of life: the deity was replenished in order to continue his favors for the family or individual; secondly, the proffered food implied an act of communion between the petitioner and the deity.[67]

But two offerings were unique to the Genius—flowers and greenery, and wine. Tibullus, for example, insists that Genius sate his appetite with honey-cake and wine and don soft garlands (2.2.5–8); Apuleius (c. A.D. 158) in *De Magia* weaves garlands and songs for a young boy and his Genius (9). Flowers and green plant life were appropriate gifts for the deity—supporter of life, continuity, and the perpetuation of the species (earlier representations, as we have noted, portrayed the god with an offering in his right hand and a cornucopia in his left, or they depicted a snake twined around an altar bearing fruit).

Wine is mentioned even more frequently than flowers and plants. Libations were poured to the Emperor's Genius; Horace in his *Epistles* alludes to flowers and wine offered to the god, "mindful of the shortness of life" (2.1.144). In another place, he speaks of appeasing the Genius on festal days by drinking wine,[68] considered by Trimalchio in the *Satyricon* to be life itself—"vita vinum est"—and enjoyed during the festivity Ovid called a "festum geniale." [69] The association was made explicit by Censorinus (c. A.D. 238) in *De Die Natali:* a libation of wine instead of a sacrificed victim was offered to the Genius because, according to an ancestral custom, supplicants should refrain from shedding blood (or ending life) on their birthday.[70]

The sharing of wine and cake with the Genius was later amalgamated with the rites of Christian communion; they continued to symbolize "life"—although placed in a different context. The elaborate descriptions of the celebration of the Genius envisioned by Horace, Ovid, Tibullus, Persius, and Apuleius (all of whom were very popular in the Middle Ages [71]) very likely influenced later literary allegorizations of the Genius who appears in a garden with lush flowers and perfumed air, a setting whose decorum appealed to Bernardus Silvestris, Matthieu de Vendôme, Alanus de Insulis, Jean de Meun, and Edmund Spenser.

The purpose of such sacrifices offered to the Genius, "voltu mutabilis, albus et ater," was two-fold. The deity was rejuvenated, which meant the devotee also received new life and energy; secondly, the Genius, who knew everything about the individual's future and who controlled his fate, was encouraged to provide good fortune for him. Ovid complains at one point in *Tristia* that his Genius has been cruel to him (3.13.15); Tibullus begs Cerinthus' Natalis, "quoniam deus omnia sentis," to grant their mutual prayer, even if unspoken (4.5.19). When the Genius acceded to requests, he was appropriately thanked; libations of wine were poured on the birthday in part to express gratitude for the birth-god's gift of yet another year of life. Thus Persius advises his friend Macrinus, "funde merum Genio," in appreciation for his many years (*Satura* 2.1–3).

The parental figure of the Genius usually granted favors when properly propitiated. At the birthday celebration, it was common then (as now) for the individual to make a wish—only he addressed his Genius. Tibullus, speaking to Cornutus about an imaginary celebration, instructs him to make a request (to which the Genius must assent) at the appropriate moment—apparently after the offerings had been accepted by Natalis, and when he was making his bow (2.2.9–10). Thus Tibullus' Cornutus will ask for his wife's true love and for offspring, "turba novella," suit-

able requests to direct to one's Genius (2.2.11–12, 17–22). If the suppli-
cant were female, she invoked "Natalis Iuno," as Tibullus relates of Sul-
picia (4.6.1–2). Also, it was entirely possible to beg for good fortune for
a friend; in *Tristia,* after performing rites in honor of his lady's Juno,
Ovid petitions the natal goddess for her long life, protection, and happiness (5.5.13).

It should be emphasized that this deity held no moral sanction over the
individual; he was merely an agent of personal luck and fortune. One
might ask without opprobrium to have evil or selfish desires fulfilled by
his Genius. However, in public one spoke only "good words" to the
birth-god: Tibullus cautions, "Dicamus bona verba: venit Natalis ad
aras" (2.2.1). Wicked wishes were expressed to the gods, especially to
one's Genius, in private (Persius, *Satura* 2.3–4).

This sensitivity enforced the sanctity of an oath sworn upon the Genius
of another person in order to attest to the truth of a statement, like that of
the bailiff who vowed upon Seneca's Genius that he was working as hard
as he could on his behalf (*Epistle* 12.2). To lie while uttering such an
oath was to court the ill-will of the gods. Similarly, an appeal to another
person was strengthened by a protestation upon his Genius: Volteius,
duped into buying a country estate by his creditor Philippus, later entreats
him to permit a return to his former life; the vow accompanying the plea,
according to Horace, was made upon his Genius, his right hand, and his
household gods (*Epistle* 1.7.92–95). If the other person was a woman,
one swore by her Juno: Tibullus professes his faith and loyalty to his mis-
tress by invoking the holy power of her divine tutelary (4.13.15–16).

Previously, a member of the family swore by the Genius of the paterfamilias; the good citizen, by the emperor's Genius; and now, one individual protested his good intentions by an oath upon the Genius of the
other. In every instance the sacredness of the birth-god lent credence to
the oath.

The context of the Genius has changed markedly from its inception,
yet through every phase of development the Genius has retained vestiges
of its initial meaning. The parental Genius worshipped by the family
safeguarded its present and future renewal, and represented the begetting
spirit of the father. The Plautive *genius,* patron of individual *sucus,* life-
fluid, virility, and, by transfer, energy, protected the "life" of each man.

The extension of the *genius* to cities, things, and gods corroborated the earlier meanings of the spirit; the ultimate apotheosis of the Genius, concomitant with the deification of the emperor, pointed to a higher element born with each man, sexually differentiated, and controlling the course of one's life—the vagaries of luck and fortune.

CHAPTER TWO

The Late Classical Genius: Philosophical and Cosmological Conceptions

Having investigated the early and popular religious beliefs in the Genius, we turn now to philosophical and cosmological conceptions based upon the popular beliefs, and directly influencing the manifestations of the Genius in medieval philosophy, theology, literature, and popular belief. These cosmological conceptions, originating in Greek and Egyptian sources of the sixth century B.C., flourished in the first five centuries A.D. They share two features, despite differences in *Weltanschauung*—a Genius, or its analogue, is attributed to the cosmos and to the microcosm, man. Secondly, the cosmic Genius acts as an agent of generation or of fate or of both.

The frequently bewildering array of cosmological systems populating the universe with *genii* influenced one another, directly or indirectly. For this reason it is difficult to distinguish influence from analogy. The blending of systems occurred both in this late classical period and then again in the twelfth-century revival of pagan naturalism and humanism. In discussing the four major cosmological systems of astrology, Stoicism, Platonism and Neo-Platonism, and Christianity, this chapter will attempt to provide one or more of the following: the system's relationship with and development from early popular beliefs in the Genius, its influence upon or relationship with other systems, and, when appropriate, its influence upon medieval (especially twelfth-century) conceptions.

THE ASTROLOGICAL STAR AND INDIVIDUAL TEMPERAMENT

The Genius born with each man controlled his fortune and destiny; Horace says, in fact, that he "temperat astrum" (*Epistle* 2.2.187). During the Augustan period, the concept of the *genius* accrued an astrological meaning.[1] It controlled the guiding star, the natal constellation, of each individual, and thus also his uniqueness—the personality or temperament, and fortune, determined by this star. When Juvenal declares that "nemo mathematicus genium indemnatus habebit"[2] ("no astrologer will [be believed to] have prophetic skill [*genius*] unless he has been exiled or condemned"), he is alluding to the close association of the *genius* and the stars: only the competent astrologer, having knowledge of the stars (or *genius,* by metonymy), will be sentenced for his apparently illegal activities.

The horoscope of a man—the position of the planets and zodiacal signs at the hour of birth—influences a person's temperament and destiny, so that some men are born to pursue riches and fame, ignoring their own desires in the process, and others, in contrast, are pleased with a more leisurely pace of life, enjoying the sensuous gratifications produced by good food and simple pleasures. Whether one indulges his *genius* or denies it therefore becomes a choice relegated to fate and the stars. Persius (A.D. 34–62) made famous this choice granted to each of us: in one satire, he describes men who grow thin and bent in the quest for money, although he himself chooses to delight in spicy food and good wine. Indeed, even twins born under the same star or horoscope will have different attitudes toward life, different *genii* or temperaments: "geminos, horoscope, varo / producis genio."[3]

In another passage, which like the latter appealed to the medieval imagination, Persius suggests that the star controls the personality and also the destiny of each man, although he is not certain which one is specifically responsible for the affinity shared by Cornutus and himself ("nescio quod certe est quod me tibi temperat astrum," 5.51). Their capacity for close friendship results from the influence of either Libra (whose symbol is a scales or balance) or Gemini (whose twins remind him of their friendship); or else the position of Jupiter in the horoscope has overcome the generally malefic power of Saturn, thereby allotting jovial instead of saturnine temperaments (or fortunes) to the pair. Firmicus

Maternus (c. A.D. 337) later describes the place of Jupiter in the horoscope as a good *genius,* and that of Saturn as an evil *genius* or *daemon.*[4] Although the *genius* retains its astrological association for Firmicus, its function has been reduced and has become specialized: it no longer denotes the total horoscope or star originating at birth.

Macrobius (b. A.D. 360) explains the role of the Greek *daemon* (analogue to the Roman *genius*) in the process of the individual's conception, birth, and destiny in the *Saturnalia,* a valuable source of information concerning pagan beliefs. Each human being, according to the Egyptians, is the product of the conjunction of Eros, Necessity or Fate, a *daemon* (related to the zodiacal position of the sun at the individual's birth), and a *tyche* (related to the position of the moon at the individual's birth).[5] Macrobius etymologizes "daemon" as either "knowing of the future" or "burning, sharing"; the latter etymology links it with the sun, *mens mundi,* the regulator of the planets and pivot of the other eleven zodiacal signs (as it always occupies the remaining twelfth sign, 1.23.5–7). When the sun passes through a particular sign of the zodiac at the time of an individual's birth, it designates a temperament or *daemon* for him, and establishes, through its position in relation to the moon, his fortune or *tyche.* Contingent upon the season in which a man is born, i.e., a warm or cold one, indicating the extent of the sun's warming power and its relationship to other planets and signs, his *daemon* or *genius* will be warm or cold, good or bad, jovial or saturnine.

These astrological associations of the *genius* disturbed Prudentius, who wrote his *Contra Orationem Symmachi* in the early fifth century. By this time the *genius,* the star of life and destiny arising upon creation, had been allotted to cities, places, and even walls. Symmachus, whom Prudentius attacks, had said, "just as different *animae* fall to the lots of children at birth, so the hour and the day when city walls are first built impart to those cities a destiny or *genius* under whose direction they will prevail." [6] Fate, he continued, has also assigned such a *genius* (or destiny) to Rome, analogous to the individual character stamped upon the soul newly-arrived in the human body (2.370–74). However, Prudentius cannot fathom this notion of an unchangeable fate accorded to the city by its horoscope; the destiny of Rome, he believes, is determined by her mind or soul, her inhabitants, not her *genius.* And why, he questions, is there only one *genius* envisioned for Rome, when every door, house, public bath, and tavern has its own *genius,* and when no corner exists without a shadow or ghost (*umbra,* 2.409–10, 445–49).[7] It is clear that the credibility of the *genius* as a guiding star had been weakened by this time. Yet this simplistic relationship between the individual and the natal star, or man and the heavens, established at birth and continuing during his life, grows increasingly more complex in other cosmological systems. A macrocosmic analogue to the role of the *genius* in the generation and fate of the microcosm man is provided by the Stoic concept of the World Soul.

THE UNIVERSAL BEGETTER, THE COSMIC MIND

It was previously noted that *genii* had been ascribed to various gods, including Jove. The concept of the *genius Iovis,* affected by Etruscan beliefs in the phallic Mutinus Titinus, represented the begetting spirit of the universal paterfamilias. The cosmos was regarded as a great household occupied by Di Penates, certain gods of whom Jove or Jupiter was chief.

However, there was an important difference between the Etruscan Mutinus Titinus and the Roman *genius Iovis:* the latter was predicated upon the Stoic belief in the World Soul. The Stoic World Soul, like the Etruscan deity, was equivalent to Creator, hence, archetypal father: responsible for universal generation, it was identified as a cosmic "seed-power." But in addition it also signified Generative Reason or *logos spermatikos* to the Stoics: *logos,* meaning "word," "reason," and *sperma,* meaning "semen," denote the two functions of the seed-power or primary fire from which all life and reason, shape and form, have sprung.[8] The seed-powers, emanations of the fiery spirit of the World Soul, were actually the various gods and spirits who assisted the World Soul in shaping, creating, producing, and designing.[9] The operation of the Generative Reason or World Soul, the life of the world which produces all life on earth, is described, for example, by Virgil (70–19 B.C.) in the *Aeneid:* "First, the heaven and earth, and the watery plains, the shining orb of the moon and Titan's star, a spirit [*spiritus*] within sustains, and mind [*mens*], pervading its members, sways the whole mass and mingles with its mighty frame. Thence the race of man and beast, the life of winged things, and the strange shapes ocean bears beneath his glassy floor." [10] This heavenly procreative force, composed of fiery, burning particles or seed ("igneus est ollis vigor et caelestis origo / seminibus," 6.730–31), later became associated with the Genius of the universe.

We are indebted to Augustine for preserving the fragments of Varro (116–27 B.C.) on the relationship between the World Soul, Jupiter, and the universal Genius because his discussion was very influential during the Middle Ages. Augustine, elucidating Varro's remarks on natural theology, explains, first, that the universe itself is God, and that God is the soul (anima) of the universe. Just as the wise man, having both a body and a mind (animus), is called "wise" because of his mind, so the universe, by analogy, having both a "body" (material world) and a "mind," is called God because of its animus or guiding principle. [11] The World Soul, in Varro's terms, is therefore Jupiter, highest of gods.

Described as a progenitor of kings, things, and gods in two lines of Valerius Soranus (c. 133 B.C.) cited by Varro and again by Augustine, Jupiter becomes a Prime Mover or First Cause responsible for everything that exists in the world (" 'Deus est . . . habens potestatem causarum, quibus aliquid fit in mundo,' " 7.9). He is both the soul of the universe and the universe itself, both Father and Mother, and is accordingly addressed as Jupiter Progenitor and Genetrix (7.13). The male emits seed, the female receives it, but Jupiter, both masculine and feminine, emits seed (semina) from himself and receives it into himself (7.9, also 7.13).

Augustine equates Genius with Jupiter, the World Soul, in two ways. First, because each man has his own genius, his individual god or higher self (Varro had called it a rationalis animus, a Greek concept to be discussed at length in the next section), so then this World Soul must also be understood as a universal Genius: Varro thinks "that we should believe the world soul itself to be the universal Genius. And this is what they call Jupiter" (7.13). Augustine adds that this universal Genius, as distinguished from the individual genius, is "uniquely and outstandingly god" (7.13).

Secondly, Varro had defined Genius as "The god . . . who has command and control of everything that is begotten" ("Quid est Genius? 'Deus,' inquit, 'qui praepositus est ac vim habet omnium rerum gignendarum,' " 7.13). This older Roman belief in the Genius as a generation spirit is incorporated by Augustine into his concept of the World Soul: Jupiter Progenitor and Genetrix, father and mother of all that exists in the world, is equated with the universal Genius. Like the other gods, Genius is only part of the World Soul or Jupiter (7.16); Augustine does not understand this Stoic belief, and scoffs at its illogic. But the universal Genius represents a specialized function of the world or of Jupiter—universal begetting—in precisely the way the Genius of the paterfamilias controlled his power of begetting. These correlations between Genius, Jupiter, and the World Soul were very important in the Middle Ages: Varro's definition of Genius was repeated almost verbatim by Isidore, Paulus Diaconus, and Rabanus Maurus; it also influenced certain twelfth-century concepts of the World Soul.

The two definitions of the universal Genius—as a World Soul analogous to man's *rationalis animus,* and as a cosmic begetter—in effect duplicate the functions of the Stoic World Soul or *logos spermatikos,* which Varro identifies as Jupiter. Genius apparently acts as Jupiter's active agent in begetting all life, that is, as Jupiter Progenitor in emitting seeds from himself. Although Varro (and Augustine) do not explain the nature of this process, the Stoics believed that Jupiter in the aether (fiery heaven) penetrated the lower air (the realm of Juno) to become germinating seed, the source of life and agent of universal reason.[12] Juno, therefore, is the name given to that part of the World Soul which receives the seed—Jupiter as Genetrix. Varro's universal Genius, as generative agent of Jupiter, interacts on his behalf with the female cosmic Juno in order to produce all things. These macrocosmic forces, deified in Genius and Juno, mirror the male and female spirits (Genius and Juno) of the microcosm man.

Indeed, Augustine relates that Varro and the pagans, recognizing that Jupiter as both Progenitor and Genetrix is responsible for first causes, nevertheless credit Juno with the second causes of things ("et ideo ei [Juno] secundas causas rerum tribuunt," 7.16). But in Augustine's account, Juno rules the realm of earth, not the lower air (although he says later that she is both the lower air and the earth, 7.16). He has previously explained that the universe is divided into two main parts, heaven (aether and air) and earth (water and land, 7.6); if Genius as a heavenly agent of Jupiter controls all begetting (the emanation of seeds from the aether, or from aether into air), then Juno, Genetrix of Jupiter, must act as an earthly (or aerial) recipient for those seeds.

Juno, who is also known by the names "Ceres" and "Magna Mater," apparently does govern seed (although Augustine reveals it is the dry seed of females, not the wet seed of males, 7.16). Ceres was commonly associated with the seed in the cornstalk; Cerus, the masculine form of the word, meant "engenderer," and both names stemmed from *cereo* or *creo,* "I beget, engender." [13] Also, Genius, we remember, was often depicted holding a cornucopia of seeds; the seed was passed from father to son by heredity.

This cosmic seed and the fiery seed-powers who produce all life from it constitute a complex philosophical view of conception and creation. The seed-powers (loosely termed Genius and Juno in their role of universal generation) inhabit the four regions of the world—aether, air, water, and land. Thus Paulus, in his eighth-century epitome of Festus' second-century abridgment of Verrius Flaccus (c. 10 B.C.), glosses Varro's definition of Genius as a god who controls all begetting by declaring that water, earth, fire, and air are called "genial gods" (*"Geniales* deos dixerunt aquam, terram, ignem, aerem"").[14] It is these genial gods, he continues, who are the "seeds" or causes of all things ("ea enim sunt semina rerum").

Although Paulus is speaking of the four regions of the universe and not the four elements per se (for he will later inform us that the Greeks reckoned the twelve zodiacal signs, the moon, and the sun among these genial gods, 95), the four elements may also be regarded as the seed or germ of creation—the components of material life, of matter ($\sigma\tau o\iota\chi\epsilon\hat{\iota}\alpha$, primary elements, and $\dot{\alpha}\tau\delta\mu o\iota$, atoms, in Paulus, 94). Thus fire, air, water, and earth are "genial gods," the seeds of all things, in a second sense. Macrobius (c. A.D. 410) elucidates the genial process of material creation in his commentary on the *Somnium Scipionis,* although he does not mention either Genius or Juno.[15] He explains that the human body is constructed from elemental matter whose four parts are mirrored in the four divisions of the universe (he will later explain the origin of the human soul). First, Necessity, the line of demarcation between earth and water, binds the clay of which bodies are composed. Next, Harmony, at the border between water and air, joins the lower, the dross, with the upper, the pure. Finally, Obedience, the interstice between air and fire, completes the union of the four elements in the body. Human bodies, therefore, are produced by the three interstices acting on and fusing the four elements in a hierarchical sequence. Paulus' four regions and also the four elements, the seeds (or causes) of all things, are rightly termed "genial gods."

Macrobius amplifies this discussion of cosmic generation in a symbolic and mystical interpretation of conception and birth delineated in the *Saturnalia*. His summary stresses the astrological influence on creation, particularly with respect to the origin of individual temperament and fortune. Four forces are involved, those of Eros, Necessity, the sun, and the moon, all of which are symbolized by the caduceus (1.19.16–18). Two serpents, male and female (Genius and Juno?), unite their upper parts in a kiss, which signifies Eros or Amor, and their lower coiled parts in a knot, called the knot of Hercules, which signifies Anangke or Necessitas. Necessity, one of the three interstices in his discussion in the commentary, suggests, with its fatalistic implications in this passage, a bond with the gods comprised by the World Soul, or, because of the coiled tails forming the knot, a bond with the stars and heavenly spheres which translate divine dicta and laws into earthly events and happenings (i.e., the alignment of the spheres, in an astrological sense, governs the time of birth and the disposition of the person born). Macrobius likens the coiled bodies of the snakes to the serpentine movements of the sun and moon: the sun's progression through the signs of the zodiac designates different horoscopes or natal stars (temperaments, or what Macrobius calls *daemones*) for all men, and the changing nature of the moon, imprinting the sublunary realm with mutability, allots different fortunes (what Macrobius calls *tychai*) to all men.

That is, conception or creation is initiated and controlled by cosmic forces—the World Soul, whose agents are Genius and Juno, the various gods, who are part of the World Soul and who are also identified as planets or stars (Mercury, Saturn, Venus, etc.), and also the sun and the moon, which are both luminaries and gods. Augustine in fact lists the primary parts of the World Soul or Jupiter as Genius, the Magna Mater (Juno), and Sol and Luna (the sun and the moon, but also Apollo and Diana, 7.16). Arnobius (c. A.D. 295) defines the cosmic household gods similarly: to the Genius Iovialis and Ceres he adds Fortune (equivalent to

Augustine's Luna, or perhaps the gods in general), and Pales, apparently a male attendant or bailiff of Jupiter.[16] Finally, Paulus explicitly associates Genius, god of all begetting, not only with the "genial gods" of earth, water, air, and fire, who are the seeds or causes of all things, but also with the twelve zodiacal signs and the sun and the moon: "they reckoned the twelve signs [constellations], the moon, and the sun among these [genial] gods" ("Duodecim quoque signa, lunam et solem inter hos deos computabant," 95).

The influence of these "seed-powers"—Genius and Juno, the gods or planets, the twelve signs, and the sun and the moon—determines the temperament, fortune, and even the mind of the individual at birth. Macrobius, in his commentary on the *Somnium Scipionis,* declares that "By the words of Paulus it becomes clear that of all the creatures on earth man alone has a common share in Mind, that is *animus,* with the sky and the stars. And that is why he said, *Minds have been given to them out of the eternal fires you call fixed stars and planets.*" [17] *Animus* originates from the World Soul: the soul descends from the Milky Way through the various spheres at the time of birth. Each planetary sphere affects one attribute of the soul—Saturn's affects reason and understanding; Jupiter's, ability to act; Mars', boldness of spirit; the sun's, sense-perception and imagination; Venus', passion; Mercury's, rhetorical ability; and the moon's, growth and propensity for physical change (1.12.13–14).

The world, its body (four regions, stars and planets) and its soul (Genius Iovialis, Jupiter, the gods), help to knead and shape the human mind and body. This Stoic and astrological interpretation of the World Soul will be altered in the Middle Ages; as early as Calcidius (c. A.D. 300), changes occur in the concept of the World Soul. His Neo-Platonic orientation provides three universal principles or substances (*substantia*)—Ineffable God, Providence, and Mind or Intellect; the task of administering divine law in the lower regions is allocated to Nature, Fortune, Chance, and *daemones.*[18] No Genius Iovis appears, no Juno (except perhaps as Magna Mater in the guise of Nature), although slightly later Martianus Capella (c. A.D. 423) portrays Jupiter in *De Nuptiis* describing Genius as "the faithful reflex and interpreter of my mind, o sacred *nous*" ("fida recursio / interpresque meae mentis, ὁ νοῦς sacer," 1.92). Calcidius' "Mind" (*Mens*) resembles Genius, sacred *nous* of Jupiter, but nowhere does he make such an explicit equation.

The cosmic Genius, agent of universal begetting, resembles the Genius of each man, formerly conceived as a generation spirit, virility, "life," temperament. But the individual *genius* also mirrors the cosmic power's other major function, one only mentioned briefly in the preceding discussion. Augustine, drawing a parallel between the macrocosm and the microcosm, defines the individual *genius,* analogous to universal Reason, as the rational soul of each man: Varro says that "a *genius* is the rational soul of each man [". . . genium . . . esse uniuscuiusque animum rationalem"], so that each individual has one, while the corresponding world soul is a god ["talem autem mundi animum Deum esse"]" (7.13). The statement, clearly, is not derived from popular beliefs in the Genius; it has developed, instead, from the Platonic concept of the individual *daemon.*

THE RATIONAL SOUL AND THE PROBLEM OF GOOD AND EVIL

The Greek *daemon* assumed two forms according to Plato: it was a cosmic messenger of the gods, and it was also the highest form of the soul, housed at the top of the human body. The former phenomenon will interest us later in this chapter; for the present, we shall investigate the nature of the human *daemon.*

In the *Timaeus* Plato speaks of the *daemon* which lifts us from earth to heaven and to our kin therein.[19] He says that the man who indulges in concupiscence acts mortally, but he who devotes himself to learning and wisdom, that which is divine and immortal, magnifies his *daemon,* the divine part of man. Thought is the "food" of this part, which seeks to understand the intellections of the universe; therefore, man should offer his *daemon* such food (90B–90C).

Plato's internal god resembles the Stoic principate of the soul, that part governing the remaining seven parts (the five senses, and the powers of speech and generation) which were functions or aspects of the principate. Known by various names—*logike psyche* (λογικὴ ψυχή), *nous* (νοῦς), *dianoia* (διάνοια)—it represented the reason or intellect, "also the 'ego,' that is, the will, the energy, the capacity for action. It is in one aspect the divinity in us, world-wide, universal; in another the individual man with his special bent and character; so that we may even be said to have two souls in us, the world-soul and each man's particular soul.'' [20] The first passage from the *Timaeus* was instrumental in changing the meaning of the Genius in the late classical period and in the Middle Ages; the catalyst for this change in meaning was the Neo-Platonic Apuleius.

When Apuleius (c. A.D. 158) first encountered this Platonic *daemon*, he must have been confused. He was aware of the meaning of the Roman Genius, born with each man, but he also realized that the *daemon*, rational soul, differed. Therefore, in *De Deo Socratis* he cleverly synthesized the Greek and Roman concepts of the spirit by introducing two lines from the *Aeneid* (9.184–85) which provided a link between the figures. The question Nisus addresses to Euryalus concerns the source of "dread desire": is it inspired by the gods, or is it actually a god within man (" 'diine hunc ardorem mentibus addunt, / Euryale, an sua cuique deus fit dira cupido?' "). Apuleius believes that such desire is prompted by the human soul in the body, the *daemon* (". . . animus humanus etiam nunc in corpore situs daemon nuncupatur") or, in Latin, the *genius*, although he is not convinced that his interpretation is wholly accurate.[21] A good desire of the soul is a good god ("igitur et bona cupido animi bonus deus est"), and the good *daemon* is the mind perfectly virtuous (". . . daemon bonus id est animus virtute perfectus est," 15.150). The good *daemon* may be identified with the *genius*, he continues, who is both a god and the soul of each man, immortal, although begotten in some way along with man (*genius* is "deus, qui est animus sui cuique, quamquam sit inmortalis, tamen quodam modo cum homine gignitur," 15.151).

The first consequence of Apuleius' equation of the *genius*, born with each man, with the *daemon*, rational soul, was the merging of the two concepts. *Genius* and *daemon* became synonymous terms; the former lost its original meaning of individual virility, life, temperament, personality. Augustine, as we have noted, speaks of the *genius* as the *rationalis animus* of each man. Ammianus Marcellinus (c. A.D. 392), drawing upon the works of unidentified theologians and of Greek poets and writers (Menander, Homer, and others not specified), describes the *daemon* or *genius* as a guardian spirit born with each man to guide his conduct during life, but visible only to the most virtuous of men.[22] (Here he confuses the Greek *daemon* as an internal rational soul with the external Greek *daemon*-messenger, a slightly different spirit which will be discussed in the following section.) Ammianus declares that the *daemon* described by Menander as the guide and leader of each man's life is the same guardian *genius* which has attended, supported, and instructed such famous men as Pythagoras, Socrates, Numa Pompilius, the elder Scipio, Marius, Octavianus, Hermes Trismegistus, Apollonius of Tyana, and Plotinus (21.14.5). The latter three, Ammianus continues, attempted to discern the nature of the bond between *genii* and men's souls, and also the reason they offer protection and moral direction only to men entirely virtuous and pure (21.14.5). This Greek concept of the *daemon* as rational soul similarly influenced a definition of the *genius* presented by Martianus Capella (c. A.D. 423): "this most faithful tutelary and brother protects the minds and souls of all men" ("hic tutelator fidissimusque germanus animos omnium mentesque custodit," 2.152).

The second consequence of Apuleius' identification of the Roman *genius* with the Greek *daemon* was more subtle but more important. In that same passage, Apuleius concludes that the prayer addressed to the *genius* of another person, performed while embracing his knees (*genua*), symbolizes in two words ("Genium et genua") the conjunction of soul (*genius*) and body (knees) through which we exist ("quibus Genium et genua precantur, coniunctionem nostram nexumque videantur mihi obtestari, corpus atque animum duobus nominibus conprehendentes, quorum communio et copulatio sumus," 15.151–52).[23] That is, the *genius* is immortal, like the soul, but is begotten with each man and exists within his body only until death; thus the *genius* and *genua* symbolize man's paradoxical nature, spiritual yet corporeal. This notion was later misinterpreted: the *genius* and *genua* were apparently envisioned as the good and evil sides of each man. If there is a good *daemon*, representing the good desires of the soul, to which the *genius* corresponds, then there must also be an evil *daemon*, representing the evil desires of the body, to which a bad *genius* corresponds. Servius (c. A.D. 389), for example, commenting upon the same Virgilian passage (9.184–85), distinguishes the Genius, the familiar *numen* which desires only good, from the evil desires which originate in man. Like Ammianus, he turns to Plotinus to amplify his comments: we are motivated to perform good acts by our individual Genius, who has been allotted to us at birth ("ad omnia honesta inpelli nos genio et numine quodam familiari, quod nobis nascentibus datur"), but it is our mind which prompts evil desires or longings ("prava vero nostra mente nos cupere et desiderare").[24] In his conclusion he alters the sense of the Virgilian lines by rephrasing them: Nisus then asks Euryalus whether the gods have inspired these desires, or whether we have made desire a god ("o Euryale, dine nostris mentibus cupiditates iniciunt et desideria, an deus fit ipsa mentis cupiditas?"). This particular passage, like several others of Servius, was repeated verbatim by Mythographus Tertius, and strongly influenced the medieval moralizations of the pagan Genius.

The opposition of the good desires of the Genius to fleshly *cupiditas* was very likely enhanced by Servius' awareness of the meaning of *genialis*. Although the Genius in the Servian passages cited above represents moral and even sapiential longings of the soul, Servius glosses *genialis* (from *genialis hiems,* the farmer's pleasant and workless winter celebrated with festivities and feasts) as *voluptuosa* and *convivalis*, explaining this by means of the old ideas of indulging and defrauding one's *genius*. Indulging one's *genius* is pleasurable, denying it is not: "nam quotiens voluptati operam damus indulgere dicimur genio, unde e contrario habemus in Terentio suum defraudans genium." [25] The pleasure-seeking *genius* of this passage, which surely helps man to make a god of his longings, is the "malus genius," opposed to the "bonus genius" (or good *daemon*) in Servius' gloss on *Aeneid* 6.743: "when we are born, we are allotted two *genii:* one exists which strongly urges us toward good things [*qui hortatur ad bona*], the other which corrupts us toward evil things [*qui depravat ad mala*]." The consequences of such assistance determine whether we are led after death to a better life, or condemned to a worse: through the efforts of the two *genii* we either earn our freedom from the body, or are eternally chained to it (by lingering over the body, or by seeking out incarnation in a new one, 6.743). It is for this reason, Servius concludes, that *genii* are also called *manes* (shades, or *genii*-after-death). This passage, like the others cited, was repeated by the Third Vatican Mythographer; we shall return to his compilation of definitions later in the description of the medieval view of the *genius*.

Servius, however, introduces a new element to our understanding of the *genius*—the concept of the after-life and the function of the *manes* both in this life and thereafter. The Di Manes from the earliest of times represented the unindividualized family dead, becoming personalized only later with the rise of individuality in Roman religion and philosophy. The Greek *daemon* which rose to the heavens after death resembled the Roman Di Manes. The popular Greek belief in this tutelary spirit influenced the development of the Platonic *daemon;* all three, *manes,* popular *daemon,* and Platonic *daemon,* fostered the identification of the *genius* with the (immortal) soul of man.[26]

Servius explains that our life on earth and the good or evil use we make of it determines our life and position after death, that is, the fate of our *manes.* What exactly are these *manes* he speaks of, and what is their relationship with the cosmological demons?

THE DEMONIC MESSENGER, "MEDIOXUMUS"

The Di Manes constituted one class of demons. There were three kinds [27] in addition to the *daemon* (soul) of each man on earth. Highest in rank were the divine messengers, who observed the affairs of men and reported back to the gods. These good *daemons* were contrasted with the second class—the careless and idle spirits, employed as the executioners of the gods. The third and last class consisted of the *manes*—the good or evil souls of men which had departed from their bodies.

Apuleius (c. A.D. 158) in *De Deo Socratis* provides the most ample and influential discussion of *daemones,* based upon the Platonic tripartite division of nature.[28] The highest part of nature comprises the gods—the twelve intelligible gods perceived by the understanding (Juno, Vesta, Minerva, Ceres, Diana, Venus, Mars, Mercury, Jove, Neptune, Vulcan, and Apollo), and also the sensible gods perceived by the senses (the sun, moon, and five planets or stars). Although there seems to be no way for the lowest part of nature, earth and her inhabitants, to communicate with these divinities, Apuleius contends that the *daemon,* who is *medioxumus,*[29] provides the means for such communication: it carries messages between the gods and man; to it man addresses prayers, makes vows, sacrifices victims.

Neither divine nor mortal, *daemones* share immortality with the gods and rational minds and passions with men; however, they possess aerial bodies, a facet peculiar to themselves. This very popular description of demonic nature was later echoed by Augustine and Calcidius.[30]

There is some discrepancy concerning the precise cosmic location of *daemones,* although most writers, like Apuleius, place them in the air between aether and water. Augustine does not mention the word *daemon,* but he admits the four parts of the world are full of souls, immortal ones in the aether and air, mortal ones in water and on land (7.6). In the aether reside the most important "souls," the stars or planets, which are visible; between the sphere of the moon and the highest region of clouds and winds dwell invisible souls—"heroas et lares et genios" (7.6). The fullest and most detailed account of the cosmic position and hierarchy of the various spirits is presented by Martianus in *De Nuptiis;* his discussion spurred subsequent amplification in many other works throughout the Middle Ages.[31]

Augustine's invisible souls or spirits, intermediaries between the stars and planets and man, aid the World Soul in its functions. According to Macrobius (who alludes to Plato and Posidonius) in the *Saturnalia,* the term *daemones* (Greek δαιμονες), applied both to spirits and to gods, springs either from the word δαήμονες, "gifted with knowledge of the future," or from the word δαιόμενος, "burning, sharing," in reference to their nature, which shares in heavenly substance (1.23.7). The *daemones,* "burning" or "sharing" spirits, resemble the fiery seed of the World Soul: they help to animate the cosmos. Their precise function, however, is to transmit the knowledge with which they are gifted by the gods, the stars, and Jove, or by man, to the appropriate recipient.

In the *Symposium,* the cosmic *daemon,* neither mortal nor immortal, but sharing attributes both of the gods and of man, conveys petitions and news of sacrifices from man to the gods, and commands from the gods to man.[32] The most famous instance of the latter is related by Socrates in the *Apology:* he speaks of a divine spiritual voice that has accompanied him from boyhood, discouraging certain acts, but never encouraging others.[33] Plutarch (c. A.D. 46–125) in *De Genio Socratis* suggests that Socrates' oracular *daemon* (*genius* in the Latin), who guided him from the very beginning, was a vision lighting his way in the exploration of difficult matters beyond most men. Such prophetic messages were transmitted from the gods to many men, but only an individual like Socrates,

with a mind free of distracting and tumultuous passion, could fully comprehend such *daemonic* instruction. His pure mind allowed the soundless
utterance of the *genius* to reach him via revelation: they communicated
mentally.[34]

Socrates' *daemon*, in Apuleius' *De Deo Socratis*, is ascribed to the
third and highest class of *daemones*, ranked above the *daemones* of the
after-life (soul-without-the-body) and the *daemon-genius* (soul-within-
the-body). This class of spirit, to which "sleep" and "Love" belong,
understands all things. Socrates, with his untroubled mind, needed neither the dreams accompanying sleep nor the blissful ecstasy of love to
communicate with his *daemon*.

Although Apuleius distinguishes between the Socratic *daemon* and the
genius-daemon (soul-within-the-body) of men on earth, Tertullian (A.D.
150–230) defines this external Socratic *daemon* as a *genius*. The *daemonic* spirit (*spiritus daemonicus*) visited Socrates when he was still a
boy; "so to all men *genii* are assigned, which is the name for *daemones*"
("sic et omnibus genii deputantur, quod daemonum nomen est").[35] Both
Ammianus and Annaeus Florus view the message-carrying spirit as a *genius*. In Ammianus (c. A.D. 392), the Genius brings both good and bad
news to Julian. As the Genius of the State (*Genius publicus*), he appears
in Julian's dream in order to reproach him: the Genius has wished to aid
him by increasing his rank because many men have agreed he is worthy
of advancement, but each time he approaches Julian, he is rebuffed. He
threatens to leave forever if Julian does not receive him (20.5.10). Apparently Julian aceedes, for he later becomes Augustus. It is interesting to
note that this *Genius publicus* brings good luck or news like the Greek
messenger *daemon*, but that he frequents the vestibule of Julian's house
like the earlier Roman *Genius domus*.

But the Genius of the State, serving as the "executioner" of the gods,
can also bring bad news: one night Julian sees the same Genius who
visited him when he was rising to power, but now—signalling his fall—
he appears with a veiled head and cornucopia (25.2.3). Julian's reign
ended shortly thereafter. Annaeus Florus (c. A.D. 137) describes the appearance of a Genius to Brutus before imminent disaster—the deaths of
both Brutus and Cassius in the war against Caesar and Antonius. In this
case, the role of the Genius as executioner of the gods, representative of
bad luck, is clearly differentiated from that of the Genius bringing good

news: the figure appears to Brutus during the night when he is meditating and confesses that he is his "malus genius." [36] Evil and ill-fortune are clearly linked.

The mistaken identification of the *daemones,* messengers of the gods conveying good or bad news to men, with the *genius,* either good or bad, born with each man to guide his conduct, was an easy one for Florus and Ammianus to make. The difference between the two concepts, or classes of *daemones,* can be resolved only by distinguishing between the nature of the *daemon*—internal or external, moral or fatalistic. This confused situation was complicated by the nature of the third type of external *daemon,* the spirit lesser in rank than the messenger of the gods, but greater than the *daemon* (indwelling power) of each man on earth—the *daemon* or soul, shade, of each man after death.

This species of *daemon* included several sub-types. Plutarch does not classify the *daemones* he discusses; he merely mentions that such *daemones* appeared after the deaths of Lysis and Trophonius (16, 21, 22). Apuleius, however, explains that the soul ("animus humanus") after death is called a *lemur* (15.152). If it has proven to be good, i.e., relatively uncontaminated by the flesh, it becomes a *lar;* if bad, a *larva;* and if its condition is uncertain, a *manes* (15.152–53).

Martianus (c. A.D. 423) also categorizes these spirits inhabiting the airy region below the moon, the underworld ruled by Pluto, or Summanus ("summus Manium," he explains), and the moon (Proserpina: "hic Luna, quae huic aëri praeest, Proserpina memoratur," 2.161–62). However, his classification differs slightly from that of Apuleius: Martianus calls the *genius* of Apuleius (soul-in-the-body) a *manes,* which is either good or evil ("ἀγαθούς et κακούς δαίμονας" in Greek). Also, Martianus does not list a name for the neutral *lemur* whose condition is uncertain (Apuleius' *manes*). But the remainder of his classification is identical with that of Apuleius: after leaving the body, the *manes* becomes a *lemur.* The good *manes* is then regarded as a *lar,* and the evil *manes* as a *larva* (2.162–64). The good and evil *manes* do not differ essentially from Apuleius' good and evil *genii* born with each man and living until his death. The difference between the good and evil messenger *daemones* and the *manes* and *genii* should be clear: the former perform as agents of fate, the gods, and the stars, but the latter depend upon man's "free will," so to speak, the choices he makes during his life.

Virgil (70–19 B.C.) described in the *Aeneid* the spirit or *mens* animating the world and creating all things; but, he added, "Fiery is the vigour and divine the source of those life-seeds [*seminibus*], so far as harmful bodies clog them not, nor earthly limbs and mortal frames dull them" (6.730–32). The flesh dulls and corrupts the heavenly spark; when life departs, the retarding flesh frequently inhibits that spark. Thus the spirit is punished according to its corruption: "quisque suos patimur Manes" (or "Manis," 6.743). Macrobius (c. A.D 410) discusses in his commentary on the *Somnium Scipionis* the alternatives available to a soul after it has quit the body: if virtuous, it ascends into the heavens; if, however, it has been overwhelmed by the bestial nature of the body, it dreads its departure, and before entering the underworld of the shades, hovers over the corpse, or seeks a new body, human or animal (1.9.4–5).

Much of this sounds very Christian. The soul, sent to heaven, hell, or purgatory, bears a suspicious resemblance to the *lemur,* which is either good (*lar,* good *manes, agathos daemon*) or evil (*larva,* evil *manes, kakos daemon*), or uncertain (*manes* in general). What influence did the corps of *genii, daemones,* and *manes* have upon Christianity?

THE CHRISTIAN ANGEL AND DEMON

The Christian soul is analogous to the classical "soul" which became a *manes* after death; the Christian saint, celebrated on certain days, resembles the virtuous *manes,* what Apuleius and Martianus called the *lar,* and what had been, during its sojourn on earth, an *agathos daemon.*[37] But the pagan *daemones,* messengers of the gods and the stars, most spiritual of all three classes of spirits, received the greatest attention from the Christian apologists. First, this cosmic *daemon* was transformed into a very Christian *angelus;* secondly, the pagan *genii* and *daemones* were regarded as demons perpetrating evil and havoc.

The cosmic *daemones* carrying their messages and commands from heaven to earth had been previously divided into two classes—the fortunate *daemon* with good news and the careless and idle *daemon,* the executioner of the gods, with bad news. Calcidius (c. A.D. 300) in his commentary on the *Timaeus* describes these messengers, who are called *daemones* because they know all things. But then he discusses the *angelus,* intermediary between God and man, who interprets and reports to God our prayers, innermost wishes and needs, and who delivers divine help to us: it is a type of *daemon* (*angeli*—"tamquam daëmones dicti," 132). Called *angeli* from the Greek ἄγγελος, *angelos* or announcer, messenger, they assiduously perform the duty of announcing and reporting ("officium nuntiandi," 132). An even stronger connection between the *genius* (*daemon*) and *angelus* is established by Martianus (c. A.D. 423): the *genius,* "this most faithful protector, . . . since he announces to the heavenly power the secrets of thoughts, will even be able to be called Angel" ("hic tutelator fidissimusque . . . quoniam cogitationum arcana superae annuntiat potestati, etiam Angelus poterit nuncupari," 2.152–53). The Greeks, Martianus continues, call these spirits *daemones* (*Medioximi* in Latin) from the "the sharing one" (δαιομένος), presumably because, as mediators or intermediaries, they share the secrets of heaven and of earth.

According to the Christian apologist Lactantius (fl. A.D. 297), there were two kinds of angels, the heavenly and the fallen. In relating the story of their fall, Lactantius relies heavily upon the concept of the careless and idle *daemon* to explain their fallen nature. God, observing the deception and harassment caused by the diabolic Serpent, sent angelic messengers to warn and to protect men. However, the Devil enticed the negligent angels into the enjoyment of earthly pleasure: they copulated with women, and earthly "angels" were born of the union.[38] The fallen angels, *depravati angeli* or *daemones caelestes,* became minions of the Devil, the ultimate *daemoniarch* (2.14.5). Calcidius calls them *desertores angeli:* having been contaminated by their own earthly passions, they henceforth inhabit the aerial region instead of heaven, and promote evil and impiety on earth (135). There are, then, two kinds of messengers—the angelic messenger sent from God, and the demonic messenger, or the depraved angel, sent from the Devil.

The product of the union of angel and man was neither immortal nor mortal: these spirits, *daemones terreni,* encouraged the workings of evil on earth by acting like demonic messengers. This type of *daemon* Lactantius uses to amalgamate the Greek and Roman spirits—the *daemon,* the *genius,* and even the *manes.*

Lactantius' long description of the *daemon* is divided into two parts, the first dealing with the Greek spirit, the second with the Roman (2.14.6–14). He alludes to the *daemones* described by Hesiod, Plato, and Minucius Felix and explains their etymology as Macrobius has: they resemble "indwelling powers," δαήμονες, who are "gifted with knowledge" (from δαήμων, "knowing") because they are almost omniscient (not entirely, for they do not know of God's hidden plan, 2.14.6).

However, the *genius* receives greatest emphasis. Lactantius disparages the *genii* of houses and of individual men, the libation of wine poured to the *genius*, the veneration of the spirit as a god. The evil of the *genius* infects man's body with disease and unbalances his mind with terrible dreams, causing madness. This vitriolic attack, in effect recapitulating the evolution of the *genius* and *daemon*, does provide new information which will later be incorporated in the medieval popular belief in the demon: the spirits' knowledge of magic arts, designed to delude men's minds, encompasses astrology, augury, divination, necromancy, casting of lots, and oracular pronouncements (*Epit.* 28). He draws upon the late classical belief in the *genius* as natal star (horoscope) to develop the astrological link; the *daemon* and *genius* who were associated with individual fortune (*tyche*) or messages from the gods or Jove (World Soul) here become associated with augury, divination, omens; and the *manes* of the dead man is apparently summoned by the necromancer. In the Middle Ages the *genius* and *daemon* condemned by Lactantius will be called "demons," but will continue to allow men to read the secrets of the future in the omens and auguries they manipulate.[39] The fondness of the Lactantian *daemones* for communicating by means of dream visions whose nightmarish qualities terrify or whose prophecies impress will later be incorporated into the medieval definition of madness as the state produced by a possessing demon.[40]

The Greek *daemon* and Roman *genius* have been completely denigrated by Lactantius, yet they live on in disguise: for the Greek *daemon* (good *genius*), he substitutes by analogy the Christian angel, and for the Roman *genius* (begetting spirit, inclination, bad *genius*), the pagan *daemon* or demon, agent of evil skilled in the black arts.

To summarize, we find that the *genius* and *daemon* developed cosmological and philosophical affiliations—with astrology, Stoicism, Platonism and Neo-Platonism, and Christianity. Despite differences among these systems, a pattern linking *genii* and *daemones* emerges. The *genius,* representative of the forces of fate and generation, is associated with the star, the horoscope; occasionally with Jove and the *anima mundi;* with the stars and planets, including the sun and moon; with Fortuna and the Magna Mater. The Greek *daemon,* "medioxumus," residing in the air, is a messenger of the gods, bearing good news (like the Christian *angelus*), or bad news (like the evil fallen angel); it is also a *manes,* a good or an evil soul of the dead; finally, it is the *genius* and soul of the man on earth, frequently split into two parts, good and evil. And from this pattern we note another: from the supernal regions come the messages of inexorable fate and fortune affecting the lower regions, but from the depths, from the earth, comes a challenge to this force—a chance to determine one's personal fortune during life and after death, what might be termed a classical form of "free will."

The patterns we have discussed evolved from the earlier popular worship of the Genius; they bear unmistakable signs of their origins. The begetting spirit of the paterfamilias, ensuring the continuity of the family, has been metamorphosed into the generational and fatalistic force of the universal household. Jupiter, father of the gods, and the stars and planets, authors of fate, govern the continuity and life of the world. The individual *genius,* born with each man, and signifying his life, energy, and later, his personal luck and temperament, has been transformed to represent his individuality, personality, soul, "free will."

How much of this is transmitted and retained in the Middle Ages? Was the medieval view of the Genius the same, or were changes made? We have, in passing, noted the popularity of various quotations, definitions, and concepts concerning the Genius during the Middle Ages. We turn now to a broader overview of the figure's influence in this later period.

CHAPTER THREE

The Classical Genius in the Middle Ages

The pagan *genius* or *daemon* survived in the Christian world of the Middle Ages in three states: alive, in the popular medieval belief in angels and demons, the latter always associated with astrology, the black arts, dreams, and madness; fossilized, in classical literature, commentaries on classical literature, and aids for the reading and understanding of classical literature, e.g., mythographic manuals; and moralized, in the writings and literature of the twelfth and later centuries.[1] The latter phenomenon, to be discussed in this section, most concerns us, although all three states are related. The moralization and allegorization of the Genius from fossilized classical definitions was also affected by its popular manifestation as a demon. When a twelfth-century writer encountered Horace's definition of the Genius as "natale comes qui temperat astrum, / naturae deus humanae," he immediately associated it with the demonic pagan gods, magic, evil. And yet this eminent *auctor* had presented a different and less pejorative meaning for the god. To resolve his dilemma, this hypothetical Christian writer, after examining very carefully other classical definitions of the Genius, synthesized the many, frequently divergent, meanings, attempted to make some sense of them by envisioning an over-all pattern, and moralized the figure. The moralization made the god palatable to the Christian reader. It also affected the allegorical and literary appearance of the Genius for the next four centuries.

The number of classical authors defining or using the Genius in some way, and accessible to a twelfth-century writer, was very large. Terence, Persius, Horace, Ovid, Tibullus, Juvenal, Virgil, Cicero, to name a few, were copied, recopied, and read during the period from the sixth to the twelfth century.[2] Apuleius, Augustine (and through him, Varro), the Christian apologists, Calcidius (and through him, Plato), Macrobius, Servius, Martianus Capella—many writers of the late classical and early medieval period found a receptive audience in the scholars of the Middle Ages. The renaissances of the ninth and the twelfth centuries, characterized by a revival of interest in the classics, stimulated their transmission;[3] many other classical authors, in addition to those listed above, were cited copiously in *scholia, florilegia,* glosses, commentaries, cyclopedias, and *libri manuales.*[4] Most of the ideas and definitions of Genius—with the exception of those involving the State cult of the imperial Genius, the Genius of the city, and related popular beliefs, which did not appeal to the medieval mind—were available in some form in the twelfth century. Frequently, however, *scholia* from the classics were used to define Genius without acknowledgment of authorship and understanding of all of the philosophical and religious implications of the figure. We shall see, in later examinations of specific literary works, most of the classical concepts of the Genius, but often misunderstood.

With such a plethora of definitions from which to choose, the medieval compiler favored, hence copied and circulated, only a few. Most perplexing to the medieval mind, with its passion for unity and clarity, were the differences among them. Two twelfth-century writers, Bernardus Silvestris and Guillaume de Conches, discovered a means of synthesizing divergent views, reconciling classical concepts of the deity with the medieval belief in demonic forces and spirits, and rescuing Virgil and other classical *auctores* from the charge of devilish inspiration. This means was provided by their interest in Aeneas' descent into the underworld, delineated in the sixth book of the *Aeneid.*

In the preface to this sixth book in his commentary on the first six books of the *Aeneid,* Bernardus Silvestris (c. 1145) explains that the world is divided into two fixed spheres (*aplanes*), one superior and one inferior.[5] The superior Aplanon is called "paradisus" in Greek, "ortus" in Latin (the East, Orient or Origin: because from it things originate— *oriuntur*), and "Eden" in Hebrew. This last name, when translated into Latin, becomes "deliciae," "pleasures," because it is the very pleasant home of souls. The inferior Aplanon—the lower, fallen, inferior realm ("caducam et inferiorem regionem")—is identified as the infernal regions ("inferos dixerunt"). This infernal underworld was previously regarded as the sublunary realm by one of the sources of Bernardus: Macrobius, in his commentary on the *Somnium Scipionis*, explained that the immutable part of the world, which ranged from the fixed sphere to the moon, effected "causes and the necessity of change" upon the passive and mutable part, which ranged from the moon to the earth.[6] The lower region derives its name, *locus mortis* or *locus inferorum*, from the fact that living souls who enter this region from above are subjected to mutability and die. The sphere of the moon therefore represents the line of demarcation between life and death.

This Neo-Platonic macrocosmic underworld is paralleled by the microcosmic underworld, an equally "inferior" region. Bernardus describes the human body as the lowest of all existing things; it is not equal to spirit (which is rational and immortal), or to the transitory bodies of beasts (which are stronger, larger, more swift), plants (which regenerate after pruning), or inanimate objects (which are not destroyed by disease or old age). This *infernum* is not only "inferior" but "infernal": Macrobius relates that ancient philosophers called the body the "tomb of the soul" ("animae sepulcrum"), the "hollows of Dis" ("Ditis concava"), and the "infernal regions" ("inferos," 1.10.10).

These two underworlds—the sublunary realm and the human body—fascinated medieval writers like Bernardus, Guillaume de Conches (fl. 1080–1145), and later, Colucio Salutati (b. 1330). Extrapolating from Aeneas' descent into the underworld, they postulated types of underworld descents from a superior region or position to an inferior. Man is introduced to the inferior regions of the world in two ways: when he is born into the sublunary realm, his soul assuming an inferior fleshly form, and also when he consults the demons of Hell. But man can descend into the underworld of the body voluntarily in a more figurative way—by gratifying excessive fleshly desires, or by understanding the way of all flesh in order to protect himself from its temptations. The birth of man they labeled "descensus naturae"; the pursuit of sensual gratification, "descensus vitii"; the knowledge of oneself and the fallen world, "descensus virtutis"; and the consultation with demons, "descensus artificii." [7] This pattern of descents was used, not only to explain the underworld, but to unify and justify the many meanings of Genius transmitted from the classical period. We shall now examine these four descents separately, relating them to the most popular medieval definitions of Genius, and to the cosmological concepts outlined in Chapter Two.

THE NATURAL DESCENT

Bernardus based his notion of the four descents upon Guillaume de Conches' glosses on *De Consolatione Philosophiae* of Boethius. Guillaume (fl. 1080–1145), after equating the infernal regions with the inferior part of the world, determines that the "natural descent" occurs "namely when the soul of someone is joined with the body" ("naturalis scilicet cum anima alicuius corpori coniungitur").[8] He qualifies his statement by adding that this union is natural, not for the soul, but for the body: "natural . . . not because it [the soul] descends from the celestial regions where it existed previously but because there are reasons why it is joined to the body" ("naturalis . . . non quod de celestibus ubi ante esset descendat sed quia sunt causa [*sic*] quare corpori coniungatur"). The divine soul, whose most comfortable residence is the heavenly region, finds its lodging in the body to be unnatural; but the body has neither life nor natural vitality without the soul, and dies at the moment the soul departs. The reason such a union is unnatural for the soul is explained by Guillaume: "the union of the soul with the body is called a descent of the soul, because it is evident that when it has been subjected to the passions of the body, it has descended from its proper dignity" (p. 42). The human body is an underworld into which the soul is compelled to descend.

Although Bernardus relies heavily upon this description of the natural descent, he stresses in contrast the soul's fall into the sublunary underworld, rather than the inferior human body, at the time of birth—"the natural descent is the birth of man: for from birth the soul naturally begins to exist in this fallen region [*in hac caduca regione*] and thus to descend into the inferior and thus to recede from its divinity and gradually to decline into vice and to assent to the pleasures of the flesh, but this is common to all" (p. 30). Birth initiates the fall of the soul from the heavens through the spheres and into the mutable underworld of life on earth; this process has been briefly discussed in Chapter Two.

The two definitions of the underworld presented in the discussions of the *naturalis descensus* serve to organize two major classical concepts of Genius. Implicit perhaps within Bernardus' description of the fall of the soul into the mutable underworld at birth is the Augustinian analysis of generation: Genius is "the god . . . who has command and control of everything that is begotten" (" 'Deus,' inquit, 'qui praepositus est ac vim habet omnium rerum gignendarum' ").[9] The universal Genius or Jupiter Progenitor was responsible for bringing to birth all of creation. This particular quotation was transmitted through the Middle Ages by Isidore (sixth century), Paulus (eighth century), and Rabanus Maurus (ninth century).[10] The same definition, slightly garbled, reappears in the words of Martianus Capella, Remigius' commentary on Martianus, and Mythographus Tertius.[11] Although Bernardus does not mention the cosmic Genius of generation in his commentary on the *Aeneid,* he elucidates its association with the natal descent of the soul in *De Mundi Universitate,* a work which will be investigated in depth in the following chapter. Human birth involves the descent of the soul from a superior region (the Milky Way according to Macrobius) through the various planetary spheres, and into an inferior one characterized by change and corruption—the region below the moon and the human body. The agent or catalyst of the natural descent, the god of Nature, is Genius. Other writers recognized the figure's affiliation with Nature, if not with the natural descent: he is called a natural god or god of nature by Servius ("genium autem dicebant antiqui naturalem deum uniuscuiusque loci uel rei aut hominis"), Remigius and Mythographus Tertius ("deus naturalis"), and later in the twelfth century, Alanus de Insulis ("Genius enim natura vel Deus nature dicitur").[12]

Genius is explicitly mentioned in other places in the commentaries of Guillaume and Bernardus as a god of *human* nature. Although his appearance is linked with the natural descent, he functions, not as a cause, but as an effect, of man's fall into the underworld; he is not a cosmic force of generation but the concupiscent soul of the microcosm, whose appetites and desires typify the union of the soul with the body, the second *infernum.* Guillaume introduces Genius to amplify his tropological interpretation of the Orpheus and Euridice myth related by Philosophy in Boethius' *De Consolatione.* Euridice, wife of Orpheus (wisdom or eloquence), represents natural concupiscence or *genius:* "His wife [*coniunx*] is Euridice, that is, natural concupiscence [*naturalis concupiscentia*] which is joined [*coniuncta est*] to each one of us: for no one, not even a child one day old, can exist in this life without it. From which again the poets imagined that there was a certain god, namely the *genius,* who is born with each one of us and dies. Whence Horace: *deus albus et ater mortalis in unum-quodque caput.* Genius is natural concupiscence.'' [13] The marriage of Orpheus and Euridice represents the union of the soul (with its wisdom derived from heavenly origins) and the body (with its inherent passions and desires).[14] In effect, the two figures illuminate the consequences of the natural descent—the imprisonment of the soul in the inferior body at birth.

Bernardus, like Guillaume, casts Euridice in the role of natural con-cupiscence, the *genius* common to all men. Glossing Guillaume's first line, he emphasizes the natural marriage of wife (Euridice, natural con-cupiscence) to husband (Orpheus, wisdom): "Huic Euridice i.e. naturalis concupiscentia coniunx est i.e. naturaliter coniuncta" ("to him Euridice, that is, natural concupiscence, is a wife, that is, naturally joined or mar-ried," p. 54). Having discussed the four descents in the Preface to Book Six, he turns to Aeneas' specific descent into the underworld, and an allusion to Orpheus in the *Aeneid* triggers this digression on the Orpheus-Euridice myth. Again, the natural descent is not explicitly mentioned here, but his comments on natural concupiscence amplify the conse-quences of the descent of the soul into the fleshly underworld. "For no one indeed exists without his natural concupiscence. Whence in poems it is read that some sort of Genius, god of human nature, exists who is born with each man and dies, from which Horace: *naturae deus humanae mortalis in unum-/quodque caput.* We understand natural concupiscence to be that which is dominant in human nature and is called Euridice" (p. 54). Euridice as a personification of natural concupiscence reappears as late as the fourteenth-century *Genealogie Deorum Gentilium* of Boccac-cio, illustrating the currency of this interpretation, but she is not explicitly identified again with *genius.*[15]

Both Guillaume and Bernardus rely on Horace's definition of Genius (*Epistle* 2.2.187–89) as god of human nature or a human god, born with each man and living until his death. These very popular lines were re-peated in slightly changed form by Apuleius (second century), Cen-sorinus (third century), Servius (fourth century), Martianus Capella (fifth century), Remigius and Joannes Scotus (ninth century), and finally, Guillaume and Bernardus (twelfth century).[16] All these writers have chosen to ignore the astrological function of the Genius, he who "temperat astrum"; among these writers, only Guillaume and Bernardus have explicitly perceived *genius* as "natural concupiscence."

But some ambivalence is expressed in the description of Euridice as *genius*. Although signifying the inherent flaw of life in the sublunary region, "Euridice" (natural concupiscence) is etymologized by Guillaume as *boni iudicatio*, judgment for good, and by Bernardus as *boni appetitus*, appetite for good. Guillaume existentially declares that concupiscence desires whatever it considers good, whether it is actually good in fact ("Sed hec naturalis concupiscentia merito dicitur Euridice, id est boni iudicatio, quia quod quisque iudicat bonum, sive ita sit sive non, concupiscit," p. 46). Bernardus, in contrast, explains that concupiscence has been given for desiring good, as if it were naturally and innately impelled toward it: "concupiscenti[a] natural[is] . . . e[s]t . . . Euridice i.e. boni appetitus dicitur: data est enim ad appetendum bonum," (p. 54). The differences in approach depend upon the definition of "good": Guillaume's concupiscence may act independently of reason, desiring a good Guillaume later equates with pleasure; Bernardus' "appetite" is always driven toward good, although he will later depict this good in two ways—as temporal good and virtue. The differences [17] can also be explained by a consideration of two varying but likely sources for these interpretations of *genius*.

Bernardus may have been familiar with Apuleius' discussion of *genius* in the gloss on *Aeneid* 9.184–85, in which Nisus asks Euryalus whether his desire for war is prompted by the gods or is itself a god within him. According to Apuleius, desire springs from a human soul or *daemon* (*genius*) within man: a "good desire of the soul" ("bona cupido animi") is either a good *daemon* (the mind perfectly virtuous) or the *genius* (a god or soul-within-the body).[18] This *genius*, "begotten in some manner with man," signifies, like Euridice, the conjunction of body and soul in that it survives only while man lives. For Bernardus, then, who has cited only portions of the Horatian definition of Genius ("the god of human nature mortal for each person," "naturae deus humanae mortalis in unum-/quodque caput"), the appetite for good or the concupiscent part of

(god of Nature), involved in the *naturalis descensus* of the soul, regenerates nature and perpetuates the species by introducing souls into the mutable underworld. As desire or concupiscence typifying human nature, he represents the consequence of the natural descent of the soul into the corporeal underworld. He acts therefore both as a cosmic generator concerned with reproduction of the species and as a microcosmic "generator" directing individual appetite or concupiscence. Bernardus and Guillaume set no precedent by implicitly uniting the two concepts: Martianus in *De Nuptiis* declares that a Genius (whom they call ruler) presides over all generation, but that he is also a single guardian for all mortals ("generalis omnium praesul et specialis singulis mortalibus Genius ammouetur, quem etiam Praestitem, quod praesit gerundis omnibus, uocauerunt," 2.152). Remigius' commentary on Martianus carefully distinguishes the two types by rearranging the word order: "GENIUS SINGULIS MORTALIBUS et GENERALIS OMNIUM PRAESUL ET SPECIALIS," "a single *genius* for all mortals and a particular ruler for all species." [20] The former, one of the minor gods, resides in the region between the sun and the moon, Remigius explains, and the latter, one of the superior gods, the realm above the sun (2.65.7). In these passages, as well as in the twelfth-century natural descent, Genius becomes a generic ruler, indeed a god of Nature who enforces natural descents at birth in order to perpetuate the species, and also an individual deity or god ("bona cupido animi") who is born with man and lives until his death.

The concept of the natural descent unifies several, but not all, of the meanings of Genius. In questioning the motivation behind the good and evil actions of man during his life in this underworld, Guillaume de Conches and Bernardus Silvestris would find a means of linking other meanings with the symbolic underworld—a means afforded by their allegorization of the Orpheus and Euridice myth.

THE VICIOUS AND VIRTUOUS DESCENTS

Each man is faced with a choice during his life: whether to succumb to fleshly temptations and thereby fall viciously, or whether to prevent such a descent by arming himself with a knowledge of *temporalia*. Both neces-

the soul granted to each man at birth is "bona cupido animi," a lin. human capacity for choosing the good.

Guillaume, who suggests that concupiscence desires whatever regards as good, whether actually so or not, may have misread the defi tion of Genius that appeared in Servius' discussion of those same line from the *Aeneid* (9.184–85); the passage was later repeated almost verba tim by Mythographus Tertius.[19] Servius altered the Virgilian lines to un derscore a point: Nisus now asks whether desires are inspired by the gods, or whether man makes a god of his desire. Arguing that no god would encourage evil, and that therefore the desire for evil must be attributed to man himself, Servius accordingly ascribes good acts to the counsel of the Genius allotted to man at birth. The human mind, not the Genius, is responsible for evil longings, which may indeed become gods for man. Guillaume's Euridice, "judgment for good," represents a synthesis of Servius' Genius who advocates the good ("for good"), and the human mind ("judgment") which transforms desire into a god ("desires whatever it considers good, whether so or not"). Guillaume's elliptical quotation of the Horatian definition underscores his interpretation of *genius* as fickle, uncertain, unbalanced: *genius* is a "god white or black, mortal for each person" ("deus albus et ater mortalis in unumquodque caput," from Horace's "naturae *deus* humanae, *mortalis in unum / quodque caput,* voltu mutabilis, *albus et ater,*" *Epistle* 2.2.188–89).

Bernardus' treatment of *genius* attempts to reconcile the classical and Apuleian definitions with his medieval understanding of human nature; Guillaume distorts the classical and Servian applications in order to render a more strongly conventional medieval view of *concupiscentia.* The two authors' interpretations are not entirely discordant: if we assume man is born with a propensity for good (stemming from the nature and origin of the soul) and for evil (stemming from the nature and origin of the body), his judgment or appetite for good (Euridice or *genius*), neither good nor evil itself, may be drawn toward real good or deceptive good (i.e., pleasure, temporal good). Guillaume is merely more realistic than Bernardus.

The different definitions of *genius* synthesized by the two writers' description of the natural descent and the figure of Euridice suggest a relationship between the world and man. Genius as macrocosmic agent

sitate delving into the underworld, but the latter choice is conscious and controlled. Guillaume de Conches declares that a vicious descent occurs when someone "directs his mind to temporal things" ("Per alia [vicia] fit dum aliquis in temporalibus totam intentionem ponit," p. 42). Such a descent is justified when a wise man desires to understand temporal things so that, seeing how little good exists in them, he will extricate his concupiscence from love of them ("Est alius descensus non vitiosus cum scilicet aliquis sapiens ad cognitionem temporalium descendit ut, cum parum boni in eis vidit, ab eorum amore concupiscentiam extrahat," p. 42). It is, in fact, virtuous to descend into the underworld in such a manner, and especially in order to learn about the nature of vice.

Bernardus, who duplicates many of Guillaume's comments, suggests in his preface to the commentary on the sixth book of the *Aeneid* that the wise man descends through a consideration of worldly things, not so that he will direct his mind toward them ("non ut in eis intentionem ponat"), but instead for two different reasons: so that, when their fragility has been learned, having cast them away he may turn entirely to invisible things ("ut eorum cognita fragilitate eis abiectis ad invisibilia penitus se convertat"), and secondly, so that he may perceive the Creator more clearly through an understanding of his creatures ("et creaturarum cognitione creatorem evidentius agnoscat," p. 30). Orpheus and Hercules exemplify wise men who have descended virtuously into the underworld. The former's foolish wife, Euridice, became corrupted by worldly delights, and now serves as an example of the vicious descent. Bernardus regards this third (vicious) descent as a common one ("qui vulgaris est"), "by which one succumbs to temporal things so that his mind is totally occupied with them, his mind is totally reserved for them, and his soul cannot be removed from them any longer" ("quo ad temporalia devenit⟨ur⟩ itaque intentio tota in eis ponitur eisque tota mente servitur nec ab eis animus amplius dimovetur," p. 30).

Bernardus' use of Orpheus and Euridice as examples of each descent developed from two lines of the *Aeneid* (6.119–20), Guillaume's commentary on the myth as it appears in Boethius' *De Consolatione Philosophiae,* and perhaps certain definitions of *genius*. The seminal lines from the *Aeneid,* which allude to the poet Orpheus' attempts to retrieve his wife's shade from the underworld, provide the opportunity for moralization: "potuit Manis accersere coniugis Orpheus / Threicia fretus cithara fidibusque canoris" ("Orpheus availed to summon his wife's shade, strong in his Thracian lyre and tuneful strings").[21] The *manes*, shade of Euridice, was rescued from Hell by Orpheus, but then lost again when he glanced back to see if she followed. The moral, as presented by Philosophy in *De Consolatione*, claims that man loses all the excellence he has acquired when he looks back at the underworld, i.e., lower things ("dum uidet inferos").[22] Transforming this moral into allegory, Guillaume de Conches shifts the focus from Orpheus to Euridice in his gloss on *De Consolatione:* she dies and descends as a *manes* into the underworld, "id est ad terrenam delectationem" (p. 46). Her spiritual death (or descent into the underworld of earthly pleasures) occurs when she flees a union with Aristeus, who represents Virtue (from *ares*, excellence, according to Guillaume): "But Euridice flees Aristeus, because natural concupiscence objects to virtue when desiring its own pleasure which virtue opposes" ("Sed Euridice Aristeum fugit, quia naturalis concupiscentia contradicit virtuti quia appetit voluptatem propriam cui virtus contradicit," p. 46). Her husband, mourning her death because he disapproves of the control of his concupiscence by *temporalia*, descends into the underworld to reclaim his wife (i.e., to rescue his desire from earthly pleasures by understanding their worthlessness). However, he fails because he returns to the things he has forgotten and looks back at the underworld of pleasure. Bernardus incorporates, but also elaborates upon, Guillaume's interpretation when he comments on the original lines from the *Aeneid*. He adds a snake (temporal good) which bites Euridice on the heel (that part of the body closest to earth, and also farthest from the head) when she runs from Aristeus. The snake's venom, the pleasure of temporal good, poisons her. The opposition between Aristeus ("virtus divina") and the venom of the snake ("boni temporalis delectatio") is more clearly presented in Bernardus' account. Euridice's fall constitutes a vicious descent, and Orpheus' (although it fails), a virtuous descent.

The description of Euridice as a shade who enters the underworld of the dead is based upon the old classical belief in *manes:* according to Apuleius and Martianus Capella, the *genius* or *daemon* of the living man was transformed into a *manes* (*lemur* in Apuleius) after death. But Bernardus and Guillaume also use the term more figuratively. Euridice or *genius* becomes a *manes* after a spiritual death, that is, when she departs from true life or celestial good: "*Manes coniugis,*" i.e., Bernardus explains, "mortuam concupiscentiam quae tunc moritur quando a vera vita i.e. celesti bono elongatur," p. 55). The metamorphosis of *genius* into a *manes* as a result of faulty judgment in making a decision is not wholly original with the two twelfth-century writers. Servius, explicating the Virgilian line, "quisque suos patimur Manes" ("we each suffer our own *manes*," 6.743), in his fourth-century commentary on the *Aeneid*, implies that the judgment of an individual after death is predetermined by his own judgments—of good and evil—during his life. That is, evil actions, "spiritual death," during life will assure his condemnation to an even worse "life" after death (". . . post mortem . . . condemnamur in deteriorem [vitam]"). In effect, *genius*, delegated to man with life, is identical to the *manes*, delegated to man at death:

> "We each suffer our own *manes*": the punishments which accompany the *manes*, just as if someone should say, "we suffer a judgment [trial]," and would mean those things which are contained in a legal investigation [or trial]. And there is also another interpretation more true. For when we are born, we are allotted two *genii*: one exists which exhorts us to good, the other which depraves us to evil. With these standing by [as at a trial] after death, we are either liberated [*adserimus*] into a better life, or condemned to a worse: through them we are either entitled to freedom from or a return to the body. Therefore "*manes*" means *genii*, which we are allotted with life.

The choices made by Euridice, or *genius*, determine her life as a *manes*: her flight from Aristeus, or Virtue, and her "delight in temporal good," or the snake, ensure an eternity in Hell. That Bernardus and Guillaume were familiar with the Servian gloss on that line and with his linking of *genii* and *manes* may be inferred from the currency of Servius' passage: it was repeated in part by Remigius in his commentary on Martianus [23] and transcribed verbatim by Mythographus Tertius, who appropriately placed this passage in the section on Pluto and the Underworld.[24]

The two choices confronting Euridice or natural concupiscence—Aristeus (Virtue) and the serpent (Vice)—exemplify those of the Servian man, counseled or tempted by his two *genii* or *manes*. The snake, formerly a totem of the begetting *genius* in the early classical period, functions appropriately as temporal good, which poisons with its pleasures. Bernardus may have been familiar with several classical definitions of *genius* having sensuous or sensual connotations: Servius' gloss on *genialibus*, which was passed to Isidore, Paulus Diaconus, and Rabanus

Maurus, mentions that the marriage bed or genial couch (*genialis lectus*) was used for the purpose of begetting ("dicti a generandis liberis").[25] Secondly, Servius employed the expression *indulgere genio* in his definition of the genial festival that occurred during the winter, associating such indulgence with *voluptas*, pleasure, gratification of desire; this passage was later repeated by Mythographus Tertius.[26] Euridice's introduction to the pleasure of temporal good by the phallic surrogate similarly exemplifies self-indulgence, indulgence of the concupiscence or *genius*. This particular moralization, in addition, may have been influenced by the sequence of definitions of *genius* perceptively organized by the compiler, Mythographus Tertius. After transcribing the Servian concept of the good Genius opposed to human *cupiditas*, he then mentions three related ideas: Genius as a natural god of generation, as the capacity for pleasure (*indulgere genio*), and as a snake. The snake, originally guardian of a place (*genius loci*) or the spirit of the father, is supposedly created from the "marrow" of the spine (i.e., spinal cord), possibly a cryptic reference to the physiological changes in the male during intercourse.[27] The association of *genius* with pleasure, generation, the father, and the snake provides a brilliant synthesis of classical concepts which may have guided Bernardus in his moralization of Euridice's behavior. Indeed, the vicious descent into the underworld occasioned by Euridice's seduction unifies several associated concepts of the *genius*—the symbolic phallic serpent; life, energy, appetite (from *indulgere genio*); and the urgings of the evil Servian *manes* (*genius*).

The virtuous descent of Orpheus into the underworld, based upon Aeneas' *descensus ad inferos*, represents the soul's introduction to *mundana* for the purpose of enhancing wisdom and better understanding God through familiarity with his creation. Orpheus enters the infernal regions so that he can recognize the nature of temporal good and remove his wife (appetites) from it. The specific means for attaining this end, according to Bernardus, is acquaintance with the *trivium* and the *quadrivium*, which enable man to study philosophy and theology, and eventually to ascend to God.[28]

Orpheus or Oreaphone, son of Calliope (best voice, "optima vox") and Apollo (wisdom), personifies both eloquence and wisdom: "Orpheus ponitur pro quolibet sapiente et eloquente." [29] He also represents the mind, *nous*, who is married to Euridice, passion or desire; reason must control passion by arming itself with eloquence and wisdom.[30] Accordingly, he descends into the underworld for this virtuous purpose, although he eventually fails. This wise man resembles Hercules, Bernardus declares (p. 30), who performed a similar descent. Such superhuman men were regarded as *heroes* or *semidei* (demi-gods) in the late classical period; they occupied the air between the earth and moon, the region described as the underworld.[31] But Orpheus as the soul, mind, *nous* also suggests the Greek concept of the *daemon*, highest part of the soul— Apuleius' *animus*, the rational soul identified as *genius* by Augustine and Ammianus Marcellinus.

Mythographus Tertius analyzes the two parts of the soul, concluding that the superior soul springs from the heavens and is incorruptible; the inferior soul is concupiscent (6.16). The former is called *rationalitas, spiritus, domina, mens, animus;* the latter, which succumbs to the desires of the body ("quae voluptatibus corporis consentit"), is called *sensualitas, animalitas, famula, mens.* Although the superior soul should rule the inferior, if it is negligent, *sensualitas* seduces *rationalitas.* Mythographus Tertius concludes, "Est etiam in hac figura Adam et Eva." The seduction of Eve by the serpent resembles the seduction of Euridice by the serpent of temporal good: Orpheus is a type of Adam; Euridice, of Eve. No *genius* appears in the Adam and Eve myth, but a discussion of the Servian good and evil *genii* follows this analysis of the two parts of the soul, or Adam and Eve. Glossing "quisque suos patimur Manes" (*Aeneid* 6.743), he includes Servius' comments on the *manes*, synonymous with the *genii* who are born with each man, exhorting him either to good or to evil, determining whether man will receive a better life after death (that is, he inserts, ascent to the supernal regions) or a worse life (6.18). In the Mythographer's terms, *rationalitas* (Adam) would be equated with the good *genius* (Orpheus as wisdom, *nous*), and *sensualitas* (Eve) with the evil *genius* (Euridice as concupiscence, passion).

Several late classical concepts of *genius* have been tightly unified and organized by this moralization. One concept conspicuously absent involves the *daemon*, not as a *manes* (soul-of-the-dead) or as a rational soul, but as a cosmic intermediary. The fourth and artificial descent entails the use of such an intermediary.

THE ARTIFICIAL DESCENT

Guillaume divides the *descensus vitii* into two parts, one vicious, one artificial: the latter, equally pejorative, occurs "per magicam artem." The example provided by Guillaume (and also Bernardus) concerns Aeneas, who wished to consult the demons about the future, and who therefore descended into the underworld through "magic art" (p. 42). Bernardus, unlike Guillaume, separates the artificial from the vicious descent, but affirms that the *nigromanticus* (necromancer) by means of his special art ("artificio nigromantico") petitions for conversation with the demons through some "execrable" sacrifice in order to consult them about the future (p. 30). The search for forbidden knowledge through demonic intercourse constituted a descent into the underworld as reprehensible as that of Euridice.

The Lactantian *daemon,* product of the fallen angel and woman, inhabitant of the underworld (aerial region between the moon and earth), possessed a limited knowledge of the future (it did not know God's plan); its name was derived from the Greek words for "knowing" or "sharing." Associated with the art of divination since the classical period, it existed as an intermediary between man and the underworld during the Middle Ages, consulted by the magician and the astrologer, and sending malefic messages to men through dreams.

The secrets of the future were obtained from the demon, according to Lactantius, through the black arts of augury, divination, necromancy, the casting of lots, oracular pronouncements, and astrology (the latter with which the Roman *genius* was uniquely linked). Demonic intervention is instrumental in three of the five kinds of magic classified by the twelfth-century Mythographus Tertius—divination (in particular, necromancy), sorcery (*maleficia*), and the creation of fantasies and illusions (*praestigia*).[32] The *genius,* cited in a line from Juvenal, is included in the discussion of *horoscopica,* casting of horoscopes, one of the branches of *matematica* (astrology), which he regards as *vanitas.*[33] John of Salisbury (d. 1180) also discusses magic in the *Policraticus,* condemning *praestigia,* the magic arts, and astrology because they are artificial and malefic, and depend upon a familiarity between demons and men.[34] Sacrifices offered to demons by the necromancer in order to obtain contact with the dead are similarly deplored (1.12, p.51). The *genius* again appears in two lines of Persius' *Saturae* used in a discussion of *horoscopica*.[35]

The practice of magic involves an art which is deceptive and unnatural. Mythographus Tertius describes *praestigia,* for example, as incredible mutations of things seen through daemonic art (''arte daemonica''), and intended to deceive the human senses through ''phantastica illusione'' (11.12, p. 235). Such magical artifice resembles the deceptive and troubling dreams maliciously directed by demonic spirits to men during sleep, or dreams which involve unnatural shapes or figures similar to the *praestigia* (illusions) created by the magician.

The demon's association with dreams, derived from various classical sources (Virgil, Apuleius, Ammianus Marcellinus, Augustine, Lactantius), was elucidated by Macrobius in his commentary on the *Somnium Scipionis* and rephrased by John of Salisbury in the *Policraticus*.[36] After classifying the five kinds of dreams, Macrobius dismisses the nightmare (*insomnium*) and apparition (*visum* in Latin, *phantasma* in Greek) because they have no prophetic significance. Both are unnatural and false. The nightmare, caused by mental or physical stress or anxiety about the future, is a deceptive dream, likened to that occurring during the disquietude of love, and sent to men by *manes:* he cites Virgil (*Aeneid* 6.897) to proclaim, '' 'sed falsa ad caelum mittunt insomnia manes' '' (1.3.6). The shades of the underworld, types of *daemon,* disseminate false dreams in order to trouble men. The apparition (*phantasma* or *visum*), which appears between waking and sleeping, is accompanied by ''vagantes formas'' (wandering shapes) which may be of unusual size or form (1.3.7). An example is the *epialtes* or incubus which presses like a weight upon a person.[37] Macrobius stresses that such forms are unnatural, ''a natura . . . discrepantes,'' and therefore, we infer, deceptive.

The three prophetic and significant dreams enable man to learn about the future, but they are truthful dreams, even if veiled by *figurae* and *aenigmata*. Although none of the three involves a demonic intermediary, the *oraculum* is presented by a divine intermediary—a venerable person, an angel, or God—and the *somnium* or allegorical dream conceals its secrets under *involucrum,* a term usually associated with twelfth-century theories of poetry. The *daemon* was instrumental in instigating dreams in Apuleius' *De Deo Socratis;* Macrobius Platonizes his theory, and John of Salisbury Christianizes it. Secondly, the demon's role in magic art (the artificial descent into the underworld) may have influenced the twelfth-century Platonic view of poetry as a type of artifice concealing truth—a positive *descensus artificii* analogous to the natural descent.

The loftiest type of dream, according to John of Salisbury, is the *oraculum,* in which a wise man, angel, or God informs the individual about some truth or an imminent event (2.15, p. 92). But, he cautions, there is only one real God: Aeneas' oracle was not a true one, because his gods (Apollo, Jupiter, et al.) were actually demons, and hence Rome, the city he founded according to their promise, became demonic—treacherous, avaricious, proud.[38] The *oraculum,* then, disguises the classical notion of the message sent from the gods to man via the beneficent cosmic *daemon.* It anticipates the Christian twelfth-century concept of the theophany, "manifestation of God," which Alanus will use implicitly in the *De Planctu Naturae* and define explicitly in other works. The second most important dream is the *visio,* in which an event portrayed (without the intervening agency of a sage or God) will later happen (2.15, p. 91). This, too, constitutes a reworking of the classical belief in cosmic intermediaries directing warnings about the future to men.

But the third prophetic dream, the *somnium* or enigmatic type, which manifests *imagines* (images or ideas) under "the coverings of things" (*involucra,* "per quaedam inuolucra rerum gerit imagines," 2.15, p. 89), clearly involves a form of artifice, although not necessarily magic art. John explains the role of the soul, analogous to the more supernal intermediaries—sage, angel, God—of the *oraculum,* in understanding the ideas conveyed by the *somnium.* During sleep, the *animales virtutes* (*animae* or senses) remain quiescent, while the soul is released from exercise so that it may contemplate truth "through figures and *enigmata*" (2.14, pp. 87–88). Interpreting the meaning or *significatio* of dreams by the "unveiling" (*revelatio*) of their figures and allegories is difficult: their meaning, more manifold or various than that of openly-direct words, may be compared to that of the works of nature, whose complexity of import surpasses that of the works of the author (*artifex*) imitating nature ("Est itaque tam ad interpretationem somniorum quam ad reuelationem enigmatum et figurarum sollerter attendenda rerum significatio, quae tanto multiplicior est quam uocum, quanto ab operibus naturae opera uincuntur artificis imitantis naturam," 2.16, p. 94). Here John distinguishes between the truths concealed by the figures and *involucra* of dreams and of the natural world, and those more plainly and openly revealed in exposition and writings. This Neo-Platonic view of Nature is derived from Macrobius: she clothes herself in *operimentum* (a covering) because she does not wish to display herself (i.e., her truths) "apertam nudam" to the senses of vulgar men; accordingly, her secrets must be disguised *per fabulosa* (through the fabulous) by prudent writers.[39] The truth of God is concealed within Nature, his creation, as the truths of Nature are disguised in dreams—and in fabulous narratives, according to Macrobius—"sub pio figmentorum velamine," under the modest veil of allegory [40] (although John's amplification of Macrobius demonstrates the greater complexity of meaning in Nature and dreams). The secrets veiled by the fictional, Macrobius continues, include those of sacred rites, the stories of Hesiod and Orpheus, the ancestry and deeds of gods, the mystic conceptions of the Pythagoreans (1.2.11), the soul, and the powers of air and aether (1.2.13). The resemblance between the sacred truths of such narrative and the lofty knowledge and venerable intermediaries (wise man, soul, angel, God) of prophetic dreams in general is striking.

The incarceration of truth in fiction (the artifice of personification, myth, allegory, various kinds of *integumentum* or *involucrum*) parallels the imprisonment of the soul in the *infernum:* this "artificial descent" of truth simulates the natural descent of the soul at birth. The philosopher discourses on the nature of human life, Bernardus admits in the *accessus* to his commentary on the *Aeneid,* but he must describe the temporal sojourn of the human spirit in the human body *sub integumento* ("Scribit enim in quantum est philosophus humanae vitae naturam. Modus vero agendi talis est: sub integumento describit quid agat vel quid patiatur humanus spiritus in humano corpore temporaliter positus," p. 3). To communicate the secrets of *human* nature, the writer becomes a kind of *daemonic* messenger or wise intermediary for the reader, skillfully manufacturing integuments—the artificial—as a poet ("artificialem poeta") and correctly perceiving the truth—the natural—as a philosopher ("naturalem philosophus"). The final product, like the *somnium* of John of Salisbury, unites both the natural and the artificial, as the soul is joined to the body at birth: "*Integumentum* indeed is a genus of demonstration clothing the perception of truth under fabulous narrative, whence it is also called *involucrum*" (p. 3).

Artifice becomes analogous to the underworld of the body or of earth; this "descent" of truth into dreams or fabulous narrative, however, does not involve demons or magic, despite the early classical concept of the *daemon*'s prophetic dream, the patristic notion of the demonic nightmare, and the medieval association of demons with "magic art." The modern attribution of "genius" to a writer perhaps evolved from these earlier associations. Indeed, the figure Genius in Alanus de Insulis' *De Planctu Naturae* represents an archetypal poet-philosopher; although Genius is not explicitly linked with the artificial descent, poetic theory, or dreams elsewhere in the twelfth century, his role in the moralizations of the Orpheus and Euridice myth discussed previously may have influenced Alanus' depiction.

This myth, used by Guillaume and Bernardus to explain the vicious and virtuous descents into the underworld, was also interpreted by other commentators as a demonstration of the relationship between eloquence or artifice and judgment or knowledge—in effect, a mythological rendering of the artificial descent. This Fulgentian (sixth-century) interpretation of the myth, although basically ignored by Bernardus, resurfaces in Remigius of Auxerre on Martianus (early tenth century), Mythographus Tertius (twelfth century), Boccaccio and Nicholas of Trivet (fourteenth century), and Thomas of Walsingham (fifteenth century).[41] The Fulgentian moralization transcribed by Mythographus Tertius, while less popular during the Middle Ages than the Boethian one he also includes, presents a view of the secrets of music which is analogous to the view of the secrets of Nature and human nature (in relation to fabulous narrative) described by Macrobius and Bernardus. Orpheus represents eloquence or "best voice" (*optima vox*); Euridice is wisdom or profound judgment (*profunda dijudicatio,* 8.20, pp. 211–12). This student of musical skill wishes to marry Euridice because he cannot be a musician without understanding the profound secrets of art ("quia qui musicae studet, nisi secretiorem artis ipsius profunditatem comprehendit, musicus esse non potest"). He wins her eventually through the skillful (*artificiosa*) modulation of his voice.

But Profound Judgment, or the height of knowledge (*scientiae altitudo*), was also loved by the best of men, Aristeus, a type of the philosopher whose relationship with truth we have previously noted in the accounts of Macrobius and Bernardus. She fled (*transmigrat*) to the underworld because of the snake's bite, a kind of rape: he came to "know" her subtle secrets.[42] Profound Judgment, like Nature, does not wish to be exposed: as the secrets of Nature (or even of the *somnium*) must be hidden from base men by clothing them in fictional narrative (and *involucra*), so the subtle secrets of the highest knowledge, we infer, must be similarly dressed (with eloquence, ornamentation, artifice) to protect them from penetration by common men (the snake's bite). Euridice even eluded the philosopher Aristeus, although she had initially succumbed to the music of the poet Orpheus and married him.

A similar interpretation is provided by Remigius: Orpheus excelled in the Thracian region through his music and poetry until he neglected the practice of his art and fell into the *infernum* of "profound study." [43] Euridice (*inventio*), after comparing the corporeal and transitory nature of the human voice (i.e., Orpheus) to the eternal thought of profound art (*profundae artis inventio*, i.e., herself), disappeared, leaving Orpheus saddened because he then retained the "voice" (*vox*) of music, but without *ratione*.

Skill is mutable and ephemeral, like life in the sublunar and corporeal underworlds; *inventio* or theory, knowledge, is eternal, like the human soul. Secrets—of music, art, Nature, the future—are enveloped by artifice in order to "live" (to be accessible to men); when they are not, or when the art is weak, too plain, too revealing, they "die" and return to their sources as *manes*. "Genius," Euridice, lives only as long as she remains happily married to the poet Orpheus: judgment, knowledge, secrets must be conjoined with eloquence, skill, artifice. This allegorization of the myth reveals the relationship between poetry and philosophy—the union of the artificial and the natural orders.

Although Bernardus does not follow Fulgentius in his explication of the Orpheus and Euridice myth, he does comment on the relationship between wisdom (the province of the philosopher) and fables (the province of the poet) in discussing Aeneas' descent into the underworld. First, Aeneas directs his ships to the sacred grove of Trivia (the *trivium*, study of eloquence) and the "golden houses" (*aurea tecta,* the *quadrivium*, study of philosophy, p. 31).[44] Achates ("tristis consuetudo," joyless study) is sent to fetch the Sibyl ("intelligentia"). Aeneas and his companions then journey to the Sibyl's cave, which represents the profundity of philosophy. Bernardus pauses to describe Apollo's temple: it houses the *quadrivium* and philosophy, but its doors are ornamented with the fables of the *auctores*. When he declares, "hae fabulae figurant omnes poetarum fabulas" (p. 37), he implies, through the iconographic description, not only that poets conceal the truths of philosophy within fable, but also perhaps that such truth must be discerned *sub integumento:* one enters the house of wisdom through the portals of fable.

The *descensus artificii,* explicitly a descent into the underworld to learn of the future by means of a demonic intermediary whose help is invoked through magic, implicitly suggests that poetic truth can only be comprehended by examining the shadowy underworld of fable, *integumentum,* allegory, *aenigma.* "Profound secrets"—of the future, Nature, music, philosophy—must not be casually revealed; they demand a buffer between themselves and common men, which is provided respectively by the *somnium,* the *umbrae* of the world, the skillful modulation of voice, the fictitious narrative. Celestial secrets, formerly communicated by cosmic *daemones* or *angeli* to the best of men through dreams, omens, or premonitions, are transmitted in the Middle Ages through *figurae,* personifications, enigmatic signs, mythological figures, the "artificial voice," in effect, to the best of men (wisest philosophers) by other wise men, Nature, angels, or God. The "intermediary," while not a "daemon" per se, may be a fictional analogue, a *daemonic* figure who will communicate a secret or truth, once fully contemplated and understood.

The earliest literary archetype is the second-century Greek *Cebetis Tabula,* which involves a Daemon as the central character and guide, and which masks Neo-Pythagorean secrets through the allegory depicted on a table in Cronos' temple.[45] A later example, the *De Planctu Naturae* of Alanus, includes the figure of Genius, a fabulous narrative, and the organizing framework of the dream vision. Indeed, the components of the dream vision genre characterizing much medieval literature show the influence of the artificial descent and related concepts: for example, the use of the dream as a structural principle; the appearance of personifications, pagan gods (often considered demonic), aerial inhabitants (e.g., the Eagle in Chaucer's *House of Fame*), or a Genius; allusions to celestial secrets forbidden to most men and disguised by fabulous narrative; an emphasis upon madness, misery, division of self, loss of identity (all marks of a possessing demon) in the narrator or central character. In the dream visions of Boethius, Alanus, Guillaume de Lorris, Jean de Meun, Deschamps, Marot, Machaut, the Pearl poet, Chaucer, and Gower, among others, an instructive guide paralleling the demonic intermediary leads the dreaming protagonist, beset with anxieties, into self-knowledge or truth. Such characters descend into an artificial dream world peopled by strange figures, as the reader enters the artificial world of the fabulous narrative, in order to discern truth and wisdom.

In conclusion, the four descents served as a loom upon which were woven the different threads of meaning for the classical Genius, transmitted by various means through the Middle Ages. The natural descent incorporates the Stoic view of Genius as a universal generation god and the astrological concept of *genius* as star or temperament born with each man and influencing his destiny; the latter is transformed into concupiscence by the twelfth-century humanists. The moralizations inherent in the vicious and virtuous descents, which explain the nature of good and evil, unify the Roman good and evil *genii* or *manes* and the Greek *daemon* as rational soul. The artificial descent, explicitly based on patristic associations of demons, dreams, and magic, is implicitly founded upon the Greek notion of the cosmic intermediary or messenger—the *daemon*. Finally, the underworld linking all four descents was originally inhabited by shades—*manes*.

The unification of the various classical definitions of Genius, derived in part from the Orpheus and Euridice myth, also influenced the portrayal of the figure in the twelfth-century *De Mundi Universitate* of Bernardus and the *De Planctu Naturae* of Alanus, the thirteenth-century *Roman de la Rose* of Jean de Meun, and the fourteenth-century *Confessio Amantis* of John Gower. Alanus' Genius, for example, becomes an Orpheus figure in his descent into the underworld of fallen man; Gower's Genius, an Orphic poet whose eloquence masks philosophical truth.

Finally, this moralization of pagan concepts, affected by the medieval belief in the infernal demon (*genius*), offered a way of structuring and unifying several medieval works of literature through the principle of the *descensus ad inferos*. The second book of the *De Mundi* of Bernardus constitutes a fabulous rendition of the descent of nature; the *De Planctu* of Alanus, which delineates man's fall into depravity, also depicts, through its organization and motivation, the artificial descent.

In examining these works of literature, we shall indicate the respective usage of the four descents as a structural principle, their influence upon the presentation of the figure of Genius, and finally, the influence of the many classical definitions discussed previously upon the description and symbolic associations of this figure.

CHAPTER FOUR

The Fertile Universe: Genius and the Natural Descent in the "De Mundi Universitate" of Bernardus Silvestris

The *De Mundi Universitate,* or *Cosmographia,* of Bernardus Silvestris, written between 1145 and 1153,[1] decisively influenced the later literary conceptions of Genius in the *De Planctu Naturae,* Jean de Meun's *Roman de la Rose,* and the *Confessio Amantis.* For the first time in medieval literature, the classical Genius reappears in many of its forms, but organized by a cosmological framework based upon the two principles of plenitude and hierarchy, and allied with Bernardus' concept of the natural descent of the soul from the spheres.

If Bernardus had omitted all references to a Genius in his elaborate *prosimetrum,* it would still provide an elucidation of the natural descent—a description of the origins and nature of archetypal man.[2] It is divided into two books entitled *Megacosmus* and *Microcosmus.* The first book offers an account of the creation of the world—the placing of form upon matter. After Natura complains to Noys (*Nous* or Noûs, intellect of God) of the shapelessness of primordial matter, and begs for the superimposition of form and order upon this chaos, Endelechia, the World Soul, arrives to implement the task. The remainder of the first book describes the hierarchy of the informed world, beginning with the angels, stars and constellations, zodiacal signs, and planets, and ending with mountains, animals, rivers, trees, vegetables, herbs, fish, and birds. The second book, *Microcosmus,* deals with the origin of man, whose creation requires the cooperation of Natura and her sisters, Urania and Physis. The former first ascends to the farthest reaches of the firmament to find Urania, then both descend through the spheres to the garden of Granusion, home of Physis and her daughters, Theory and Practice. After this literal descent of Natura and Urania, which parallels the descent of the soul from the heavens, man is created by Noys, Natura, Urania, and Physis. As a product of heaven and earth, "he will draw his mind (*mens*) from the heavens (*caelum,* firmament), this body from the elements, / So that he may inhabit the earth with his body, the poles (heavens) with his mind." [3] Bernardus then describes man's body from head to ignoble feet, distinguishing all the bodily organs and their functions. Although this body is frail and mortal, the soul is divine and immortal: by "legibus astrorum" (laws of the stars), the limits of man's life are prescribed; its ending entails the casting off of the body and a return of the soul "ad astra" as a god added to the host of supernal powers ("Additus in numero superûm deus," 2.4.25–50). In this second book, Bernardus' purpose is clear: he intends to trace the archetypal process of the natural descent outlined briefly in his commentary on the *Aeneid:* "The natural descent is the nativity of man: by which indeed the soul begins naturally to exist in this fallen region and thus to descend into the underworld and so to recede from its divinity and gradually to decline into vice and to assent to pleasures of the flesh; but this is common to all." [4] The latter half of *De Mundi Universitate* describes the birth of the First Man, Bernardus' fabulous Adam.

Genii appear throughout this second book. Although Bernardus had cited the Horatian definition of Genius as "god of human nature" to support his interpretation of Euridice as natural concupiscence (that appetite for good characteristic of the soul joined to the body) in his commentary on the *Aeneid,* in *De Mundi* he is more interested in Martianus' definition of Genius as "generalis praesul," a god of nature or a universal begetter. The figure primarily assists the descent of the soul into the corporeal underworld; it does not merely represent the consequences of that descent. Unlike the Stoic *universalis Genius* aiding the World Soul, Jupiter Progenitor and Genetrix, the Silvestran Genius is not one but many: the entire universe is animated by *genii,* each of whom rules a single sphere and aids the descent of the soul into flesh. This perception of generation enables Bernardus to organize the different species of classical *genii* into a unified coherent system, predicated upon the principles of plenitude and hierarchy.

Although several scholars have commented upon isolated examples of *genius* in *De Mundi,* no one has considered all of them consecutively and individually, noting their differences (from varying classical traditions), and at the same time attempting to see a relationship among them predicated upon Bernardus' recognition of their similarities.[5] In the course of *Microcosmus,* a *genius* (or an analogue) rules each of the twelve parts of the Calcidian universe.[6] The Genius Pantomorph[7] governs the fixed sphere; the sun is located between celestial *oyarses* and *genii,* presumably the other six planetary rulers; there are *angeli* in the aether, *genii* in the air; the garden of Granusion with its own Genius is situated in the moist lower air; finally, the twin *genii*[8] presiding over the genitals perpetuate the species on earth. All of these *genii* are mutually involved in the genesis, earthly life, and regeneration of mankind. This *schema* is noted by Brian Stock, but it is not explicitly delineated: he declares only that "each of the divisions of the heavens, and presumably of the earth, is governed by its own *angeli, genii,* or *numina,* which mediate all generated things including the ungenerated life-force itself."[9] Also, he uses the term "genius" very loosely to describe even Natura, Noys, Physis, Imarmene, and Urania, as if it stood for an undifferentiated essence or spiritual quality associated with generation.[10] Yet the specific *genii* of *De Mundi* are actually products of very different classical traditions assimilated gracefully by Bernardus: the astrological *genius,* the Stoic universal Genius of generation, the Greek cosmic and *daemonic* intermediary, the various spirits of the underworld, the *genius loci,* and the begetting Genius of marriage, among others. This chapter will examine each of the appearances of *genius,* distinguishing its role and function, and tracing its origin to classical sources.

Bernardus' synthesis of *genii* is based upon the unifying theme of the natural descent. That is, the *genii* of the heavens ruled by Urania (the stars and planets) contribute individual form for the soul descending into the first underworld—the sublunary realm. The Genius of Physis' Granusion (the moist lower air, which man can breathe), representing a vegetative force, aids the descent of the soul into the second underworld—the body. Once this First Man has been created—at the point *De Mundi* ends—he must fulfil his obligation to Natura by perpetuating the species, and ensuring the viability of the natural descent for later generations. The *genii* protecting the reproductive organs of man aid him in this function by initiating the descent of future souls from the spheres at the moment of conception. Man is truly a product of his parents and of the stars.

When the First Man begins his earthly sojourn, his soul successfully incarcerated in the two underworlds of the body and of the earth, he will re-enact the drama of the original descent to the *infernum* by rehearsing other descents (virtuous, vicious, artificial). Bernardus does not employ these descents significantly in *De Mundi;* he only hints obliquely that they will occur subsequent to the archetypal natural descent outlined in *Microcosmus*. This promise is conveyed by the externalized projections of good and evil impulses usually found within man—the aetherial and aerial angels and *genii,* messengers between the stars and planets and man.

Microcosmus mirrors Macrocosmus: his *genii* of reproduction duplicate and initiate the generative tasks of the universal *genii* in their respective spheres; the parts of his soul, directing him to good or evil actions during his life, are influenced by and externalized in the good and evil angels and *genii* of the cosmos. His soul, drawn from and through the heavens, and his body, created from the elements and produced by the sublunary region, resemble the soul of the cosmos (Urania, Natura, Physis, and the *genii* and *oyarses* animating the spheres) and its body (the stars, planets, earth). The mythologization of the natural descent in *De Mundi* admirably synthesizes the various classical concepts of Genius while presenting a view of the cosmos unusual for the Middle Ages.

THE GENIUS OF THE STARS

The descent of the soul begins at the sphere of the fixed stars, the Aplanon [11] where Natura is introduced to Urania by its ruler, the Genius Pantomorph. Inspired by a similar figure with an astrological function in the Latin *Asclepius,* this Genius is a thinly disguised personification of the classical *genius* that controlled the star and temperament of the individual. The metaphoric and symbolic description of this fixer of forms, however, expands his celestial importance: like the Stoic cosmic Genius, he becomes an instrument of universal Generative Reason, or Jupiter

Progenitor and Genetrix, whose functions Bernardus allegorizes in the activities of Noys and her three daughters, Natura, Urania, and Physis.

Pantomorph or "All-Forms" is described as a god, an aged figure, an "Oyarses," and a Genius: "Therefore in this all-forming region a personage appears, a god of venerable aspect and with the appearance of decrepit old age. Indeed the Oyarses there was that Genius engaged in the art and office of painting and forming" ("Hoc igitur in loco pantomorpho persona deus venerabili et decrepitae sub imagine senectutis occurrit. Illic Oyarses quidem erat et genius in artem et officium pictoris et figurantis addictus," 2.3.89–93). The Oyarses ruling this *circulus* (sphere) is called Pantomorphos or Omniformis because he ascribes all forms to all things ("formas rebus omnes omnibus," 2.3.97–100). Both "Oyarses" and "Pantomorphos" are names derived from the Latin *Asclepius*.[12] "Ousiarchs" (Bernardus' Oyarses), invisible gods or rulers of material substance, govern the three parts of the aether: Zeus controls the outermost sphere, Pantomorphos the sphere of the thirty-six fixed stars or Decani of the horoscope, and Heimarmene (Imarmene for Bernardus) the seven planetary spheres.[13] The thirty-six Decani separate the outermost limits of the universe from the circle of the zodiac.[14] A different Decanus appears on the eastern horizon every forty minutes, at which time it becomes Horoscopus. Originally, the Horoscopus was identified with the star rising at a particular hour and governing all events occurring during that time, including births; astrologically, it indicated the point of the zodiacal circle intersecting the eastern horizon at the moment of a child's birth.[15] Thus, in the Latin *Asclepius,* Trismegistus informs Asclepius that all living beings bear the likeness of kind (*genus*) and sameness of form, but each man's appearance differs from another's, for "it is impossible that any single form should come into being which is exactly like a second, if they originate at different points of time, and at places differently situated" ("inpossibile est formam unamquamque alteri simillimam nasci horarum et climatum distantibus punctis," 3.35, Scott's trans.). The reason this is impossible, he continues, is that the revolution of the celestial circle (*circulus*) ruled by Pantomorphos (Omniformis) forces the forms to change every moment during each hour. Therefore the type (*species*) remains unchanged, but produces copies (*imagines*) of itself successively, which vary as much as the moments in any revolution (*conversio*) of the heavenly sphere (*mundus*).

Bernardus, familiar with these ideas from the *Asclepius,* draws upon this description of Pantomorph, both implicitly and explicitly, in his own work: after portraying the figure's task as one of "painting and figuring," he explains that the external appearance *(facies)* of things in the lower world is copied *(sequitur)* from the *caelum* according to the image or copy *(imago)* produced (figured, *figuratur*) by the revolution *(conversio)* of the heavenly sphere. He qualifies his statement by citing that clarifying line from the *Asclepius:* "inpossibile est formam unam quamque alteri simillimam nasci horarum et climatum distantibus punctis" (2.3.95–97). The verbatim transcription underscores Bernardus' stress on the astrological theory of the *Asclepius:* the forms differ because the Decanus or star which acts as Horoscopus changes continually. Pantomorph, god of the Decani, affixes the appropriate form determined by the ascendant Decanus upon each individual born.

Bernardus' interest in astrology, tempered by Neo-Platonism, is evident in his other works, in his use of sources, and elsewhere in *De Mundi.* The *Experimentarius,* translated from Arabic, examines a complicated geomantical system involving sets of tables which refer to astrological constellations; the *Mathematicus* is a narrative poem whose denouement is contingent upon an astrological prediction.[16] In addition, the sources for *De Mundi* include not only the *Asclepius,* but also the Neo-Platonic commentaries, with astrological and Neo-Pythagorean biases, of Calcidius and Macrobius, and the very important *Matheseos* of Firmicus Maternus and *De Eodem et Diverso* of Adelard of Bath.[17] Finally, in *De Mundi* itself, astrological notions appear in conjunction with the Neo-Platonic descent: for example, souls hover tearfully at the portal of Cancer immediately below the Aplanon (sphere of the fixed stars) in preparation for the descent into the lower world, "from splendor into shadows," "from *caelum* into the underworld," "from eternity into the prison of the body" (2.3.61–69).[18] The Neo-Platonic concept of the natural descent is easily linked with the Hermetic and astrological theory of the fixing of form upon matter by the ruler of the *circulus*—Pantomorph the Genius.

Although Pantomorph is not depicted as a Genius in the *Asclepius,* Bernardus' equation of the two may have been influenced by the earlier astrological associations of the *genius.* He had access to Horace's definition of the figure as "companion from birth who rules the star," for he repeats portions of it in his commentary on the *Aeneid* that his immediate source, Guillaume de Conches, does not.[19] Other late classical and medieval writers, some of whom Bernardus used as sources in his commentary and elsewhere in *De Mundi,* had also established the astrological context of the *genius.* Prudentius had reviled the *genius* or star of birth attributed to cities, places, walls and individuals; its significance for the horoscope was clarified by Lactantius, Mythographus Tertius, and John of Salisbury. After defining *horoscopica* as the reading of constellations whose stars control the fate of men, Mythographus Tertius explains that the term *horoscopi* is derived from *horoscopica,* "id est *horarum* fata *inspicientes.*" He also indicates that he understands the relationship between the star, rising as Horoscopus every forty minutes to vary the forms of individuals, and the *genius,* which controls the individual's star, by citing a cryptic line from Juvenal: "Nemo mathematicus genius indemnatus habebit." [20] ("The astrologer will not be believed to have *genius*"—by metonymy, knowledge or control of the stars, but more generally, skill—"unless he is condemned.") John of Salisbury similarly discusses *horoscopi* and human birth, including Persius' statement that twins with the same horoscope are born with a different fortune ("star") or temperament ("genius").[21] Whether the stars are controlled by a *genius* or whether they produce individuals with different fortunes, temperaments, or appearances, the usual association of the two may have stimulated Bernardus to identify the Pantomorph, ruler of the Decani, as a Genius.

But this personification who guides the soul descending from the spheres into life on earth also appears in the guise of an old man whose astrological function is masked by his scribal and artistic activity: he ascribes ("ascribit") forms for all things and is "engaged in the art and office of painting and forming" ("in artem et officium pictoris et figurantis addictus," 2.3.100, 92–93). The writing and figuring of this *senex* who provides form—generic similarity, individual difference—for matter acts not only as a "synonym for reproduction," in C. S. Lewis' phrase, but as a metaphor for the communication of God's knowledge—Providence—to the lower world. The Genius Pantomorph is thus a *daemonic* intermediary translating celestial secrets into "language" more comprehensible to man. The *senex,* a god (or god-like figure) charting the progress of souls by means of astral secrets and directions, had functioned analogously in two classical literary works; its later appearance in medieval works like *De Mundi* that develop the writing metaphor more extensively emphasizes the importance of the figure.

The first-century *Cebetis Tabula* describes a mysterious tablet, a votive offering to Cronos or Saturn, upon which a series of concentric circles have been inscribed. At the gate into the outer circle, a Daemon (Genius) addresses a multitude of souls who are waiting to enter Life. Standing in a higher place, the *senex* holds a "chart" in one hand, and points with the other toward the path to Life, and also to the innermost circle of True Knowledge and Virtue.[22] This wise figure, whom the later aged scribe of Bernardus resembles, carries a chart upon which instructions have already been written; he guides souls through a gate (like the portals of Cancer in *De Mundi*) leading into Life, a circular enclosure (a series of circular spheres arranged in a hierarchy in *De Mundi*).

A similar *senex,* but not called "Genius" or "Daemon," is introduced in the *De Consulatu Stilichonis* of Claudian (c. 395). Surrounded by souls ("animae"), he and Nature sit at the entrance of a huge old cave encircled by a serpent biting its own tail. The serpent's shape, like that of Macrobius' kissing snakes, parallels the concentric circles of the *Tabula* and the celestial spheres of *De Mundi;* the cavern itself is "annorum . . . mater," hiding the secrets of time and the various ages, golden, silver, brass, and iron.[23] The emphasis on time is significant: the tablet described in Cebes' *Tabula* is a votive offering to Saturn or Cronos (Time); Pantomorph varies individual form according to the hour of birth. Indeed, Claudian's *senex* is a scribe ("scribit") who copies fixed laws: he divides the numerous stars, and decides which will move and which will remain stable, thereby determining through their fixed laws ("legibus") what will live and what will perish. His control is not limited to the stars: he also dictates the movements and orbits of the various planets. His scribal office, like Pantomorph's, epitomizes the cosmic forces of generation and fate.

The *senex* and the writing metaphor resurface in later works. In the *Architrenius* of Jean de Hautville (fl. 1184), written after *De Mundi,* old men attend Natura while she discourses on the gods, the zodiac, and cosmology in general; although called *genii,* they are not portrayed either as writers or artists.[24] The scribal metaphor reappears in Alanus' *De Planctu Naturae* and Jean de Meun's *Roman de la Rose.* In the latter, the scribe's pen and parchment ultimately symbolize the male and female reproductive organs. The writing and book imagery of *De Mundi,* however, is used to suggest the workings of fate, for the heavens resemble a book containing pictures upon which "all earthly things are prefigured." [25] As the book imagery is traced through the text, it becomes evident that the artistic responsibility of the Genius Pantomorph, although expressly generative in an astrological sense, also implies an adherence to the laws of fate.

That is, the role of Pantomorph in the continuing formation of human beings is depicted analogously to the roles of Natura, Urania, and Physis in creating the First Man; the writing metaphor links the two relationships. The difference between the two is similar to that between *natura naturans* and *natura naturata,* only applied specifically here to human nature. The three sisters, daughters of Noys (*ratio* of God) and 'parents' of the First Man, resemble Genius, "son of the gods and parent of men." [26] Bernardus' scribal Genius, Pantomorph, fashions different forms for all things, particularly man, but he must "copy" from the book of the stars, the pages of the heavens. The Creator (Opifex, Artist, 1.3.57) imprints and adorns the heavens with stars ("Scribit enim caelum stellis totumque figurat") and thereby designates what may later come to pass through the law of Fate ("Quod de fatali lege venire potest, / Praesignat," 1.3.33–35). Noys proclaims that the heavens have been inscribed with a variety of images ("multiformi imaginum varietate conscriptum," 2.1.23–24), like a book with opened pages, containing the events of the future in secret letters ("quasi librum porrectis in planum paginis . . . secretis futura litteris continentem," 2.1.25–26). As Pantomorph writes, directed by the book of the stars, so Natura and her sisters create the First Man, guided by the knowledge of Noys or the "Word of God." The "Verbum Dei" [27] is described as a book in which the "text of time" (*textus temporis*), the events of Fate (*fatalis series*), and the disposition of the ages (*dispositio saeculorum*) have been written down (*exarata,* from *exarare,* to write with a stylus on a waxen tablet) by the finger of the Supreme Examiner (or Investigator—*supremi digito dispunctoris,* 1.2.160–61). The knowledge of the Word of God is transmitted to Urania, Natura, and Physis through three gifts—the Speculum Providentiae, the Tabula Fati, and the Liber Recordationis. The Mirror Urania receives from Noys reflects the ideal images or models of all things; the Table of Fate given to Natura outlines the process of Fate, that which is destined to come to pass through the operations of the sisters Atropos (of the firmament), Clotho (of the planets), and Lachesis (of the earth, 2.11.51–58). It also contains information expecially pertinent to Natura: the means of joining species and form, and a catalogue of all the different species of creatures, including man. The very short Book of Memory received by Physis concentrates on the way bodies of all things are composed from the four elements. The Word of God, communicated through the mirrors and books of Urania, Natura, and Physis, is not only intended to direct the formation of the First Man, but also to guide them in the regeneration of all of creation. Still, the First Man constitutes a copy of the model described in their texts (or mirror), as the informed souls of Pantomorph embody the "text," dictated by the ascendant Decanus Horoscopus, of a particular moment of time. The Artifex Natura [28] resembles the scribe and artist Genius.

Although their functions are depicted in a somewhat similar manner, Pantomorph and the sisters are not, however, directly parallel figures. This *senex* ruling the Aplanon and fashioning different *imagines* of all things from an archetypal model (*species*) under the direction of the stars most closely approximates Urania, *siderum regina*, whom he introduces to Natura. Her task, after studying the ideal forms of things portrayed in the Mirror of Providence, is "the composition of the soul from Endelechia [the World Soul] and from the edification of the virtues" ("conpositio animae ex endelechia et virtutum aedificatione," 2.11.2). The "edification of the virtues" probably occurs when the soul descends through the various spheres of the heavens, a descent triggered by the Genius Pantomorph in the subsequent regeneration of mankind, but paralleled initially by the descent of Urania and Natura from the Aplanon to the Garden of Granusion. Physis is allotted the task of the composition "of the body from the preparation of matter" ("corporis ex materiae praeparatione," 2.11.3); Natura must join soul and body so that the conjunction of the two will emulate the heavenly order ("Utrorumque corporis et animae formativa concretio de caelestis ordinis aemulatione," 2.11.3–5). Urania, queen of the stars, and Physis, goddess of the Garden of Granusion, rule the regions from which the two parts of man, soul and body, originate; Natura will unite these two parts, working from Noys' instructions. In this sense, Urania and Physis, Natura's "mind" and "body," interpret Noys to create the First Man. The Genius Pantomorph, then, a subordinate agent of Urania, duplicates only part of her original work, and yet, as instigator of the descent of the soul into the lower regions, also partly helps Natura in her symbolic task of joining soul to body.

This Genius is not identical to the universal Stoic Genius, agent of Jupiter Progenitor and Genetrix: if he contributes to the generation of all things, he does so in conjunction with *genii* in other regions of the universe, all of whom together combine to form a cosmic Genius similar to the Stoic concept. These specialized *genii* are agents of the mythological personifications, Urania, Natura, and Physis, themselves subordinate to Noys, *mens* of God. Bernardus has adapted and refined the role of Genius as "faithful reflex and interpreter of my [Jove's] mind, O sacred *nous*" in the *De Nuptiis* of Martianus Capella. Nour ("ὁ articulus, νοῦς mens, sacra mens") he personifies in Noys; but the Genius ("nomen naturale") he diversifies through a hierarchy of figures—Natura, her sisters and other selves, Urania and Physis, and their cosmic agents, usiarchs who rule the different regions of the universe.[29] So in *De Nuptiis*, Philology, bearing "sacra dogmata," travels through the heavens, her light seen clearly by means of the subordinate *numina* of Fate and the *genii*.[30]

Bernardus' heavenly *genii* also participate in a journey—of the soul. The god with the appearance of old age, the Oyarses and Genius Pantomorph who translates the secrets of the stars into the "book" of human nature, ascribes individual form to the soul according to the instructions of the stars, the Decani. Thereafter it enters the portals of Cancer and falls through the spheres, guided by planetary *genii* who are ruled by Imarmene (Heimarmene, Fortune) [31] and who are located in the general region of Clotho.

THE PLANETARY GENII

In the short account (225 lines) of the planets, we learn that Saturn and Jupiter are Oyarses (2.5.45,76); although none of the other planets are labeled with this epithet, the sun is situated "inter Oyarsas geniosque

caelestes'' (2.5.131), apparently the rulers of the planetary spheres. Bernardus' depiction of the planetary *genii* stresses both astrological and
Neo-Platonic aspects of the descent of the soul.

Saturn and Jupiter, the first planetary usiarchs encountered by Natura
and Urania, are clearly contrasted in the description of their regions, behavior, and influence. Saturn's region is barren and icy, Jupiter's, pleasant and delightful; the former usiarch, a savage and malicious *senex* who
devours his sons as soon as they are born and who also mows down
roses, lilies, and other flowers wherever they flourish, represents the antithesis of Jupiter, an agreeable and beneficent figure whose scepter and
scale suggest moderation and balance (2.5.45–89). The significance of
the two planets' influence is expressed in veiled astrological terms. The
''image'' or idea conveyed by Saturn's mythical destructiveness portends
the future ''deadly quality of his star'' for the human race soon to exist.[32]
In contrast, Jupiter, named ''Jove'' in Latin from *iuvando,* ''the ability to
aid,'' is both propitious and benevolent: the *beneficia* of Jove's indulgence are believed to pervade ''omnia mundi membra'' (2.5.75–79).

The astrological opposition of the two planets' powers as unfortunate
and fortunate had been previously established by Persius, Firmicus Maternus (c. A.D. 337), and Macrobius. Persius alludes to the helpful influence of Jove mitigating Saturn's severity.[33] Firmicus Maternus, examining the twelve *loci* (houses) of the horoscope, explains that the eleventh
and twelfth places (those of Jove and Saturn) are called, respectively, the
good *daemon* or *genius* (*agathos daemon*) and the evil *daemon* (*cacos
daemon*).[34] In the latter *locus* we find vices and physical and mental illness, which affect us and our horoscope adversely. Macrobius adds that
both Saturn and Mars are considered malefic planets, as Jupiter and
Venus are beneficent, by those *genethliaci* casting horoscopes (however,
he does not believe that the adversity or prosperity of human life is
caused by the stars).[35]

Mars' hostile influence is also underscored by Bernardus: the two goddesses discover his ''mansio'' (house) is ''seething with hostile vapors''
(''dirisque vaporibus aestuantem,'' 2.5.112). In contrast, Venus has a
felicitous effect on births conjoined by already benevolent stars. Mercury,
the last planet the goddesses encounter, is not mentioned in Macrobius'
account; however, Bernardus indicates that, alone, he has little negative

power over man's fortune. This indecisive "star" depends upon a partner for direction: if associated with Mars, for example, he will strengthen boldness or madness in the horoscope (2.5.163–68).

These planets and the two luminaries, the sun and the moon, are also presented in a way which connects their astrological importance in a horoscope with their simultaneous influence on the soul descending toward earth at birth. Bernardus proceeds by drawing upon Macrobius, who had indicated that the soul receives its share of reason and understanding from Saturn, practical intelligence or decisiveness (*vis agendi*) from Jupiter, courage, spirit, or irascibility from Mars, and then more physical qualities from the lower luminaries and planets—sense-perception or life from the sun, passion from Venus, speaking ability from Mercury, and propensity for growth from the moon.[36] Bernardus alludes or refers to most of these influences: Saturn, abhorring fertility and beauty, suggests by antithesis the importance of the higher faculty of reason; [37] Jupiter's position as a king wielding scepter and scale implies control, direction, and leadership. Mars is portrayed as fiery, bold and terrifying: he searches for an opportunity to hurl himself out of his sphere so that he may appear as a red and terrible comet (2.5.107–11). The sun is "rerum fomes sensificus," the tinder which produces sensation in creatures (2.5.134–35); Venus controls and bolsters human desires for pleasure (2.5.180–81). Of Mercury's influence Bernardus says little to associate him with Macrobius' description: in *De Mundi,* he is sexually promiscuous, effects the formation of hermaphrodites, and acts as the messenger of the gods and interpreter of their laws. The moon, finally, administers *aethericon,* which is increase or bodily growth ("quae crescendi natura est," 2.5.211), to the lower regions.

The sun and moon, in addition to Saturn and Jupiter, receive greatest attention in the account. The luminaries not only affect the descent of the soul, tempering the faculties of sense-perception (which man shares with the animals) and of growth (which man shares with plants), as Saturn, Jupiter, and Mars have conditioned the rational faculty (understanding, leadership, boldness), but they also play a major astrological role in human birth. The life-giving and generative sun and moon assisting growth ("sol vitalis et generans, luna coadiuvans incrementis," 2.11.37–38) designate personality and fortune within the horoscope. The sun, regulator of the planets and signs of the zodiac, was one of four gods presiding over human birth in Macrobius' *Saturnalia:* "the author of spirit, of heat, and of light is the genitor and custodian of human life, believed to be the Daemon [Genius] or god of the new-born" ("sol auctor spiritus caloris ac luminis humanae vitae genitor et custos est, et ideo nascentis Δαίμων id est deus creditur").[38] Bernardus appropriately depicts the sun traveling around the circle of the zodiac, changing appearance as the seasons change, and growing from boyhood to puberty to manhood to old age (2.5.114–31). The association of its journey with the stages of human life and the four seasons suggests the variety of temperaments allotted at birth through the agency of that star which is Horoscopus. The rashness and buoyancy of youth, characterizing spring signs, mellows gradually into more dispassionate, even cold and foreboding, traits, as the sun proceeds through its zodiacal cycle. Macrobius' moon, a second god of human birth, represents the *tyche* or fortune of an individual, that aspect of the horoscope determining the course of one's life, "because she is the guardian of bodies which are subjected to the change of circumstances" ("quia corporum praesul est quae fortuitorum varietate iactantur"). Bernardus hints at her Macrobian function when he describes her incessant travel into and out of each sign ("per eadem signa"), concluding that she controls the fate and business of men ("in res et fata hominum vim praesentissimam vendicavit," 2.5.220–21).

The synthesis of astrological and Neo-Platonic theories in his chapter on planetary *genii* and usiarchs is skillfully woven. By extracting the details concerning a planet's influence on the descending soul and on the generation and birth of man, we can see the relationship between the two: each planet, under the control of the zodiac and the ultimate direction of Pantomorph, affects and tempers the human faculties of the soul, which vary in nature or degree according to the time and place of birth. The sun and moon, in addition, have other responsibilities: the former determines the individual's "life" or personality through its position in one of the signs of the zodiac, and the latter, the individual's fortune. These planets and stars prefigure the individual cast of the man born at the conclusion of the soul's natural descent through the spheres and into the underworld of the body. Once he arrives on earth, his behavior and decisions are affected by other celestial forces—the *angeli* and *genii* residing in the aether and air.

THE ANGELI AND GENII OF AETHER AND AIR

After Natura and Urania have journeyed through the planetary spheres, Urania pauses at the lunar boundary to lecture to her companion on the celestial life animating the universe—the hierarchy of *angeli* and *genii*. Although the discourse breaks the continuity of the hypothetical progress of the soul, it allows Bernardus to add another dimension to his crowded cosmos. In Urania's "animate powers" we recognize that Greek messenger of the gods, the aerial *daemon,* and his Roman brother, the tutelary *genius:* indeed, the function of these *animalia* is to transmit secrets from God to the lower regions of the universe.

Urania explains that there are three kinds of cosmic spirits or creatures: the highest order, wholly rational sidereal fires ("ignes siderei," probably angels), rules the firmament; the lowest, man, inhabits the earth; and the middle order, *medioxumus,* presides over the middle region, resembling the sidereal fires in its immortality, and man in its affective passions. The middle spirits occupy every realm of the universe—the two parts of the aether, the three levels of the air, and the three divisions of earth. The syncretistic world of *De Mundi* is filled with many different concepts of spirits—Greek, Roman, and Christian.

The two parts of the aether are populated by flaming or burning spirits, perhaps Seraphim,[39] and also by *angeli.* The former, located in the space between the firmament and the sun, receive from God's mind the secrets of the future (*futurorum arcana,* 2.7.48), which will direct the course of events in the universe *per inferiores mundi species* (2.7.49). The species inferior to and less radiant than the burning spirits is lodged in the adjacent aetherial region between the sun and the moon. This spirit, gifted with *intelligentia* and *memoria,* also perceives *arcana,* thereby becoming a mediator between God and man. Because of its roles and duties, but not its nature, it is called *angelus* ("angelus officii nomen est, non naturae," 2.7.66–67): it "announces" or "reports" the petitions of man to God ("hominis indigentias ad Deum," 2.7.63–64) and the benefits of God's indulgence to man ("indulgentiarum Dei beneficia ad hominem," 2.7.64–65). Its adherence to virtue in communicating the dictates of heaven and promoting the needs of earth suggests that it corresponds to the beneficent Platonic *daemon*-messenger, the Greek intermediary which developed into the pure Calcidian and Lactantian (i.e., non-Pseudo-

Dionysian) *angelus*.[40] Bernardus adds, however, that this *angelus* will become a *genius* once man is created: its task will be to protect each man, appearing whenever virtuous practice is undertaken, but avoiding contact with the impure and dissolute.[41] Bernardus' talent for syncretism is evident here, for his qualifying statement introduces the late classical concept of the good *genius* (*manes, daemon*) espoused by Apuleius, Servius, and Martianus Capella. The *angelus* constitutes an amalgam of Greek, Christian, and late Roman figures.

Of the three types of spirits found in the sublunary region, differentiated by the names "rulers," "interpreters," and "deserter angels" (2.7.109–10), only the latter two are clearly defined by Bernardus. The tranquil and serene spirits of the uppermost air do not appear to have a relationship with either God or man. But the interpreting spirit, living in middle air, is a *genius* who is united with man from birth and who signals possible future dangers by means of premonitions, dreams, or omens.[42] In this figure Bernardus combines the Horatian *genius* born with each man and living until his death with the Graeco-Roman executioner, the *daemon-genius* delivering messages of ill-fortune from the gods to men. (This spirit, regarded as an evil offspring of man and the fallen angel by Lactantius, assumes a more neutral position in Bernardus' account.) The third and last aerial spirit, the renegade angel, cruelly and maliciously torments wicked men (often with God's consent) or disturbs men in general on its own by invading their thoughts or assuming the shapes of dead men. These *desertores angeli*, whose name and functions are based primarily on Calcidian and Lactantian accounts of the fallen angels,[43] also mask the classical concepts of the *cacos daemon* (or *genius, manes*) urging man to evil acts (Servius, Martianus Capella) and the *manes* or shade of the dead, in addition to the more important medieval concept of the demon.

Of the intermediary spirits discussed by Urania, the good *angelus*, the *genius*, and the evil (renegade) *angelus* are themselves the most "medioxumus," for they inhabit the lower aether, and middle and lower air. (Beneath these aerial regions are the three sub-divisions of earth, governed respectively by Silvans, Pans, and Nerei, figures derived from Martianus' *De Nuptiis*.[44]) Of these three middle spirits, the *genius* born with each man occupies an intermediate position: Bernardus' Chinese box opens to reveal this figure at its center. If we regard the good and evil *angeli* as cosmic mirrors of the good and evil impulses warring within man, then the neutral *genius,* like the man it accompanies from birth, constitutes a middle-ground. There is a very slight hint that this *genius* of the middle air is intended to be a macrocosmic correlative of the natural concupiscence common to all men and equated with *genius* in Bernardus' commentary on the *Aeneid.* In addition, the vicious and virtuous journeys into Hell of the unnatural (fallen) concupiscence and the soul, also described in the commentary, are analogous to those of the renegade and pure *angeli* in *De Mundi.* The poisoned and tainted Euridice descends into the underworld when she chooses temporal good; contaminated by earthly corruption, the evil *angelus,* who resembles the evil *manes* or *daemon,* descends into the sublunar underworld in order to punish man for vicious behavior with hellish torments. Orpheus (the *animus*) attempts a rescue through a virtuous descent into the infernal regions (knowledge of temporal good and the created world), but loses her when he looks back at these inferior things; the good *angelus,* who counsels man in making decisions, enters the underworld in order to reward him for virtuous behavior, but reascends if a decision is based on earthly concerns. Despite the plethora of classical concepts implicit in Bernardus' celestial hierarchy, the ordering vision is Neo-Platonic: evil is associated with the earth; good, with the heavens. But more significant, the intimate relationship between microcosm and macrocosm at birth and during man's life is definitely twelfth-century in focus.

These celestial messengers, ghosts of classical cosmology, are resurrected by Bernardus for two reasons. First, this digression indicates the plenitude and hierarchy of spirits (emanations of God) within the universe, ranging from the usiarchs and *genii* of the fixed sphere and planetary spheres and the sidereal fires of higher aether to the fallen angels in the lower air and the creatures of earth, all of whom are obligated to foster the communication of secrets or of knowledge to the lower realm. Secondly, Bernardus accounts for the existence of evil in the world by portraying the varying shades of purity and brightness in the different types of spirits in the hierarchy. This allows him to hint—perfunctorily and obliquely—at the three descents (vicious, virtuous, and artificial) into the underworld inspired by the history and evolution of Genius, but which are peripheral to his primary interest, the fable of the natural descent of the soul. At the end of the digression, Bernardus accordingly returns to the immediate topic—the creation of the First Man.

THE GENIUS OF GRANUSION IN THE MOIST LOWER AIR

Noys, Urania, Natura, and Physis meet in the garden of Granusion to create man: Urania will design the soul from *endelechia* and the *aedificatio* of its powers (that is, the influence of the various spheres upon the descending soul); Physis must shape the body from primary matter—the four elements; Natura, acting as a joiner or *artifex,* will combine soul and body in man so that the microcosm emulates the celestial order of the macrocosm (2.11.1–6). Noys' instructions are supplemented with mnemonic aids—the Mirror of Providence, Table of Fate, and Book of Memory. Despite Noys' delegation of responsibility to the three goddesses, we see only the work of Physis, who attempts to form the human body from the four elements: first assembling and controlling her materials, she then sculpts the actual body itself, beginning with the head, continuing to the breast, and concluding with the loins. The reason Bernardus does not portray the other sisters engaged in their specific tasks is clear: Urania, by descending with Natura through the heavens to this underworld garden, has already allegorically performed the journey the soul must make. Natura, who has brought Urania from the firmament to Physis, turning off at this place where she guesses Physis may be found, has also similarly performed her task—of joining "soul" with "body"—through this allegorical confrontation between Urania and Physis. She is a go-between, guided by the behests of Noys.

   The garden of Granusion is located in the sublunar realm, but beneath the region controlled by the conflicting sons of Aeolus, ruler of the winds and of human birth, in which freezing and burning alternate, hail storms vying with thunder clouds for supremacy (2.9.1–4).[45] The name "Granusion" is derived from Calcidius' description of *humecta substantia,* called "hygran usian" in Greek, whose moisture or humidity, necessary in order for men to breathe, distinguishes it from simple *aer*.[46] Bernardus' Granusion, recalling Calcidius' *hygran usian,* was named for its implicitly hothouse atmosphere, "quia graminum diversitatibus perpetuo conpubescit" ("because it allows plants of different kinds to flourish perpetually," 2.9.18–19). Ruled by Physis (whose name, Φύσις, means "Growth"), this paradisal garden with its blooming and fragrant plants, herbs, and flowers enjoys an unchanging temperate climate and a continual spring. These qualities, in addition to its location—a secret place in the East (*eous* or Orient, 2.9.14)—confirm its identity as that Paradise or Eden Bernardus defined as the superior part of the world in his commentary on the *Aeneid*. Called "Ortus" in the commentary because things originate from it, this Eden, which would be translated into Latin as *deliciae*, "pleasures," is regarded by Bernardus as the "pleasant places of souls" yet unfallen (p. 29). The Eden of Granusion, situated beneath the region ruled by Aeolus, the god of birth, and offering ideal conditions for Physis to fashion flesh from matter in creating the First Man, represents Bernardus' eclectic—classical but twelfth-century—view of Genesis' Eden. Symbolically it parallels the earlier Aplanon, the sphere of the fixed stars overseen by the Genius Pantomorph: from that sphere Urania (and the first soul, guided by Pantomorph) descends, just as Physis emerges from this Aplanon to create man's body (whose gradual formation is stimulated by the genial power of Granusion). The soul, having mythically fallen into the first underworld—the sublunary region—must now enter the second underworld—the inferior flesh.

As Pantomorph of the Aplanon assists Urania in the natural descent of the soul, so a similar Genius quickens life, implicitly aiding Physis, in Granusion. But, unlike the goddesses, both Genii are restricted to a particular place—the sphere of the fixed stars, or the place of moist lower air. When Granusion senses that Natura, *mater generationis,* is approaching, its beauty is enhanced with quickly replenished flowers and plants. This act, a form of obeisance to the great mother, is explained by Bernardus: the earth, by means of the fecundity inspired by the Genius of nature, swells with life ("De naturae igitur genio fecunditate concepta derepente tellus intumuit," 2.9.32–33).[47] As Bernardus was influenced by the Latin *Asclepius* in his portrait of Pantomorph, ruler of Decani, so he is perhaps equally influenced in his brief allusion to the Genius of Granusion. According to the *Asclepius,* the governor of earth and sea or "the underworld," Jupiter Plutonius (comparable to the ruler Pantomorph of the fixed stars, Heimarmene of the planetary spheres, and Jove Neatos of the air), "supplies nutriment to all mortal beings that have soul, and to all trees that bear fruit; and it is by his power that the fruits of the earth are produced." [48] The life of plants and trees exists in their propensity for growth, which man shares in his vegetative faculty; [49] so the Genius of Granusion typifies the power of vegetative growth, "Life." Resembling Jupiter Plutonius, he quickens the earth as Physis (=Phytikon from the moon in Macrobius) will quicken the body. [50]

The early classical Genius, generation spirit, "life" or energy, artistically depicted with a cornucopia of seed and petitioned later with flowery garlands, reappears as a personification in *De Mundi*. Bernardus has transformed the elaborate birthday ceremonies found in Horace, Ovid, and Tibullus into a naturalistic context: the lush garden, replenished upon Natura's approach, is redolent with the sweet odors of cinnamon and *amomum* (an aromatic shrub), suggestive of the incense offered previously to the approaching birth-god, Genius.

Genius presides over a fragrant flowery garden in two passages from the *Ars Versificatoria,* a rhetorical treatise written by a pupil of Bernardus, Matthieu de Vendôme (c.1175). The first set piece or *descriptio* depicts a grove or garden which appeals to the senses through its murmuring waters, singing birds, and pleasant odors exuded by flowers, and whose description includes mention of the four elements. It concludes with a Silvestran reference to the revivifying power of a diligent Genius over the flowers, which Nature uses to enhance her own lushness. [51] The second *descriptio,* again of Nature, is inserted into a preface to a discussion of poetic diction, in which preface Flora endows a *locus venustatis* (place of rhetorical elegance) with the refreshing effects of spring in order to aid weary scholars in pursuit of wisdom. The garden wherein Genius zealously applies himself ("studet in melius") is replenished with plants, herbs, and flowers from the womb of the earth by a *fons vitreus*. [52] The strong emphasis on natural fertility conveyed by both passages involving Genius suggests Matthieu's debt to Bernardus; further, the gardens of Genius in Jean de Meun's thirteenth-century *Roman de la Rose* and Spenser's sixteenth-century *Faerie Queene* were very likely influenced by these earlier rhetorical and literary descriptions.

Growth, increase, fecundity, life—these principles dominate the greenhouse of Physis' Granusion; decay, degeneration, and death have been banished. The sphere of the moon, last of the luminaries and planets, governs both forms of change: it delivers *phytikon* (*aethericon* in Bernar-dus) to the descending soul, or *natura plantandi et augendi corpora,* but it also wreaks the forces of mutability, fortune, and death upon the earth and its inhabitants. Each man, like the plants, must grow—from birth to manhood—but he must also age and die. The Genius of Granusion repre-sents an external cosmic power of plant growth which the vegetative soul of each man and the life of all trees and plants emulate—but whose eter-nal spring and renewal elude man, faced with the reality of death and decay. Still, Physis anticipates man's inability to rejuvenate like a plant by endowing him with "genial weapons" to battle old age and death.

THE GENIAL WEAPONS OF THE BODY ON EARTH

When Physis begins to shape the third and last part of the body, the loins, she forms the genitals into *genialibus armis* to be used by two *genii* who "unconquered fight against death" ("Cum morte invicti pugnant," 2.14.161) and who "repair Nature and perpetuate the species" ("Na-turam reparant perpetuantque genus," 2.14.162). These "arms" (both metaphor and pun), in particular the phallus, also tie together the threads of life severed by the hands of the Fates, in particular, Lachesis ("Militat adversus Lachesin sollersque renodat / Mentula Parcarum fila resecta manu," 2.14.165–66). Their successful battle ensures the continuity of the species and, in addition, the rebirth of the individual: during inter-course, blood from the brain, bearing the image or likeness (*instar*) of white sperm, is sent to the loins, where it is shaped and fashioned by na-ture so that at conception and birth it reproduces the likeness of ancestors ("Defluit ad renes cerebri regione remissus / Sanguis et albentis spermatis instar habet. / Format et effingit sollers natura liquorem, / Ut simili genesis ore reducat avos," 2.14.167–70).[53]

The reproductive organs are controlled by two *genii,* the classical gen-eration spirits: "Breeding and the work once assigned to twin brothers have passed to two genii" ("Ad genios fetura duos concessit et olim / Commissum geminis fratribus illud opus," 2.14.159–60). These *genii* are probably the early Genius and Juno of generation and marriage, whose duties were fulfilled on the genial couch (*lectus genialis*). The writers of the Middle Ages were not familiar, however, with the Juno, and occasionally ascribed two *genii* to a household. Even in the third century, Censorinus, for example, mentions in *De Die Natali* the belief of several (classical) authors that two *genii* had to be worshipped in the households of married people. He also cautions against confusing the *genius* with the *lares* (twin spirits or gods who safe-guarded the family, a function reflected in their totem, the dog), probably the "twin brothers" to whom Bernardus mistakenly attributes the original work of breeding.[54] This misconception of the "twin brothers" may also have stemmed from the linking (in two successive statements from the Censorinus passage) of the Roman *genii* of marriage and the Greek tutelary *genii* (actually *daemones*) assigned to each man.[55]

When man and woman conceive a child, they obey the *genii* of marriage and initiate the soul's descent into two underworlds—the region below the moon and the body. This catalytic act engages the Genius of the Aplanon in ascribing individuality to the falling soul. Thus, a child becomes a product of the stars and his parents, both of whom have superseded Urania (for the soul) and Physis (for the body) in regenerating mankind. The *Hermetica* of Stobaeus, in an excerpt entitled "Aphrodite," examines the likeness of children to their parents, concluding that the "efflux" from the more vigorous parent determines the likeness of the child to that parent, but contingent upon the Decanus rising at the hour the woman had conceived the child.[56] The interlude between conception and birth—often regarded as a seven-month period of gestation—perhaps allows the soul time to descend through the seven planetary spheres.[57]

The *genii* of *De Mundi,* generative agents of the cosmos and man, were garnered from many different classical sources in order to explain the natural descent of the soul. But the original genesis of man through the art of Noys, Natura, Physis, and Urania must be distinguished from the subsequent regeneration of the species through the copying *genii* of the spheres and of earth: the former is allegorical and archetypal, the latter is literal and repetitive. Nevertheless, parallels between the two can be established. Urania, queen of the stars, typifies the cosmic regions from which man's soul falls into the sublunary underworld of earth; the Pantomorph and the planetary *genii* participate in this descent. Physis, goddess of Granusion, represents the material regions from which the

body is created, for she aids the descent into the second inferior region—
the body. The Genius of Granusion exemplifies the spirit of plant and
animal growth shared by the human body.

Finally, man is born with a mind and a body. The aerial *genius* guides
his mind, and the twin *genii* of breeding, his genitals. The aerial *genius*
whispers the secrets of his future into his ear; the good and evil *angeli*
convey good and evil temptations and messages to him. After man is
born, he can descend into the underworld in three ways—artifically, virtuously, or viciously. And he can cause another soul to descend from the
aetherial regions by exercising his reproductive prerogative.

Bernardus' eclectic synthesis of pagan materials involving *genii* explains the origin of mankind according to a *descensus naturae*. He
touches upon the other three descents, but does not examine them fully.
This aspect of the history of Genius will bloom in the allegorical garden
of the companion piece to *De Mundi*—the *De Planctu Naturae* of Alanus
de Insulis.

CHAPTER FIVE

The Moral Universe:
Genius and the Four Descents
in the "De Planctu Naturae"
of Alanus De Insulis

The figure of Genius in the *De Planctu Naturae* of Alanus de Insulis personifies complex philosophical elements within this skillfully woven fabulous narrative. Inspired by the fertile *genii* of the *De Mundi Universitate*,[1] Alanus' Genius represents the *generalis praesul* who controls the natural descent of the soul into the underworld. However, his allegorical role is not generative but moral: as the priest of Natura,[2] he condemns and excommunicates unnatural and vicious men from her realm. In the *De Planctu,* complementary companion piece to *De Mundi,* the second and third descents are reinacted—the fall of man into the dark world of sensuality and sin, and the subsequent virtuous descent of an Orpheus figure, Genius, in an attempt to restore the human ideal.

This twelfth-century Latin *satura* reflects in its four-part structure an awareness of the descents. Following the narrator's lament over man's sexual perversions in the Proem, the first part of the work describes the character and function of Natura, and her descent from the heavens. The second part (beginning with Prose III), an account of the unnatural and licentious actions of mankind, delineates the reason for her appearance before the narrator and constitutes the actual complaint of Natura—the vicious descent. The dialogue between the dreamer and Natura also allows for extended discussion of the creation and nature of man. The third part (beginning with Meter VI) more closely examines the human vices—Fornication, Idolatry, Avarice, Pride, Envy, Flattery. The dialogue ends in the fourth part (beginning with Prose VIII), and the personified Virtues, which have been banished from human society, are introduced—Hymen, Chastity, Temperance, Generosity. After discussion and debate among these figures, Genius is summoned to perform the excommunication, and the dreamer sleeps.

Although the concept of the underworld descents explains the antithetical roles of Genius—generation god and priest of Natura—scholars have failed to recognize this reconciliation. Edwin Greenlaw views him as Natura's Sergeant Order, a priest of generation, a *gallus* of the Phrygian deity, the Magna Mater Natura: Alanus disguised his priest of Natura on the basis of old religious cults.[3] But Natura is more than an earth-mother signifying cosmic generation. G. Raynaud de Lage explains her cosmological and moral nature, and defines Genius, her other self, as a divinity of generation and a regulator of moral life.[4] Natura cannot very well be a priestess; she requires a priest to excommunicate those errant men from her realm. Alanus, Raynaud de Lage discovers, presents a new Trinity to the reader—the goddess Natura, her priest Genius, and his daughter, Veritas.[5] Yet there is a second reason that Genius, not Natura, must perform the act of excommunication. Richard H. Green suggests that, as human nature, he has been "driven away from human society by the unnatural passion of men in their choice of *antigenius;* he shares the suffering of Nature because he is in fact the part of nature which has been perverted."[6] Although Green is apparently unaware of the Horatian definition of Genius as "god of human nature," cited in Bernardus' commentary on the *Aeneid,* his perception underscores Genius' specialized natural function. "Human nature" has been perverted in two ways: first, the sexual deviancy of sodomy, homosexuality, and prostitution hinders the reproduction of mankind, rendering the *generalis praesul* idle. Genius is then the "enemy of unnatural vice because he is the patron of generation and therefore of heterosexuality."[7] But Genius has been affronted in a second sense. He controls the natural descent of the soul into the body: man's paradoxical nature combines soul and body, angel and beast, form designated by the stars and elemental matter. When man pursues the bestial and the physical, ignoring his rational and spiritual nature, he acts unnaturally, and descends viciously into the underworld of the body. Genius, "god of human nature," must accordingly descend to separate the infected portion from the healthy. Because he created man, he is ideally suited to excommunicate him—to cut him off from creation.

As a priest, he functions in the *De Planctu* like Noys in *De Mundi:* Natura complained to Noys about the formlessness of matter, and the Intellect of God ordered the cosmos. In Alanus' *satura,* Natura complains to a man (the dreamer) and to Genius about the disorderly behavior of informed matter—the microcosm man—and her priest restores order by excommunicating the offenders. In each case, Natura consults the appropriate authority. As an agent of generation, Genius resembles the *genii* in Bernardus' work. The *genii* who aided Urania and Physis in their respective tasks—edifying the soul with virtues and composing the body from matter—have been personified in Alanus' Genius. As Urania and Physis were the sisters of Natura, so Genius is her other self in *De Planctu.*

His two roles are distinguished by the two garments he wears to perform them. We first see him dressed in a purple, red, and white vestment, writing on parchment, his hands busy with creation. After Natura summons him, he dons priestly garb, and, speaking from the secret recesses of his mind, excommunicates men from natural grace. The different garments, like the use of hands and speech, argue for a dual Genius, one loftier and nobler than the other; the two tasks—creation and excommunication from creation—link the two "halves" of Genius: the writing and the speaking both communicate, through pictures or words, and also serve to unite the double roles of Genius with the double levels of *De Planctu.*

We shall first examine his relationship with Natura in his role as *generalis praesul,* agent of the natural descent of the soul; secondly, his part in the vicious and virtuous descents which constitute the heart of the fabulous narrative; and finally, his function in the fourth descent, of artifice, in this dream vision of Alanus de Insulis.

THE NATURAL DESCENT

According to Bernardus Silvestris, a human being is a product of the stars and his parents. At the moment of conception, a soul begins to descend from the spheres into the sublunary underworld and the body. This natural descent, common to all, was expressed in *De Mundi* by the two aspects of Natura—Urania and Physis—each of whom controlled *genii* appropriate to the task. It was initiated by the two *genii* of marriage—the *genius* and *juno*—who presided over the reproductive organs.

In *De Planctu,* the generative *genii* become allegorical personifications. Genius controls the descent of the soul into flesh; Venus and Hymen (marriage) represent the *genii* who perpetuate the species on earth. Venus is the handmaiden of Natura; Genius is her other self. The members of this pagan generative hierarchy—Natura, Genius, Venus— are portrayed as artists and writers: the "tablet" (clay tiles) of Natura parallels Genius' book of human nature; Venus, the scribe, merely copies by tracing Natura's orthography. Genius' pen and pages symbolize the descent of the soul into flesh; Venus' scribal tools, however, are thinly disguised symbols of the male and female genitals. An examination of the relationship among the three personifications will elucidate the meaning of Genius, focus of the study.

Natura, "mother of generation," inscribes with a reed stylus *imagines* (images) of things upon tiles ("in lateritiis . . . tabulis") made of clay or earth; unfortunately, these "pictures" refuse to adhere to the clay, and soon disappear or "die" without a trace.[8] The tiles of clay, elemental matter or the four elements, are used in building the "structures of the palaces of earth" and the human body (M—443B, W—451). All of the created world is composed of some combination of the four elements, despite generic or special differences. However, the pictures scribbled by the busy Natura are all different: what she draws are the various classes of things. The Tabula Fati of Bernardus' Natura revealed the plenitude and hierarchy of the species in creation; Alanus' *Distinctiones* cites Boethius to define Natura as the shaper of different species.[9] In the *De Planctu,* Natura describes herself as a coiner *rerum generibus,* for the types or genera of things: she forces the figures to conform to the shape of the anvil, the original model, so that the coins resemble one another, and yet are different from other coins (M—453D–54A, W—469–70).[10]

Natura is the symbolic cosmos, the visible and archetypal universe.[11] She appears before the dreamer in a garb that illustrates the hierarchical pattern of the cosmos, beginning with her sparkling diadem (the zodiac and planets) and ending with her flowery shoes (earthly plants). Her dress depicts the species of creation—animals, birds, fishes, trees. This personified mirror of the megacosmos acts as the *anima mundi*[12] who reflects the eternal ideas of Noys in the shadows of terrestrial creatures: Alanus addresses her, in part, as "speculum caducis" (M—447B, W—458). In the same laudatory passage, her role as vicar of God is clearly established: Natura, contemplating Ideas of Noys, coins species of things, clothing matter with form (". . . noys plures recolens ideas / Singulas rerum species monetans, / Res togas formis"). This intermediary between Noys and earth, as the beginning of the dreamer's apostrophe to her indicates, is truly "proles" (offspring, progeny) of God, and "genetrix" (mother) of things.

The eighth-century Paulus describes Genius as the son of the gods and the parent of men: " 'Genius' . . . 'est deorum filius, et parens hominum.' " [13] The parallel is apt: in the *De Planctu,* Genius is to the generation of men as Natura is to the generation of all things. This *generalis praesul* for mankind expresses his natural role through scribal activity. When we first encounter him, he is busily engaged in writing: in his right hand, he holds a "reed-pen of fragile papyrus" which never stops writing, and in his left, an animal skin stripped of its fur, parchment on which he gives the life of their own kind (species) to images of things when they are transformed by his pen from the shadow of a picture to the truth of being ("imagines rerum ab umbra picturae ad veritatem essentiae transmigrantes, vita sui generis donabantur," M—479D, W—517). Genius' creation is more specialized than Natura's: his medium is a parchment, originally belonging to the animal genus which includes man, not the tiles of clay (the four elements) upon which all of creation is pictured by Natura. The pen with which he writes represents the heavenly source of man's soul; as a scribe, Genius resembles Bernardus' Pantomorph, Claudian's *senex,* and the Daemon of the *Cebetis Tabula.*[14] The writing of Pantomorph designated an individual form for the descending soul and directed the influences of the planets in implementing this form. Such scribal imagery was linked in *De Mundi* with the inscriptions of the secrets of fate and Providence: God wrote the text of time in the parchment of the sky, and the stars became his cryptic handwriting. As Natura paints the secrets of God, exemplary ideas, upon her "table," composed of tiles, so Genius writes heavenly secrets in his book of human nature, composed of parchment. Man is a combination of soul and body, angel and beast, the stars and his parents.

The natural descent of the soul into flesh is expressed by the sketching of the pen: images of things "transmigrate" from the shadow of a picture to the truth of being, "vita sui generis." When these images pass away, others will be called back to life: "quibus deletionis morte sopitis, novae nativitatis ortu, aliae revocabantur ad vitam" (M—479D, W—517). This Neo-Pythagorean word choice hints at the Macrobian descent of the soul from the uppermost reaches of heaven through the spheres into the underworld. That is, other images are called back to life "from the *ortus* of new birth"—"novae nativitatis ortu." The word *ortus,* referring to the origin or birth of persons, the East, or the rising of heavenly bodies, was used by Bernardus in his commentary on the *Aeneid* as a synonym for the Greek concept of Paradise, the Hebrew Eden, and the superior Aplanon of the world: "Because it is superior it is called by the Greek name 'paradisus,' or in Latin, 'ortus,' because from it things originate." [15] Souls, then, are summoned from the Ortus of new birth for entry into the underworld.

As the controlling agent of the natural descent, the personification of Bernardus' substantifying *genii,* Genius enjoys an intimate relationship with Natura. In other writings, Alanus explains that "Genius indeed means nature or God of nature," on account of the substantifying function of *genii* resulting in the substantial natures of things ("Per substantificos genios, id est per substantiales naturas. Genius enim natura vel Deus nature dicitur").[16] Genius as cause produces the substantial natures of things as effect; this agent of creation manifests himself through his created works (thus, "Per substantificos genios, id est per substantiales naturas"). In the *De Planctu,* when his creation, mankind, fails, he too suffers. But he is also Natura's aid, "other self," mirror, and lover (she is tied to him by a knot of love, "nodo dilectionis," M—476C, W—511): whatever happens to him happens as well to Natura. Although he is not the "God of nature" here, he is her priest.

Genius does not actually perform a sacerdotal office until he exchanges his common garments for priestly vestments in order to excommunicate vicious men (M—481B-C, W—520). However, despite his vulgar and common garment, he is a priest from the moment he appears before Natura: his clothing continually changes color, from purple to hyacinth, scarlet, and white—the four colors of the Tabernacle, the breastplate of judgment, and the priests of Israel in Exodus 26 and 28.[17] Because he is

engaged in the worldly tasks of generation and creation and not the more
spiritual office of excommunication when he first appears, it is not clear
exactly how he is functioning as a priest. And if he is a priest from the
beginning, why must he change clothes later to deliver the excommunication?

At the beginning of the *De Planctu,* we learn that sexual deviants,
countermanding the order of Natura to replenish the earth, have neglected
their duties to the priestly Genius: "such [deviants], who refuse tithes and
their own vows to Genius, merit anathema in the Temple of Genius" ("A
Genii templo tales anathema merentur, / Qui Genio decimas, et sua jura
negant," M—432A, W—431). Originally, the Genius was embodied in
the paterfamilias, priest of the family, who controlled its reproductive
luck. Later, the god Genius was invoked before an altar burning with incense, and toasted with wine. This divine tutelary protected man's virility
and fortune. It is possible that Alanus' reading of Horace, Ovid, and
Tibullus inspired him to regard the generative Genius as a priest.

But Alanus' Genius, a priest with his own temple, has a broader, more
philosophic function in *De Planctu:* he is a Neo-Platonic priest of generation who works in a Temple of the Heavens, or Palace of Forms. This
"tabernacle," described in Alanus' "Sermon on the Intelligible Sphere,"
resembles Claudian's cave of time within Eternity, governed by Natura
and the *senex,* encircled by a serpent, and surrounded by flitting souls
who must soon enter the cave and mortal life. In the sermon, Alanus distinguishes (1) the eternal *diadema* or the sphere, both "beginning and
end," of the *universalis pater,* Jupiter, from (2) the *semiciclus,* time,
which originates from it.[18] This *semiciclus,* like the diadem of Natura in
De Planctu, absorbs the secrets of Eternity and comprises the zodiac and
planets. The relationship between the eternal diadem and the *semiciclus*
illustrates the process of the natural descent, for it is from the former that
man receives his own demi-diadem, the human soul.

The Tabernacle is divided into four spheres—*sensilis* (world), *ymagin-
abilis* (primordial matter), *rationabilis* (soul of the world), and *in-
telligibilis* (Divine Being). Within the four spheres, as if in various palaces, the "species" of things inhabit "mansions" (p. 300). Such species
illustrate the stages of form—*ychones* (*imagines,* Images), *ychonie* (*iconiae,* Icons), *ychome* (*ichomae,* Forms) and *ydes* (*ideae,* Ideas). In this

Temple of the heavens, Eternal Idea in the Intelligible Sphere is united by the World Soul in the Rational Sphere with primordial matter in the second sphere through an intermediate agent, the Icon. The product of this union—the Image—populates the sensible world. A similar process is described in *De Planctu:* Eternal Idea greets Ile (hyle, matter), who is studying the mirror of forms, with the "kiss" of an intermediate interpreter Icon or *iconia* ("cum Ilem speculum formarum meditantem, aeternalis salutavit idea, eam iconiae interpretis interventu vicario osculata," M—480B, W—518). The result of the process is the Truth of Being. In the sermon, the action is likened to a "genial kiss" by which the marriage of form and matter, Nature and the "natured," propagates this Truth (p. 300).

Natura, soul of the world, belongs to the sphere of reason, between those of intelligence and matter, because she originally endowed man with the mark of reason.[19] Often regarded as the efficient cause of the universe, she is responsible for the union of spirit and matter.[20] After she had first created man's body from matter, she adorned it with the senses, spies to keep watch and guard the body from assault; the body, "purpuramentis ornata," ornamented with "purple vestments," thus became more acceptable to the spirit it married (M—442D, W—450). Similarly, in the sermon the *imagines* (*ychones*) of the sensible world are dressed in purple garments, "purpuramentis ornata," to signify the marriage of form and matter (p. 300). The color of purple, in addition to hyacinth, scarlet, and white, embellishes the priestly garments of Genius. The gradation of color suggests the process by which the white light of Idea is transformed gradually into the ornamented purple of the earthly Image: Idea darkens with the incremental addition of matter. Genius, agent and other self of Natura, directs the process of the genial kiss by which pale Idea is infused with flesh and blood—the natural descent of the soul. On a cosmic scale these male and female principles, like the Stoic Jupiter Progenitor and Genetrix (universal Genius and Juno), engender life. As the active principle of Natura, who is the soul of the world, Alanus' Genius resembles the Augustinian universal Genius, who also activated generation for the soul of the world, Jupiter. Whereas her appearance emphasizes the hierarchy of the created world—from zodiac to flowers—his appearance in a four-colored garment upon which Images are brought to life and pass away stresses the creative process, the "naturing" of nature, or the natural descent of the soul. In *De Planctu,* such "naturing" primarily involves human nature.

That is, Genius is Natura's priest, marrying form and matter by means of the "genialis osculus" in the Temple of Forms. The *imagines* depicted on his multicolored clothing live momentarily and then expire (M—479C, W—517): these *imagines* are synonymous with the *ychones* (*icones*) which in the sermon fill the sensible world. Alanus declares, "In the first [or sensible sphere] reign *ychones,* i.e., subjects of their forms, ornamented with 'purpuraments,' which subjects are called *ychones* or *imagines,* because they are brought forth into the truth of being according to the likeness of the eternal exemplars which have existed eternally in the Divine Mind." [21] Genius' *imagines rerum,* given the life of their kind, transmigrate from the shadow of a mere picture into the "truth of being" (". . . ab umbra picturae ad veritatem essentiae transmigrantes, vita sui generis donabantur," M—479D, W—517). In the sermon, Truth, Essence, and Possibility are the three daughters engendered by the genial kiss; in *De Planctu,* Veritas, Genius' daughter, is begotten by the genial kiss of Natura and the natured ("hoc solo Naturae natique geniali osculo fuerat derivata," M—480B, W—518). She then assists him in his work, following him as a daughter follows her father. However, Falsity (Falsitas), like Possibility in the sermon, mars the work of Truth. As she spies on the pictures of Truth, she deforms whatever Truth forms or fashions skillfully ("quidquid illa conformiter informabat, ista informiter deformabat," M—480C, W—519). Subject to old age and mutability, and bald like the goddess Fortuna,[22] she resembles both Atropos and Fortuna. The Truth of Being, derived from the celestial and superior Aplanon, is affected by the lower and inferior Aplanon, the mutable underworld. All of creation is subject to the vicissitudes of change—illness and death—in the sublunar realm.

In addition, the union of matter and spirit, the descent of the soul into the underworld, is different for each man. No individual is a perfect copy of the Eternal Idea: astrology, for example, explains the differences of human appearance and temperament as the result of specific planetary conjunctions and influences. In the *De Planctu,* Genius is not only a generic agent ensuring the likeness of form for all men, but also a Pantomorph providing differences among them.

As a personification of human nature, Genius himself embodies the idea and ideal of mankind. When we first meet him, we discover that his stature adheres to the mean: he is neither too short nor too tall, too thin nor too fat (M—479C, W—517). He is both young and old simultaneously; he has a youthful face, but draped with white locks. At first he appears to be a type of *puer senex,* perfectly appropriate if he is a god.[23] But he represents all men in one form, neither young nor old, and yet both young and old. Perhaps Alanus is aware of this Horatian description of Genius, transcribed by Guillaume de Conches: "mortalis in unum / quodque caput, voltu mutabilis, albus et ater" (*Epistle* 2.2.188–89). The god of human nature reflects the influence of mutability in his appearance. Indeed, his height and stature, regulated by the "canone mediocritatis," and his young-old mien suggest two basic limitations of man's sojourn in the underworld: he occupies space (the incarceration of the soul in the body), and he is subject to time and mutability (his life in the sublunar underworld). Finally, the word "mediocritas," the norm to which his stature conforms, implies not only a middle state, but also moderation: the *virtuous* mean allows neither subtraction nor excess.

The youthful *senex,* like Bernardus' decrepit Pantomorph and Claudian's fixer of laws, ascribes individual form for each person, changing the characteristics of the ideal to differentiate men. As Natura organizes all of creation into different classes or species, permitting each species its own unique appearance, so Genius orders mankind into different types or "species," allotting each man his own special character. Alanus highlights this function of Genius through the writing image: as long as the right hand inscribes and the left hand holds the animal skin, then individuals of a true and good nature are conceived. But if his right hand should tire and his left hand start writing, evil and deficient men whose bodies control their souls are born. The left hand, having less control over the pen and its sketching, exerts a less positive influence on human potential.

In *De Mundi,* the pen of the scribe Pantomorph, who ruled the Decani, paralleled the finger of God which traced secrets in the stars; in *De Planctu,* it symbolizes the process by which the soul, celestial part of man, is united with flesh, the animal skin upon which the pen writes. Genius' right hand signifies a beneficent supernal power; the left hand, a malefic infernal power. Natura herself admits that the pen in her hand is guided during her creative work by the "right hand of supernal majesty"

so that it will not deviate in any way (M—454A, W—470). The efficacy
of the right hand, as opposed to the harmfulness of the left, was mentioned during the classical period in several discussions of *genius;* more
directly pertinent is a passage transmitted from Servius to Mythographus
Secundus describing the effects of the hands of Isis, generative Genius of
Egypt, upon the Nile waters.[24] Her right hand promotes fertility, hence
good; her left hand quashes it: both hands control Egypt's fate. Similarly,
when the right hand of Alanus' Genius designs, good "species" or types
of men are created: Helen, a type of beauty; Turnus, boldness; Hercules,
strength; Capaneus, height; Ulysses, shrewdness; Cato, virtuous sobriety;
Plato, "genius" (in the modern sense); Cicero, eloquence; and Aristotle,
thought (M—479D, W—517). These "images" of the Eternal Idea of
mankind typify kinds of human excellence. Natura's great Chain of
Being—the species of things—is paralleled by Genius' chain of human
being: the hierarchy begins with types of physical excellence—beauty,
boldness, strength, height—and culminates in spiritual and intellectual
excellence—shrewdness, sobriety, genius, eloquence, thought. The ladder of types also suggests the characteristics of man influenced by the
seven planets and luminaries in Macrobius' commentary on the *Somnium
Scipionis:* reason and understanding (from Saturn: Aristotle and Plato);
the power to act (from Jupiter: Ulysses); boldness of spirit (from Mars:
Turnus); passion (from Venus: Helen); speaking ability (from Mercury:
Cicero); sensation (from the sun: virtuous sobriety of Cato); and growth
(from the moon: Hercules and Capaneus).

When the right hand tires and the left hand accepts the pen, perverse
and licentious individuals—*larvae*—are conceived: it creates through incomplete picturing ("semiplena picturatione") the "figures of things"
("rerum figuras") or the "shadowy *larvae* of figures" ("figurarum larvas
umbratiles"). Both Apuleius and Martianus Capella define *larvae* as evil
ghosts or specters representing evil men after the death of the body.[25] In
Servius, such ghosts are identified as evil *manes* or *genii*. The *manes*
produced by the left hand of Genius are clearly evil *genii* or *larvae:* Thersites, a type of disgrace; Paris, carnal love; Sinon, trick and subterfuge;
Ennius, metrical license; Pacuvius, wrong order (M—480A, W—518).
Again, a ladder of types is described, from the lowest and most bestial—
disgrace and carnality—to the highest—wrong order. These evil "genii"

are antitheses to the good "genii" produced by the right hand. The soul descends into the "underworld" as an image of potential good or evil: the stars or spheres determine its human temperament and designate its best or worst possible characteristics.

Genius, agent of Natura, controls the generation and birth of men—the fall of the soul into the nether regions. His pen, symbol of the heavens' influence upon the descent of the soul, acts as a Urania in the creation of man; his animal pelt, symbol of the underworld of the body, acts as a Physis. He is both *generalis* and *specialis praesul* for mankind: to each man he accords a special image, contingent upon the benefic or malefic influences of the heavens (i.e., the right or left hands).

The actual physical reproduction of the species, however, is controlled by Venus, Natura's deputy, who is assisted in her work by her husband, Hymen, and their son, Cupid. Their goal is to maintain and continue the human race, thereby healing injuries inflicted by the hands of the Fates (Parcae, M—454B, W—470). The goddess of love, the god of marriage, and their son, sexual desire, represent Alanus' version of the *genii* of marriage at the end of *De Mundi,* who directed the sexual organs, genial weapons battling death and Lachesis, to repair Nature and the species.

Venus' creative tools, given to her by Natura to facilitate her work, symbolize the sexual organs: two hammers which should be applied properly and faithfully to their anvils, and a very potent reed pen, a "calamum praepotentem" with which she will figure the "rerum genera" upon small leaves of paper begging for the writing of the pen ("ut in competentibus schedulis ejusdem calami scripturam poscentibus, . . . rerum genera figuraret," M—457A, W—475). Venus, like Genius and Natura, is a writer, but her scribal role is restricted to the tracing of the natures of things according to Natura's rules of orthography ("juxta meae orthographiae normulam"). She merely figures (*figurare,* to embellish with rhetorical figures) and shapes the classes of things, especially the animal genus to which man belongs. Natura accordingly instructs her pupil in the rules of grammatical art, whose connections and constructions of unlike things emulate the proper embrace of the two sexes obeying the rule of genial coition ("genialis concubitus ordinatis") that results in offspring. Venus' careful grammatical exercises prepare her for joining other unlike things: Natura describes the two genders, the placement of the adjective

(the masculine sex) next to the noun (the feminine sex), proper conjuga-
tion, and the fleshly connection of subject and predicate in the conclusion
of the syllogistic argument.

The scratching of the pen on "desirous leaves" is prompted by love
(Venus) in the context of marriage (Hymen). The latter, whose garments
depict idealized events of marriage and the nuptial ceremony, exemplifies
manliness and virility (the early classical Genius, correlative of the feminine Juno): his beard changes very rapidly from boyish fuzz (at puberty)
to a wild growth (full maturity), at which time it is sheared. His age
ranges from youth to maturity to old age; his stature alters quickly from
very short to very tall; he wears clothes which vary from a poor to a fine
material. Marriage is possible for any man at any age, of any height, rich
or poor. He is the brother of Natura in more than one sense: he is the god
of marriage for all men, as she is the goddess of "marriage"—for form
and matter.

He is also the husband of Venus. When Venus grows bored with his
attention and seeks excitement elsewhere, trouble brews and Natura complains. For, the genial work of Venus ceases, and Nature, especially
human nature, is not perpetuated. At this point, Genius must be summoned.

THE VICIOUS AND VIRTUOUS DESCENTS

Venus grows tired of her reproductive role in marriage in the *De Planctu;*
she deserts Hymen and their son, Cupid, and commits adultery with Antigenius, or Antigamus,[26] producing a bastard son, Jocus. That is, man
turns to degenerate sexual practices for the sake of variety in play
(Jocus). At the beginning of Alanus' work, the narrator laments the sexual perversions—homosexuality, sodomy, and prostitution—which have
generated the sterile mirth of men. In this manner men twist the laws of
nature and pursue an evil Venus. There are two immediate consequences:
first, man no longer advances the reproduction of the species through the
use of his sexual organs (*"Idaea* of the womb impresses no matter, but
rather the plowshare ploughs on a sterile seashore"); second, man sub-
verts his nature ("Having become a barbarian in the art of nature, he re-

fuses to be a man,'' M—431B, W—430). This refusal rightly upsets Natura, initially because Venus allies herself with Atropos, and the human race is not renewed (M—459C, W—480). But more important, the idleness that induces man to search for novel and unnatural sexual diversions is usually accompanied by drunkenness and gluttony, all of which eventually make him ill with ''acuta Veneris febre''—lechery (M—460B, W—481-82). The lesser sins of sloth, gluttony, and lechery ultimately lead to the greater sins of avarice, pride, envy, and hypocrisy (M—476C-D, W—511-12). These are the sins Genius will mention in his excommunication of vicious men at the very end of the work: the Virtues have been banished from human society, and the deadly sins reign in their place. The consequence, therefore, of dissipation through sterile adultery (Antigenius-Jocus) involves both sensual and spiritual degeneration; man ''adulters'' his soul, passion overcomes reason, and he is unmanned in another sense—he becomes a beast or a barbarian.

Basically, Alanus has traced the stages of the vicious descent: the adulterous liaison of Venus with Antigenius allegorizes the fall of man. She is an Eve who betrays her Adam (Hymen) for Satan (Antigenius); she is also a Euridice who flees Aristeus (virtue) and who is poisoned by the venom of the serpent's bite (pleasures of temporal good). Bernardus' juxtaposition of Aristeus and the serpent is reflected in Alanus' personifications, Hymen and Antigenius. Although two Venuses, one heavenly, one evil,[27] seem to appear in the poem, there is actually only one, who may be defined allegorically as natural concupiscence, the *genius* or Euridice designated by Bernardus in his commentary on the *Aeneid* as the ''appetite for good.'' This *genius,* born with each man and living until his death, differs from the generative Genius who controls the natural descent. When Venus obeys the laws of Natura, using the sexual organs not for pleasure but for procreation, she chooses natural or rational good, but when she disobeys, enjoying fornication with Antigenius, she indulges herself in the pleasures of temporal good.

We have previously discussed Hymen, the god of marriage; regarded in the fourth part of the *satura* as one of the banished Virtues, he is introduced before Chastity, Temperance, and Generosity. He might be considered as archetypal Virtue, or Bernardus' Aristeus. His original relationship with his wife and son suggests the proper marriage of man's spirit and flesh during his life on earth. His rival, his wife's lover An-

tigenius or Antigamus (Enemy of Marriage), represents that adultery of
the flesh which provokes chaos and disharmony—the overthrow of the
spirit by the passions.

Venus' fornication with Antigenius, "ignobilitatis genere derivatus"
("descended from a race of ignobility," M—459D, W—481), activates
man's descent into the underworld of the seven deadly sins, just as the
seduction of Euridice by the phallic surrogate, the serpent, thrusts her
into the underworld of temporal good. His name has been carefully chosen: he is the evil *manes* or *cacodaemon*. In the *Distinctiones,* Alanus
distinguishes between the good angel and the evil demon, declaring that
"evil *daemones* are called *cacodaemones* from *caco* which is 'evil,'
because they employ their knowledge in an evil way" ("mali vero daemones dicuntur cacodaemones a *caco* quod est *malum,* quia male scientia
sua utuntur," 759). Evil and the *genius* have been associated from the
earliest times: the Servian evil *genius* (*manes*) promoted *cupiditas* and
fleshly indulgence; the *luxuria* and *avaritia* discussed in Persius' *Saturae*
are related to the dilemma, whether "indulgere genio" or "defraudare
genium." Alanus, in fact, defines *daemones* as the seven deadly sins:
Christ exorcized "septem daemonia, id est septem peccata mortalia,"
from Mary Magdalene (*Dist.* 759). Antigenius, then, corresponds to the
seven demons, the seven deadly sins, as Alanus' Genius parallels Christ,
the ideal man or the "angel" who must exorcize the demons.

It is significant that Natura herself cannot cut out the diseased part of
human nature, "because I cannot exceed the limit of my power,"
(M—476A, W—510). Instead, she calls upon Genius to assist her in the
sacerdotal office by excommunicating fallen man from the natural order
and from grace.[28] When man chooses the way of Antigenius, he affronts
Genius by leaving him idle, for he is no longer engaged in the task of
generation, and by perverting the proper nature of man, that part of nature which is the generic province of Genius. It is appropriate, then, that
the *generalis praesul* exchanges the common garments of his generative
office for the vestments of the priest in order to excommunicate from the
realm of human nature the bestial and barbarous men whom he originally
created, but no longer considers human.

The perverted and sterile pleasure (the bastard Jocus) produced by
Venus' affair with Antigenius contrasts with the natural desire to procreate (Cupid) characterizing Venus' marriage to Hymen. The seven

deadly sins engendered by this liaison also promote a spiritual sterility and eventual "death." According to the Silvestran interpretation of the Orpheus-Euridice myth, each man "dies" when he falls into the underworld of temporal pleasure; for Servius and others, man is judged and punished after death by his *manes* ("quisque suos patimur Manes"), which are actually *genii* relegated to man from birth. The priest Genius, as if a general *manes* for fallen men, announces their punishments after this spiritual "death": each specific sin merits an appropriate punishment—for example, the drunkard will suffer eternal thirst, the glutton will become a beggar (M—482A, W—521).

As a priest, Genius functions antithetically to the lecher, Antigenius. The latter acts like an evil demon or *manes,* instigator of the vices. Genius performs the office of the good angel or *manes,* instigator of the virtues and communicator of knowledge, i.e., the message of the excommunication. Alanus defines good angels as *"calodaemones* from *calo,* which is 'the good,' that is, knowing good, and doing good, because they convert their knowledge into good deeds or uses" (". . . boni angeli dicuntur calodaemones a *calo,* id est *bonum,* id est bona scientes, et bene, quia in bonos usus convertunt scientam suam," *Dist.* 759). This agent of the excommunication is employed as a messenger between fallen man and the Eternal, Natura, and mankind: he will be divorced from the Eternal, "a supernae dilectionis osculo," from Natura, "a natura gratia," and from mankind, "a naturalium rerum uniformi concilio" (M—482A, W—521). Man's adultery after the original marriage of body and soul at birth is followed by a divorce. The genial kiss of Idea (from the Intelligible Sphere) and Hyle (from the Imaginable Sphere) through an intermediary Icon engenders man, but he is now alienated from that kiss of supernal love (Intelligible Sphere), from the grace of Natura (Rational Sphere), and from the uniform design of natural things (the Imaginable Sphere). The wedding of Natura and her offspring has been dissolved by the figure who presided over the nuptials.

The good angel conveys messages to men from God. Such messages are described as "theophanies" by Simon de Tournai, a contemporary of Alanus: "Theophany means 'manifestation,' from 'theos,' which is God, and 'phanos,' which is an apparition; whence 'theophania,' apparition of God; but in which God appears, by it he is manifested." [29] Theophanies are divided into three classes—epiphanies (seraphim, cherubim, thrones), iperphanies (dominations, principates, powers), and ypophanies (virtues, archangels, angels).[30] In other words, the theophanic messengers comprise the nine orders of the Pseudo-Dionysian angelic hierarchy mentioned in the first book of *De Mundi,* residents of the highest sphere and superior to the *angeli* between the sun and the moon. The function of the theophanic angel, like that of the *angelus,* is to communicate. Alanus cites Joannes Scotus to clarify the way in which knowledge of the future is transmitted by theophanies: Divine Nature illuminates the mind of man by means of theophany, an illumination itself likened to that of the sun in the sensible world.[31]

Such divine sanction is accorded to the words of Genius during the excommunication: he speaks with the authority of Superessential Usia and Eternal Idea, the assent of the celestial militia, and the approval of Natura and the Virtues (M—481C-82D, W—520-1). Accustomed to writing in the book of human nature, he now communicates by intoning the excommunication—in effect, the word of God (Usia). So he is an angel, a *calodaemon* or emanation of God: "For God is called a *daemon,* thus in Asclepia: 'Those who in the present are unwilling to believe words, in the future will be compelled to believe punishment; for they will pass into the power of the Highest Judge,' that is, of God, whence good angels are called *calodaemones"* (*Dist.* 759). The words he utters are themselves the punishments promised to wicked men, those who refuse to believe in the Word.

However, Genius is literally neither angel nor theophanic messenger in *De Planctu.* In *Quoniam Homines,* Alanus carefully distinguishes the symbolic theophany of the angel from the natural philosophy associated with Genius: the phenomenological mode of each differs. The secrets of God, conveyed by the angels, are manifested through symbols or "consequential signs" perceived by the senses; the secrets of Nature, the "substantial natures" of things known through her "substantifying *genii,"* are apprehended by the intellect as it investigates natural philosophy.[32] Thus Alanus concludes that "Genius indeed means nature or the God of nature. However, this manifestation pertains to natural philosophy, which examines the natures of things." [33] Genius in *De Planctu,* the personified substantial nature of mankind, "substantifies"—and perpetuates—the human race by performing as Natura's agent in the descent of the soul through the spheres and into the body. This natural process must be understood by natural philosophy (according to Bernardus in the commentary, that which is used by the philosopher to understand the "natural order," i.e., that pertaining to the life of man). However, at the end of the *satura,* Genius does carry a message, not from God, but from the Platonic Intelligible Sphere: he functions as a fabulous theophanic messenger. As excommunicating priest, he is the agent of Usia, the celestial militia, Natura, and the Virtues; his communication involves knowledge of the future instead of knowledge of human life. Further, because he ejects demons (sins) from mankind as Christ did from Mary Magdalene, he becomes a masked Verbum Dei, or a Platonic analogue to Christ. Disguised by Alanus *sub integumento,* he resembles Noys, a fabulous Verbum Dei, and Natura, a fabulous Spiritus Sanctus, in *De Mundi.*[34]

Like the theophanic angel, he descends into the underworld—of fallen man. So the grieving Orpheus, rational soul or *nous,* descended into the underworld of temporal good to retrieve his concupiscence, Euridice. Genius' descent is rendered by means of a psychological metaphor: because the vices of men have deformed his mind so deeply, it has descended into the *infernum* of sorrow, and no longer knows the *paradisus* of joy ("Quamvis enim mens mea hominum vitiis angustiata deformibus, in infernum tristitiae peregrinans, laetitiae nesciat paradisum," M—481A, W—520). This depression, his mind's descent into the underworld of sorrow paralleling man's vicious descent into the *infernum* of the body, is equivalent to the misery of the souls in *De Mundi,* who wait at the portal of Cancer to enter the spheres and, eventually, corporeal life. In fact, the sublunary region, the inferior part of the world, is full of misery and dolor, according to Guillaume de Conches.[35] The "falling" of Genius' mood, then, reflects the fall of man into viciousness and parallels the fall of the soul at birth. The ideal of human nature has been besmirched; although he is saddened when he approaches Natura and the Virtues, the promise of vengeance guarantees a restoration of paradise (joy)—for himself and for mankind.

He has figuratively and literally descended from the spheres. Hymen, to whom Natura gives a letter summoning Genius, is appointed to deliver it. But he goes nowhere: instead, he rouses his companion Virtues and they create "harmonious discord," "concordant dissension," on various musical instruments—trumpet, horn, cithara, lyre, pipe, drums, cymbals, etc. (M—477D, W—513). This musical interlude constitutes the "mysteries of his mystic embassy" during which Natura reviews and reiterates her complaint. Genius appears while the music of the festivity still sounds, as if he had been invoked to descend from the heavens by the music of the spheres. Bearer of eloquence and wisdom, he descends like Orpheus, son of Calliope, that "optima vox" whose music conceals heavenly secrets and is linked with the music of the seven spheres.[36]

Orpheus, whose name is derived from *orea phone* and means *optima vox,* is both a poet and musician; his eloquence and wisdom enable him to make a virtuous descent into the underworld in order to rescue his concupiscence, Euridice. Genius' role as priest—performing an excommunication of concupiscent men through his solemn voice—indicates that he too personifies eloquence and wisdom. His first, generational, role was symbolized by the scribal activity of his hands, busily designing the journey of images from sketch into truth of being; his sacerdotal task now is symbolized by the anathema he pronounces from the secret thoughts of his mind. Having shed the worldly vestments of the "priest" of the Palace of Form for garb befitting his higher office, he must now leave the incessant scribbling performed by *hands* and actually communicate by *voice.* The hideous vices of mankind have afflicted his mind, and he must search his thoughts carefully for the proper words to use in communicating his anathema.

Genius addresses the minds of men, leaving them a message (the excommunication) that explicitly demands man learn to know himself better. His virtuous descent, like that of Orpheus, reveals man's need to understand his human nature and, by protecting himself from sensuous pleasure and excess, to maintain the wedding of body and spirit. Elsewhere philosophy and the seven liberal arts provide the means for such understanding: Bernardus defines the virtuous descent of Orpheus as the knowledge of nature implied by the arts and natural philosophy.[37] Martianus uses the seven liberal arts and Philology's ascent through the heavens to structure *De Nuptiis;* in its offspring, the *Anticlaudianus* of Alanus, Natura ascends by means of the arts. Alanus epitomizes ultimate knowledge in the Verbum Dei, whose incarnation is related to the seven liberal arts in "Rhythmus de Incarnatione et de Septem Artibus." [38] The *Anticlaudianus* with its ascent becomes a companion poem to *De Planctu* with its descents.

The two roles of Genius—in the natural and virtuous descents—are carefully distinguished by Alanus. Genius, priest of the Formal Tabernacle, wears two different garments to reflect his tasks—generation and excommunication. The priest of generation uses his hands to write and create; man sins against him by failing to reproduce his kind, and by perverting his sexuality through the magic art of Venus Scelestis. He uses his mind and voice to excommunicate; man sins against him by failing to govern his appetites with reason. The adultery of spirit symbolized by the union of Venus and Antigenius leads to the perversion inherent in the seven deadly sins. Genius descends to rescue mankind from Antigenius: he takes back the word he bestowed on his creation—"man." The motif of communication and excommunication, writing and orating, creating and dissolving, which links the two roles of Genius, is amplified in the rhetorical metaphor pervading the *satura*. This metaphor illuminates *De Planctu,* handbook for the *trivium* and archetype for the artificial descent in which Genius again participates.

THE ARTIFICIAL DESCENT

The classical demon revealed the secrets of the future through the medium of the dream; the medieval demon transmitted its underworld knowledge of the future when consulted through magic art. The former concept was translated by John of Salisbury into a more viable medieval form: an angel, wise man, or God appeared in the *oraculum,* highest form of the dream, to forewarn an individual. But in the *somnium,* or enigmatic dream, *imagines* (images, ideas) are manifested under the *involucra* (coverings) of things: this inferior form of dream resembles the fabulous narrative used by the poet to conceal the truths of Nature *sub integumento*. The wisely and skillfully fashioned artifice of the fabulous narrative represents an antithesis to the magic or black art used to contact the demons of the underworld.

In the dream vision of *De Planctu,* Genius enters at the end to pronounce excommunication and anathema upon all vicious men. His promise of eternal thirst to the drunkard, humiliation to the proud man, beggary to the glutton, poverty to the miser constitutes a vision of future

damnation which would have been conveyed earlier by the Greek messenger *daemon* or even the late classical *genius*. Because the narrative is
structured by the concept of the visionary dream, Genius, speaking with
the authority of Usia, Natura, and the Virtues, more closely resembles
the divine or quasi-divine agent of the medieval *oraculum*. The *satura*
moves toward this final brutal communication of Genius, which ends both
the work and the dream of the narrator simultaneously.

But this dream vision is also fabulous narrative: it presents ideas and
images under *involucra*—Venus, Natura, Hymen, Antigenius, Jocus,
even Genius himself—the *figurae* of the *somnium*. And within this *somnium,* the secrets of Natura concerning the proper activity of man and of
art are disguised *per fabulosa*. We have discussed Natura's definition of
the human ideal which men have abused and perverted through their
viciousness; she is almost equally anxious about the artistic ideal which
too many weak and inferior poets have twisted and distorted. Her dual
concerns are linked in the explanation of the rent in her tunic (*tegumen-
tum*): it occurs at that place "in which the *insomnia* [dreams, fancies] of
painting [or art] represent the image of man" ("in qua hominis imaginem
picturae repraesentant insomnia," M—452B, W—467). The one flaw in
creation has been caused by men: they have assaulted and raped Natura,
tearing her garments, stripping her, and in so far as they can, compelling
her to live like a whore, instead of clothing her with honor (M—452C,
W—467). That is, they have prostituted their human nature. But the tear
in her garment also suggests men have violated "the *insomnia* of art"
depicting human life. Indeed, the metaphor she uses to describe the
affront to her dignity is Macrobian: in his commentary, he declared that
Natura's secrets must be hidden by the prudent man under appropriate
"vestments" (i.e., fabulous narrative) to prevent their exposure to base
men. And she explains her torn garment in a dialogue with the dreamer
concerning poetic theory—appropriate artifice, or the *"insomnia* of art."

Natura's discourse on art differs from Macrobius' in that she describes
poetic abuses by common men, whereas he had outlined the poetic ideal
for the wise man. First, she declares, inferior poets have prostituted a
naked Falsity to their listeners ("auditoribus nudam falsitatem prosti-
tuunt") without any cloak ("sine . . . palliationis remedio") in order to
enchant them with melody (M—451C, W—465). Delight in the sound of
poetry becomes an end in itself, so that bare Falsity (an enchanting

whore) replaces Truth (noble Natura). Having given their audience what it wishes to hear, these poets do not bother to cover Falsity with the honor and dignity of *integumenta* and *involucra,* presumably because all men "know" her and she has no secrets (no truth) to hide. Secondly, they may cloth Falsity with credible artifice (i.e., "per exemplorum imagines"), but only in order to sway men to their point of view; she is still an untrue and deceptive whore, no matter how she is dressed. Finally, however, there are some poems whose surface *cortex* (shell, body) is false, but which conceal a sweet kernel of secret truth ("dulciorem nucleum veritatis secrete"). Alanus' Natura, here repeating the poetic technique espoused by Macrobius, nevertheless respects philosophy more than poetry: she has no faith in the "shadowy fancies of the poets" ("umbratilibus poetarum figmentis") and prefers the "saner reflection of philosophy" ("senior philosophiae tractatus"). The reason is apparent: natural philosophy deals with the truths of the world created by God; however, many poems deceive through their depiction of false gods and their exploits. Despite this preference for philosophy and truth, Natura does admit that she herself must "cloak her form" (" faciem palliare," M—445B, W—454) to preserve her mystery and to prevent a contempt for her induced by familiarity. Also, she concedes that a "cloak of euphonious oration" ("euphoniae orationis . . . pallium") should be provided when the subject is "monstrous vice," not to shelter truth from vulgar men, but to protect good men from vulgarity (M—453A, W—468).

In spite of Natura's basic anathema to poetry, much of *De Planctu* delineates the proper shape and techniques of poetry—artifice. Indeed, the *artifex* Natura not only provides form for the species of the world, but in masking her own form, this *artifex* herself becomes poet and fabulist. The "artificial descent" emulates the natural descent: as the soul is joined with the *infernum,* the body, so that sweet kernel of secret truth is united with a protective *cortex* (both shell and body)—a false exterior. The truth of poetry reflects the truth of Nature, but it is masked with the artificial by the poet-*artifex.* Genius, agent of the natural descent, typifies as well the agent of the artificial descent—the poet; Venus, whose control of the reproductive organs initiates that descent upon conception, represents the control of the artist's pen—that is, technical knowledge of proper artifice. Genius as philosopher-poet becomes a mediator between Natura and

Venus, Nature and Artifice, Truth and Falsity. The scribal metaphor linking all three figures engaged in the task of generation now appears to
have a more literal significance.

Venus' scribal role consists of transcribing according to Natura's rules
of orthography. The latter provides her with tools—the hammers and
anvil, the pen and leaves—and also with instructions for their use—her
own theories of grammatical art and dialectic. Venus should join the
masculine gender with the feminine, and place the adjective (masculine)
next to the noun (feminine). Natura's instructions to Venus concerning
the dialectical art also exemplify the nature of the proper sexual union:
the syllogistic argument includes three terms, the major extreme (predicate), minor extreme (subject), and conclusion (the fleshly merger of subject and predicate). The sexual act had been described by grammatical
metaphors throughout the Middle Ages; [39] in *De Planctu,* they are also
used to explain the nature of artifice (whose successful creation depends
upon the poet's knowledge of the *trivium*). Grammar, that art dealing
with words, the mark of man's reason that separates him from the beasts,
and dialectic, that art which describes the way man reasons, both mirror
the natural. Only rhetoric, the third art of the *trivium,* which involves the
embellishment and adornment of man's speech, is forbidden to Venus.
The arts of rhetoric, or the "metonymic principles of the rhetoricians,"
although not evil or unnatural in themselves (they honorably grace
Mother Rhetoric's *rationes,* speeches), may tempt Venus, Natura fears,
into changing the true relationship of masculine subject and feminine
predicate (M—458D-E, W—479). That is, such arts may become an end
in themselves, thereby diverting Venus from her real goal.

Unfortunately, this is exactly what happens. Her boredom leads to fornication with Antigenius (the anti-poet, the opposite of Genius). As a
consequence, "destroying herself in grammatical constructions, inverting
herself in dialectical conversions, having discolored her art into *figura*
with the colors of rhetoric, she thus transforms her *figura* into vice." [40]
The product of this new union is the bastard Jocus, whose name also
suggests jest and verbal artifice.[41] Allegorically, Venus' actions depict
the conversion of art into artifice, unnatural and magic art. In the Proem
to *De Planctu,* the homosexuality of man, the making of man into
woman, is attributed to the "magic art" of Venus (M—431A-B,
W—429), which allows active nature to become passive, and man to

become both predicate and subject. When this occurs, delight in artifice (*tropus*) supplants art (*ars*). This form of artifice transcends mere metaphor (*translatio*), however, for the *figura* actually descends ("cadit") into vice (M—431B, W—430). The vicious descent of the *figura* into the underworld of rhetorical artifice resembles the descent of Euridice, initiated by the pleasures of temporal good (the snake's bite). Also, the "magic art" of Venus echoes the "magic art" used to consult the demons of the underworld. Alanus' point is that the *tropus* and *figura* are unnatural when they subvert the right order of the grammatical and dialectical arts. That is, when the body controls the soul, a process illustrated by the vicious descent, reason is controlled by passion; accordingly, when rhetorical embellishment becomes more important than the fundamental principles of grammar and logic, the trope controls the art—a *descensus artificii*. Venus' lechery for Antigenius produces this magical art, the abuse of rhetoric; classical *luxuria* was often defined as stylistic excess and rankness. Alanus, in his discussion of *daemones* and the seven deadly sins incarnated in Mary Magdalene, says of *luxuria,* "This species of *daemon* cannot be exorcized except by eloquence and abstinence," i.e., by eloquence without ornament.[42] It is Genius who will exorcize stylistic excess with his stark eloquence at the end of the poem.

His anathema is described as an "oration"; his short speech to Natura, also called an *oratio,* is shaped by Genius using the fewest possible words ("Dum hoc verborum compendio Genius suae orationis formaret excursum," M—481B, W—520). Previously an *artifex* who creates man, Genius now becomes an *artifex* who fashions words: "he coined the matter of his voice into this form of locution" ("in hanc locutionis formam suae vocis monetavit materiam," M—480D, W—519). Matter is still granted form, but Genius' creation is now eloquent, not vital. When he announces the excommunication, the process is similarly described: "under this image (form) of words, he called forth from the secret places of his mind the preordained orderly sequence of the excommunication" ("sub hac verborum imagine, praetaxatam excommunicationis seriem a penetralibus mentis forinsecus evocavit," M—481C, W—520). The process by which the excommunication is brought from the secret places of his mind into life as an *imago verborum* parallels the way in which spirit and matter enter life as an *imago* of Eternal Idea. The descent of idea into speech emulates the rhythm of the Incarnation: the word is made flesh,

coined into life. The stylus Genius used in the creation of mankind is
exchanged for carefully chosen words in his excommunication: the quill,
stylus (and plow), was also used throughout the Middle Ages to signify
the Logos.[43] Alanus does not stress the carefully-fashioned speech of any
other figure in *De Planctu* with as much detail: the emphasis on Genius'
eloquence marks him as an archetypal orator-poet—like Orpheus. Bernardus Silvestris defines the cithara of this poet-musician as "rhetorical
speech" in which "colores" resonate; the strings of the cithara are
explained as rhetorical embellishments.[44] Although Genius carries no
cithara, he descends from spheres to the discordant harmony of the music
of the Virtues in order to present his rhetorical oration.

He is both the archetypal or ideal poet-philosopher-orator and the
agent of art and inspiration (i.e., modern "genius"). The description of
his appearance with pen and parchment epitomizes his role as *artifex,* the
"other self" of Natura in a different sense (in that the artifice of the poet
should mirror nature, the artificial descent emulating the natural descent
of soul into body). Indeed, when he writes with his right hand, images
appear—beautiful Helen, bold Turnus, strong Hercules, gigantic Capaneus, foxy Ulysses. All of these are poetic figures from the *Aeneid.* The
remaining offspring of Genius' incessant writing are not poetic fictions,
but real orators and philosophers—Cato with his virtuous sobriety, Plato
with his *ingenium* (modern genius), Cicero with his eloquence, Aristotle
with his *sententiae* hidden by *aenigmata* (M—479D, W—517).

Similarly, when the left hand writes, shadowy figures arise, "ab orthographiae semita falsigraphiae claudicatione recedens" (M—480A,
W—518). Thersites, Paris, and Sinon are deficient and vicious poetic figures from the *Aeneid;* the artists mentioned, Ennius and Pacuvius, are
false and ignore the rules of art. Ennius' verses exhibit the licentious
abuse of metrical art, while suffering from a paucity of thought; Pacuvius
does not understand order or structure, and places the beginning of his
story at the end (M—480A, W—518). Note, too, that Ennius and Pacuvius are poet and fabulist, not philosophers like Plato and Aristotle.

Two extremes are portrayed by the parallel hierarchies. The poetic figures conceived by the right hand are true images of the ideal (physical
and spiritual); those of the left are incomplete (hence false) depictions of
evil types. The orators and philosophers of the right hand exemplify the
highest eloquence, virtue, and wisdom; the false poets of the left hand,

beset by ignorance, create art that is deformed and empty of thought. The ideal types and the antitypes together suggest that true poetry occupies a middle ground: the philosopher disseminates the highest truths of Nature, but the poet disguises his truth under a veil; the inferior artist allows perversity to govern his metrics or the order of his narrative, but the wise poet realizes the rules of art reflect the laws of nature. Essentially Alanus duplicates the thoughts of Bernardus concerning the philosopher-poet, who as philosopher must observe the natural order of the narrative—as poet, the artificial.[45] Finally, the figures he creates must effectively disguise an interior nucleus of truth under a surface false *cortex*. Thus Helen and Hercules, both fictional and therefore untrue, cloak ideas of beauty and strength respectively, whereas Thersites, equally fictional, requires a better artist (or so Alanus declares), perhaps because he himself represents no hidden truth, but instead his "ragged dress" signifies disgrace. The other shadowy *larvae,* Paris and Sinon, display a similar incomplete and unfinished artistry. Like Thersites, they can be understood only on the literal (i.e., integumental, fictional) level, although things associated with them have meaning: Paris is overcome by carnal love, Sinon's weapons are those of trickery and subterfuge. There is little truth concealed *sub integumento*.

The art of poetry resembles Genius' creation, man. The true soul (inner meaning) is plunged within a false body, the poetic *cortex*. As long as Truth contributes to the creation of poetic figures and the inspiration of wise philosophers, as long as she aids her father Genius, the resulting work is true; but often Falsity mars this work, just as she mars human nature. That is, when the body controls the soul, viciousness and falsity ensue; when the "body" of poetry—poetic fancy and *licentia*—governs its "soul"—truth—then incompletely drawn figures result. Ignorance produces metrical license, disordered structure, and paucity of thought.

As the natural descent of the soul from the spheres begins when a soul is conceived by the reproductive organs, so the artificial descent of truth into its fictional cortex is triggered by adherence to the rules of grammar and logic, which mirror the laws of Natura. Rhetorical art embellishes the superficial covering of poetry; it concentrates on its "body" or underworld. Accordingly, the poet may descend into this underworld, forgetting the secrets of Nature, and the *figurae,* tropes, and metaphors may become ends in themselves, so that this magic art leads to vice and ignorance. Inferior artistry emulates the vicious descent: Remigius' Euridice (*inventio* of profound art) leaves Orpheus (the poet and musician) when he descends into the *infernum* of "profound study"; he retains the *vox* of music, but without *ratione*. Alanus adds his own rendition of the Orpheus and Euridice myth to the Fulgentian tradition, shared by Remigius, through the figures of Venus and Genius. When the poet tires, when he is seduced by the attractiveness of rhetorical tricks and forgets his obligation to Truth, integument triumphs, leaving his artistry incomplete. Venus, guiding the reproductive organs in the natural descent and the poet's awareness of grammar and dialectic in the artificial descent, must serve Genius properly. As god of generation, he endows the soul with corporeal life; as agent of eloquence and wisdom, he grants man "immortal life" through his creative endeavors. Genius as "inventive powers" or "mental ability" begins to sound very modern.

The creative "trinity" of Natura, Genius, and Venus guides the descent of truth and secrets into the underworld of fiction and fabulous narrative and discloses the role of *De Planctu* as a handbook for the aspiring poet. The three figures parallel the generative "trinity" which directs the descent of the soul into the underworld of flesh. The moral "trinity" maintains the wedding of body and soul, or at least attempts to prevent man's descent into vice.

Genius is both priest of the Palace of Forms and a more conventional priest. Although he creates man, he must excommunicate him from creation when man refuses to reproduce the species and when he fails to act like a man, naturally both beast and angel. Genius then descends into the underworld like Orpheus, who represents eloquence and wisdom, and deprives the vicious part of mankind of heavenly and natural grace. His condemnation of the seven deadly sins is couched in an oration which is both eloquent and wise. As the archetypal poet and agent of eloquence and wisdom, he also inspires the artificial descent of wisdom into the eloquence of poetry. As intermediary of this *oraculum,* he brings the dreamer a prophetic message; Alanus the poet translates this oracular truth into the fabulous narrative of *De Planctu Naturae.*

CHAPTER SIX

The Later Medieval Genius:
Implications and Conclusions

The influence of twelfth-century concepts of Genius upon later medieval allegorizations was first recognized by C. S. Lewis: the Pantomorph of Bernardus "sufficiently explains the Genius in the *De Planctu Naturae,* who is the enemy of unnatural vice because he is the patron of generation and therefore of heterosexuality. From him the Genius of Jean de Meun and of Gower directly descends." [1] Certainly the thirteenth and fourteenth-century conceptions of the figure depend heavily upon twelfth-century treatments, although there are many differences between the Genius of Bernardus and of Alanus. Bernardus' *genii* function as cosmic agents of the natural descent of the soul; Alanus' Genius, although associated with all four descents, primarily represents a moral and rational standard ("priest") for mankind. In effect, the twelfth-century Genius, Horatian "god of human nature," is developed and amplified in the pattern of the four descents described by Guillaume de Conches and Bernardus. Three of the descents center on the major events and changes inherent in human life—birth, introduction to sin and the pleasures of the temporal world, and the attempt to raise oneself (concupiscence) by immersing oneself (reason) in a knowledge of the created world. The fourth, the descent into hell artificially induced by demonic consultation, constitutes an extra-terrestrial exploration forbidden to the Christian; the magic art employed in this descent invites a comparison with the fabulous artifice used by the poet to conceal truth. The thirteenth- and fourteenth-century Genius, his roles determined by the pattern of the four descents, is described by means of symbols and metaphors, and in terms of ideas, mostly borrowed from Alanus' *De Planctu.* In addition, Jean de Meun and Gower provide their own singular versions of the figure by reinterpreting the descents, and elaborating upon various aspects of them. It is not, then, simply Bernardus' Pantomorph that inspires their portraits of Genius—but instead, the general figure of Genius, god of human nature, intimately associated with this more broadly-based analysis of Original Sin.

GENIUS IN JEAN DE MEUN'S *ROMAN DE LA ROSE*

Two discordant interpretations have been presented to justify and explain Jean de Meun's Genius: first, that the figure is comic and ironic, expressing views that do not belong to the author; and second, that he does reflect the author's views, and therefore should be regarded seriously. Rosemond Tuve points to the iconographical figures accompanying the text to support the first point; Charles Dahlberg, echoing her interpretations, believes that the figures of Nature and Genius function as "mirrors" of the Lover's condition, not of the author's philosophy.[2] John Fleming has advanced this argument one step further: Genius, concupiscence or the "badge of vitiated nature," is a fraud and buffoon whose sacerdotal services to the God of Love illustrate the conventional view of courtly love as a religion.[3] However, other scholars, notably Gérard Paré and Alan Gunn, view Genius more seriously: the philosophy expounded by Nature and Genius, a combination of thirteenth-century Aristotelianism and various Chartrian concepts, provides a rich scholastic and learned backdrop for the poem.[4] Gunn interprets the figures of Genius and Nature as instructors in the "meaning of love," which is based upon the principles of plenitude and replenishment, the primary themes of the poem.[5]

The critical divergence stems from the difficulty of relating the two roles of Genius—generation god and priest. Tuve, Dahlberg, and Fleming perceive his widely contrasting roles as proof for their thesis: Jean de Meun must be poking fun at the figure. A "priest" who advocates incessant devotion to the reproduction of the species and the good use of generational "tools," but who condemns the Christian virtues of chastity and abstinence, is surely ironic. Economou, who agrees, explains that Genius, sexual power or procreative instinct, condemns chastity, but as an ironic priest of Love, does not realize his actual enemy is cupidity, Venus and Amor, or the act of love as an end in itself.[6] However, these critics do not distinguish between irony and allegory: Genius' fabulous role as priest in the *De Planctu,* for example, was not treated ironically. Also, they do not fully realize Genius' allegiance is pledged to Nature and to God, not to Amor. As "god of human nature," he becomes a priest of Nature advocating reproduction, and a bishop of God preaching the rational necessity for virtuous behavior. Jean de Meun carefully links both roles by using the natural and virtuous descents as analogues, and contrasting them with the similarly analogous vicious and artificial descents.

The two roles of Genius are underscored by his changes of clothing, an emblematic device used originally in the *De Planctu.* When Nature first goes to her priest to confess, she finds him wearing a chasuble, rochet, and alb while delivering a Mass of generation. After hearing her complaint concerning man's unnatural behavior (i.e., his failure to reproduce and his inability to live virtuously and rationally), he dons more worldly garments in order to descend to earth. When he appears before the God of Love, he substitutes the accoutrements of a bishop—chasuble, ring, cross, and miter.[7] His two earthly vestments—the worldly garb and the bishop's dress—parallel the two major parts of his speech, the exhortation to reproduce (a less celestial process on earth), and the excommunication and sermon. The confession of Nature introduces the reader to her Macrobian secrets—knowledge of a universal cosmogony aided by Genius and similar to that of Bernardus; the excommunication by Genius and his sermon on the two gardens disguise the concepts of the vicious and virtuous descents, or the two choices open to the judgment (concupiscence, *genius*) of each man.

In the first instance, Genius is a generative priest modeled upon Alanus' priest in the Tabernacle of Forms. Nature finds her priest celebrating an old Mass in her chapel; it is one he has recited ever since he first became priest of her church.[8] This service, derived from a book he had written (apparently under Nature's guidance), records "Les figures representables / De toutes choses corrompables" ("the representative figures of all mutable things," 16281–82). Certainly Jean's description involves parody, but parody need not be ironic: in the Church (or Tabernacle of Forms) of the goddess Nature, her "priest" reproduces the species of the original creation (i.e., that inscribed in the book). The writing met-

aphor is borrowed from Alanus' depiction of Genius, and the book symbol from Bernardus' "Table of Fate" and "Book of Memory" (which
Noys gives to Natura and Physis in *De Mundi*). Here Nature's book
suggests the archetypal cosmos, and the Mass of Genius based on this
book suggests the process of the regeneration of nature. Further, Nature
goes to him to confess: her priest is the appropriate authority to consult
because he is "god and master of this place" (the "chapel"—of forms)
and because he directs "all creatures in the works to them assigned"
(16285–88).

Her "confession," like the costume of Alanus' Natura and the description of the created world in the first book of Bernardus' *De Mundi,*
reveals the secrets of Nature: the way in which the world was first formed
by God out of primordial matter, and the hierarchy of the world produced
by that generative act, beginning with the Aplanon and the planets and
ending with mankind. Gunn outlines the hierarchy of her confession: she
has no complaint to make of the fixed stars, planets, sun and moon, the
weather, four elements, plants, fishes, birds, and other animals.[9] Only man
has disobeyed her laws. Her long confession converts at the end to
complaint: as in the *De Planctu,* man has fallen, affecting nature as well as
himself.

Genius has prefaced her confession with a warning concerning loose-
tongued women who cannot keep a secret; he admits that this does not
apply to Nature, who is "wise without end," according to Scripture.
Tuve believes the warning is ironic, and that it does apply to the garru-
lous goddess.[10] But Nature has not revealed her secrets—or God's—in-
discriminately to vulgar men; they are released only to her priest during
confession. Genius contrasts most women with this figural "woman" in
her relationship with her "husband," God: as master, he rules and governs her, he has taught her everything she knows, and he is her "beautiful mirror," "C'est li beaus miroers ma dame" (19900). The "mirror"
image has been carefully chosen:[11] it suggests Urania's Mirror of Providence (given to her by Noys and reflecting exemplary forms or ideas), the
similar mirrors of the *Anticlaudianus,* the Intelligible Sphere containing
Eternal Ideas in Alanus' sermon, and the Mirror of the Beau Parc. Nature, deputy and minister of God, acts then as an intermediary between
the eternal and the mutable: she translates the commands of the stars into
actions and brings all things to birth (19511ff.).

Genius, her priest, functions as an intermediary between Nature and earth; it is his responsibility to ensure that man fulfils his physical and spiritual obligations to Nature, and ultimately to her master, God. She had originally endowed man with existence, shared with minerals; feeling, with plants; and life, with beasts; although God, not Nature, apparently granted him understanding, shared with the angels (19035–70). Nevertheless, she repents having created man, for, as a slave to vice, he suffers the sins of pride, avarice, gluttony, wrath, envy, sloth, and dishonesty, among others (19225ff.), and as a pederast and hypocritical celibate, he denies proper tribute to Nature and to Love (19323ff.). After this confession, Genius flies in his earthly clothing to the God of Love and his barons, to whom he initially addresses his rather worldly request that they reproduce so that his genial work in the chapel may continue.[12] This counsel is directed toward his earthly agents—Bernardus' twin *genii* protecting the sexual organs and Alanus' Venus with her hammer and anvil, stylus and parchment. That is, he condemns those who refuse to perpetuate the species by properly using their styluses, tablets, hammers, anvils—and Genius adds plowshares and fallow fields (19543–52). The purpose of the exhortation to fecundity is clear: "Pour doner estres pardurables / Aus creatures corrompables" ("In order to give enduring being to mutable creatures," 19581–82). As Bernardus' *genii* of reproduction provided genial weapons in the battle with Lachesis, and Alanus' Venus provided them in the battle with the Parcae, so Jean's Genius opposes Atropos, who severs the "living thread" that Clotho bears on the distaff and that Lachesis spins (19763ff.). The proper use of genial weapons will guarantee the continuance of the natural descent and of the human race.

Men sin against the goddess Nature when they choose to plow desert wastes instead of blooming fields, thereby wasting their seed, or when they refuse to plow at all (19629–56). Genius demands that these men be excommunicated and also castrated: "May they lose the pendants on which the purse hangs!" (19669–70, Dahlberg's trans.). He amplifies by suggesting their "attached hammers" be ripped away, their styluses seized and carried off, and their bones broken if they do not plow properly with their shares (19671ff.). Such sinners will be doomed to death and damnation, and they will be denied offspring, a form of immortality ("enduring being") provided by means of the genitals, which will be removed.

But Genius is not only speaking of sexual sin and generic damnation.

Jean de Meun uses the plowing metaphor to depict the means of obtaining racial immortality, thereby combatting death and Atropos, and also, by analogy, the means of obtaining heavenly immortality. The castration of sinners is intended literally and figuratively: man will be "cut off" from natural grace (racial immortality) and divine grace (spiritual immortality). Jean de Meun distinguishes the two levels by explaining castration myth- ologically and by allegorizing the plowing imagery in his portrayal of heaven as the Shepherd's Park or the Park of the Lamb.

That is, Genius, priest of Nature in the chapel of forms and bishop of God chastizing man for his sins in the sermon, realizes man must fulfil his obligations to his own kind, to Nature, but also to God, Supernature. Venus laughs at him when he appears before the God of Love and is dressed as a bishop—not because he is a comic fraud or buffoon, but because the procreative instinct and the "appetite" for spiritual good at present are disrespected and ignored. Cupidity, perversity, and false ab- stinence reign throughout the world. Such sexual degeneration, as Alanus had shown, leads to a more general corruption of the soul and alienation from reason. Genius as the personification of ideal human nature wants to help man restore himself to his rightful position in the natural order. For such restoration, Genius advocates the pursuit of good, adherence to reason, and obedience to God; reproduction of kind constitutes obeisance to Nature, and, in the sense that stopping it frustrates God's work and purpose, to God.[13] Thus in one part of his sermon, he twice exhorts man to think—"Pensez"—in following the good, defined as both natural and spiritual. Man should "Pensez de mener bone vie," "Think of leading a good life," and "Pensez de vous bien confessier, / Pour bien faire e pour mal laissier," "Think of confessing yourselves well, in order to do good and avoid evil" (19885, 19893–94, Dahlberg's trans.). The "good life" he interprets as the embracing of lovers, the first step in obeying the in- junctions of Nature concerning racial immortality. But the life of good, or the pursuit of good and avoidance of evil, ultimately leading to God and salvation (spiritual immortality), begins with the confession. The concept of the good life unites the two kinds of immortality: the natural and sex- ual embrace of lovers results in racial immortality, as the harmonious and proper embrace of body and soul in pursuing the good results in spiritual immortality. In this same passage, Genius concludes by declaring that God is Nature's master and mirror: he is the salvation of body and soul

("Cil est saluz de cors e d'ame," 19899), as she is the "salvation" of the human race. Accordingly, the "good life" of God, who is Nature's mirror, is superior to Nature's, although his "reflects" hers.

The threat of castration, then, is an appropriate punishment for man's affront to Nature, who must be regenerated. But castration also serves as a figural representation of man's original fall. Jean's Genius uses the myth of Saturn's castration by Jupiter to render the vicious descent of man *sub integumento*. When the son castrated the father, the Iron Age was exchanged for the Golden Age, the four seasons for eternal spring-time, evil for good, division for unity (20027–20220). Before Jupiter ruled, no one had ever plowed or even held a plow; there was no need to cultivate the fields. The plowing image used previously to suggest inter-course reappears to demonstrate that Jupiter's subsequent reign is postlap-serian. The descent into this underworld—suggested by the passage of the Four Ages from gold to silver, brass, and iron—introduces the simple people of an earlier time to divisive boundaries and demarcations of the land, venomous snakes and malicious wolves, shortages of honey, wine, fire, the appearance of birds of prey, and hunting.

Indeed, a description of the life of the blessed in Paradise precedes the myth of Saturn's castration and its consequences (19931–20026). The Beau Parc, over which presides the good shepherd, Bon Pasteur, is a strikingly Christian Eden, clearly a version of Bernardus' superior Aplanon. Although man must labor with great difficulty to produce "crops" (offspring, virtues) in the fallen earthly fields, in the Shepherd's Park flowers maintain an eternal bloom, and no work is demanded of its inhabitants. Genius informs Love's barons that entry into the bounteous fields of this Eden, where it is eternally spring, is contingent upon obe-dience to the laws of Nature—presumably by proper plowing (a "virtu-ous descent" into furrows). That is, man's use of the plow in cultivating fallow fields (adherence to Nature's law by reproducing) produces "entry" into the perfect garden, whose pasture of grass and flowers offers the snowy sheep inhabiting it eternal nourishment. To procreate is to lead the good life, that is, to obey reason and fulfil Nature's laws; to obey reason is to pursue moral good and fulfil God's laws. The conse-quences of Genius' injunction to "increase and multiply" crops, off-spring, and virtues (by using the plow) are perfectly prefigured in the Beau Parc. Natural grace (the "crops" of the plowman) is analogous to supernal grace (the eternal flowers and pasture of the Bon Pasteur); castration (no plow, no children, no crops, no virtue) is analogous to alienation from God (no Eden).

The image of the plow and stylus had been used during the Middle Ages to typify the Logos, Verbum Dei.[14] In the *Roman,* man's plow and woman's fertile field signify the genitals which must be used to reproduce kind and ward off Atropos (mutability); in the Shepherd's Park, there is no mutability, and the replenishment of meadows is produced, if not by a Divine Plow, then by a related symbol—the fountain of life. This fountain nourishes the olive tree's fruit of salvation, the most important "crop" in the Parc. Within the fountain flowing from a triple well lies a three-faceted carbuncle, or ruby, whose perfect reflection of eternal light makes the day last forever.[15] The latter permits any man to see his face, and simultaneously, the whole garden, reflected in the spring beneath. This is Nature's mirror, God, who reveals perfect truth, and who, as source of exemplary forms or Eternal Ideas, may be called the "father" of all things.[16]

This Beau Parc is contrasted by Genius with the Garden of Deduit, also containing a fountain. After describing the paradisal Shepherd's Park, and the fall from Eden under the mythical integument of Saturn's castration, he turns to this false and deceptive garden, where nothing is stable and all is subject to mutability. Described by Guillaume de Lorris in his portion of the *Roman,*[17] this garden belongs to Deduit—Diversion or Delight. When man enters, he descends into the underworld of temporal good to which Euridice fled after being poisoned by its pleasure (the snake). Deduit or Delight also resembles Venus' bastard son, Jocus, in the *De Planctu:* his garden accurately portrays the sterile mirth which results from the body's betrayal of the soul. Its fountain, called a "perilous mirror," is murky and unclear: no man can see his face in its dark waters, and the two clouded crystals at the bottom reflect merely part of the garden, and then only if the sun is shining very brightly. The crystals represent the eyes of the Lover in Deduit;[18] the fountain is the same that killed Narcissus. When man looks into this fountain, he descends into the second *infernum,* that of the body—which the Lover sees as "himself." Comparing the two fountains of this garden and the Beau Parc, Genius declares, "The other makes the living drunk with death, while this fountain makes the dead live again'' (''Cele les vis de mort enivre, / Mais cete fait les morz revivre,'' 20625–26, Dahlberg's trans.). Man ''dies'' spiritually from the intoxication of this garden, but is renewed by the fountain of the Beau Parc.

The underworld of the Garden of Deduit is characterized by the vices, spiritual ''death,'' and by falsity and deception, artifice. Outside the Garden, painted figures are inscribed—Hate, Felony, Villainy, Covetousness, Avarice, Envy, Sorrow, Old Age, hypocritical Pope Holiness, and Poverty—comprising, in part, the seven deadly sins. Genius comments on these figures: ''Il vit dis laides imagetes / Hors dou jardin, ce dit pourtraites'' (''Outside the garden he saw ten ugly images called portraits,'' 20303–4, Dahlberg's trans.). But outside the paradise of the Beau Parc one sees the entire universe—first hell with its devils, then earth with its inhabitants, and finally the heavens, with their wandering and fixed stars (20305–34). The vicious and artificial *figurae* outside the Garden of Diversion contrast with the natural and true expanse of the created world outside the Beau Parc of the Bon Pasteur. The eternal truth inside the Shepherd's Park is similarly juxtaposed with the ''trufles e fanfelues'' inside the Garden: everything one sees is ''corrompable'' (20350–54). The artificial garden is subject to the force of Atropos: the dancers who play within its limited boundaries will all pass away (20355–68).

Man's choice of this false image of the good keeps alive delight in temporal things, as the ''perilous mirror'' of the fountain, which poisoned Narcissus and which reflects the Lover's own image, revivifies the false garden. Narcissus-man frequently becomes enamored of his own illusions and distortions, the path away from the truth. Thus Deduit also means ''Diversion'': his followers have been diverted from the truth and follow crooked ways. Genius accordingly condemns those plowmen blinded by pride (''Par leur orgueil'') who refuse the ''straight furrow'' (''la droite reie'') of the fold and prefer to waste their seed in the desert, and those who do not follow the ''dreite rue,'' the ''straight track,'' and overturn the plow, affirming their evil ''through abnormal exceptions'' to the rules (''Par excepcions anormales,'' 19640–50). The celibate, the courtly lover, the pederast, the evil man culminate in the figure of Orpheus, who, says Genius, would not plow or write or forge ''on the right forge,'' ''en la dreite forge'' (19651–53), and who established evil rules against Nature for his false followers. Orpheus was not only a pederast [19] but also a poet, as we have seen in twelfth-century accounts: the rules he creates contrary to Nature are false and artificial.

Art is described pejoratively throughout Jean's *Roman:* its falsity contrasts with the truth of Nature. Jean prefaces the dialogue between Genius and Nature with a description of the differences between Nature and Art (15891–16082). By perpetuating the species, Nature battles Death and grants a type of immortality or "eternal life" to her forms, but Art can never grant her figures life or make them natural: despite her skill in constructing figures, she cannot make them "live, move, feel, talk" (16062–64). Thus the "ten ugly images," called "portraits," adorn the outside of the wall of the garden of Deduit: their lack of life or liveliness, the natural, is underscored by their ugliness—they are *figures* of the sins, including the seven deadly sins. These external images correlate with the primary source of false images, reflections in the "perilous mirror" of the fountain inside the garden. Artistic images, like psychological illusions and deceptions, are distortions of the true and the natural. Such artificiality is demonic: halfway through Nature's long confession to Genius, after describing the planets and aerial disturbances, but before absolving the heavens, elements, plants, birds, animals, and insects of sin, Nature "digresses" on implicitly demonic properties of mirrors and glasses, dreams and frenzies. The position of this digression within the hierarchy is important. Demons were usually believed to occupy the sublunar region, and Nature has just finished discoursing on aerial turbulence, which she attributes to demons.[20] Mirrors and glasses, she declares, distort things: some objects are made to seem larger, some smaller.[21] These artificial and deceptive mirrors can pervert man's vision, even excite him to lie, e.g., to exclaim that he has seen demons (18237). The "perilous mirror" of the fountain allows man to see neither himself nor the world clearly or truly. Dreams during sleep often carry with them phantoms that seem real, thereby deceiving the five senses. Finally, such images, like those of mirrors, also appear during fantasy: some melancholy people who think too much or who are "irrationally fearful" often create images within themselves, but imagine these images as actually outside them.[22] This discourse—on "dreams," "visions," and the artifice of mirrors—suggests obliquely that literature itself, peopled by phantoms and images, is artificial, and even deceptive. Both Nature and

Genius (not necessarily the poet Jean de Meun) deny the existence of truth in flights of fancy from the real or natural world. Nature divests the universe "of its Chartrian Platonic veil" [23] through the secrets she confesses and through her condemnation of artifice.

Genius' involvement in the system of descents offers an explanation for Jean's choice of images, symbols, and ideas. The reproduction of the species (man's obedience to Nature) and the virtuous entry to the Shepherd's Park (man's obedience to God) are linked by the figure of Genius, priest and bishop. Man can achieve immortality—generic or individual—when he obeys the teachings of Genius; man falls, however, when he chooses the benefits of the temporal world, the underworld of sexual perversion, the senses, vice, self-indulgence, diversions, half-truth, distortion. All of these types of evil are unnatural and untrue, contrasted with the eternal Truth of good in the Shepherd's Park. Jean combines the artificial and vicious descents, and also the natural and virtuous descents. Replenishment of nature and the regeneration of man are associated with the figure of Genius, truly a "generation god" (in more than one sense) and a priest, whose two roles are united by Jean de Meun through the image cluster of plowing/fertile fields/garden. The synthesis of the ideas of Bernardus Silvestris (the *genii* of reproduction, Physis' paradisal garden of growth, the four descents) and the ideas of Alanus de Insulis (Venus-Antigenius-Jocus; sexual perversion, vice, sterility, artifice) is brilliantly realized in Jean de Meun's figure of Genius and the two gardens.

GENIUS IN JOHN GOWER'S *CONFESSIO AMANTIS*

John Gower's *Confessio Amantis* focuses on the descents of vice, virtue, and artifice, while apparently ignoring the natural descent of the soul from the spheres. The confession of the lover, unlike Nature's confession of the original creation of the cosmos and of the microcosm's transgressions in Jean's *Roman,* reveals only his own fall and sins. Amans has been behaving unnaturally, that is, unlike a man. Yet his fall is not so much vicious as artificial: "Amans has committed a crime against Nature. In his love fantasy he has set himself apart from the mutual plea-

sures of her domain. He has no interest in the beauty of May or the har-
monies of the birds; his singular concern is pampering his secretive
emotions.'' [24] Amans resembles the melancholy man described by Nature
in Jean's *Roman:* his emotions, springing from the illusions and deceptions of love, distort his vision, as mirrors and dreams were believed to
pervert truth in the *Roman.* The unfulfilled and courtly love for his lady
has jeopardized his emotional stability, and he seems possessed—almost
demoniacally. He throws himself upon the ground, weeping and longing
for death; his complaint to Venus and Cupid describes his plight as a
''maladie'' that may eventually change into madness:

> Now doth me pleinly live or dye,
> For certes such a maladie
> As I now have and longe have hadd,
> It myhte make a wisman madd,
> If that it scholde longe endure.[25]

This descent into the hell of unrequited (courtly) love by means of
demonic passions and illusions is artificial, but can become vicious as
well. A morbid preoccupation with the fantasies of love leads to more
dangerous problems: indulgence of the self or the will allows the lusts of
man to overwhelm his reason (8.2130ff.); he becomes a beast, and loses
his manhood (1.3043ff.). In the *De Planctu,* boredom and sloth led to
drunkenness and gluttony, and ultimately sexual perversion and lechery
(Venus sought diversion with Antigenius); these sins resulted in the
greater sins of avarice, envy, wrath, and pride, which dehumanized man.
Similarly, in Jean's *Roman,* the celibate and pederast gamboled in the
garden of Deduit (Diversion or Delight), and eventually succumbed to the
deceptive and unnatural pleasure of temporal good (vicious descent). But
Amans' fall is not pleasurable: the artificial fantasies he constructs engender pain and division of self, making him into a ''caitif'' alienated from
Nature and from man. As an archetypal divided self, he resembles the
divided world described in the Prologue: ''For Senne of his condicioun / Is moder of divisioun / And tokne whan the world schal faile''
(1029–31). The world has fallen, suffering the pain of sin and mutability;
the multiplication of sins has divided the world even further, so that each
age becomes progressively more degenerate. Thus in Nebuchadnezzar's
dream, the figure of time appears with a head of gold, breast, shoulders

and arms of silver, "wombe . . . doun to the kne" of brass, legs of steel and feet of clay—comparable to the ages of man following the descent from Paradise after Jupiter's castration of Saturn in Jean's *Roman*. The sin dividing the world is analogous to the courtly "sin" (love fantasy) dividing and perverting Amans: at the beginning of the first book, Gower explains that "loves lawe is out of reule, / That of tomoche or of tolite / Welnyh is every man to wyte" (1.18–20). Unfortunately, there seems to be no one so wise in all the world who can "Of love tempre the mesure" (1.23). The *Confessio Amantis* provides a solution to this problem through Amans' confession to Venus' "oghne Clerk": Genius will make him whole, natural, and human again by ridding him of his demonic phantasms and sins, both courtly and deadly, and by teaching him to temper the measure of his love.

Amans beseeches Venus to relieve his sorrow with her grace; she sends him to Genius, to whom he complains about his "destourbed" heart and blind wits. As her "Prest . . . touchende of love," Genius has been appointed to manifest the properties of love, and how they "stonde be degrees / After the disposicioun / Of Venus, whos condicioun / I moste folwe" (1.258–61). However, because he is also a priest, he must speak of vice too:

> I mot algate and nedes wile
> Noght only make my spekynges
> Of love, bot of othre thinges,
> That touchen to the cause of vice,
> For that belongeth to thoffice
> Of Prest, whos ordre that I bere.
>
> (1.238–43.)

His relationship with Venus indicates that he should be a type of reproductive force, similar to Alanus' Venus and Jean's Genius, the latter of whom was sent to the God of Love. But he appears to be primarily a priest, and of love, not of generation.[26] Thus it is to Venus' priest that Amans as courtly lover confesses his sins. Genius also instructs him in Gower's version of the seven deadly sins—pride, envy, wrath, sloth, avarice, gluttony, and finally lechery and incest—within the remaining seven books of the *Confessio*. After describing each sin and its many variations, he uses a classical tale as an "essample" of each variation, and concludes by hearing Amans' confession of guilt over the courtly equivalent of the sin, or his protestation of innocence or ignorance of any such guilt. His priestly role is clear from the beginning: he will demonstrate each of the sins, so that Amans "myht take evidence / To reule with thi conscience" (1.247–48).

Yet there is one sense in which he does serve as a priest of "generation." His reason for providing "essamples" from these old books is carefully worded to suggest the original transformation of matter with idea by Natura in the *De Planctu:*

> Mi Sone, that thou miht *enforme*
> Thi pacience upon the *forme*
> Of olde *essamples,* as thei felle,
> Now understond what I schal telle.
>
> (3.1753–56, my emphasis.)

Indeed, he is a "generation god" in the *Confessio:* he seeks to regenerate the fallen Amans, to make him natural again, to give him "life." The virtuous course he advocates is modeled upon the natural descent: [27] Genius must heal the division of self, informing Amans' patience with the form of old "essamples," thereby uniting body and soul as Nature originally united them at birth. He must bring Amans back from hell: the wits can be blinded while the body incarcerates the soul, for "That on desireth toward helle, / That other upward to the hevene" (7.504–5). Genius appears to be an Orpheus figure who wishes to rescue Euridice (concupiscence, or Amans) from the underworld of demonic and disruptive love fantasy. Not only does Genius discourse on virtue and vice by providing poetic "essamples," but he instructs the lover in philosophy, as if he were a philosopher-poet. In the long digressions on alchemy, dreams, and rhetoric in the fifth book (demonic secrets involved in the artificial descent), and the description of rhetoric, practique, and theoric in the seventh book, Genius becomes an Orpheus figure, the exemplar of eloquence and wisdom, who makes a virtuous descent into the underworld of vice so that the concupiscent Amans may know himself better and protect himself from temptation. Also, as an Orphic poet, this clerk of Venus descends into artifice—the classical tales—to describe each sin. The poetic, philosophic, and priestly roles of Genius, regenerating catalyst for Amans, are linked by the constant emphasis on "shriving" him: the word is derived from *scribere,* meaning first "to write down," then "to prescribe," finally, "to prescribe penance."

The process of regenerating or healing Amans, the "phisique for the seke," is manifold: the confession of courtly sin is the first step, as it was for the sinner in Jean's *Roman,* followed by instruction in deadly sin, the application of the "physik" of the virtue (e.g., charity for envy, humility for pride), the introduction to wisdom (*trivium* and *quadrivium* in Book Seven), and finally, an Augustinian love of oneself and of God, that is, *caritas,* which supersedes the early definitions of love as courtly or sensuous. This last form of love actually exemplifies the harmony achieved through the marriage (or remarriage) of body and soul (Venus and Hymen in the *De Planctu*). Gower rejects earthly love, "Which no phisicien can hele," at the end of the *Confessio* (8.3156), and affirms the importance of charitable love: "Such love mai the bodi save, / Such love mai the soule amende" (8.3166–67). Gower begs "hyhe god" to send us love, "Forthwith the remenant of grace" (8.3168–69). Such love begins with man: he must rule his own "kingdom" well, for if he does not, "He lest himself . . . / For what man that in special / Hath noght himself, he hath noght elles / . . . Whan he his herte hath noght witholde / Toward himself, al is in vein" (8.2115, 2118–19, 2124–25). Man must love himself before he can love others: Gower anticipates modern psychology, which has determined that a lack of self-love and self-confidence is characteristic of the schizophrenic.[28] When he learns to love and accept himself, he is cured. Thus, at the end of the *Confessio,* Venus tells Amans that he has become old and can no longer love (presumably in the sexual and earthly sense); he faints ("dies"). After anointing his reins, heart, and head with medicine, she gives him a mirror: when he sees himself, he does not faint, for he accepts what he has become. His reason has returned to peaceful coexistence with his senses. The mirror serves as a symbolic mirror of forms, similar to that of Urania in *De Mundi* and of God in the *Roman:* Amans is reborn, reconciled to himself, informed by the form of classical "essamples."

Genius, the ideal of human nature and agent of this remarriage of body and soul, is an Orphic poet or scribe rewriting Amans. Like the Orpheus of Bernardus and Guillaume, this poet-philosopher weds wisdom to eloquence—as the priest reconciles soul to body. In the Prologue, after describing Heaven (peace) and Hell (discord), Gower introduces Arion, a type of Orpheus. Like Orpheus, he tames beasts with his harp; like Christ, saviour of man, he brings the lord and shepherd to accord, and introduces love to the world, so that melancholy disappears (Prol. 1057–58, 1062–69). Arion unites the three estates of the world, as Genius will unite the divided parts of Amans, the microcosm. He makes Amans' bestial self "tame and milde." What Arion accomplishes with his harp Genius achieves with his information of Amans' patience upon the form of old "essamples"—classical tales. Both are "poets" of peace and harmony: Gower seems to find consolation for the troubled man and world, not in philosophy alone, but also in poetry. Even Amans by the end of the poem has become a poet—John Gower.

The unnatural or artificial condition of Amans, the courtly lover, at the beginning of the *Confessio* contrasts with his "artificial" role as poet at the end of the poem. His initial demonic fantasies spring from within himself, but he imagines that they constitute a reality existing outside him. Essentially Amans has entered the unreal garden of Deduit (Diversion), and peered into the well of Narcissus, that mirror of distortion and fantasy. At the end of the poem, after accepting the truth of Venus' mirror, he is reborn and becomes a poet, agent of truth and harmony, but an artificer, like Orpheus and Arion. Gower clearly differentiates the two types of artifice. The lover's descent into the hell of fantasy and excessive melancholy is also a vicious descent (courtly love sins, the deadly sins); but his descent into the underworld of classical tales is virtuous, intended to arm him with a knowledge of the nature of sin so that he may protect himself from its temptation. This virtuous descent results in a rebirth of Amans: the process is described in terms of the natural descent (the information of patience by the form of classical examples). Gower's interpretation of the first artificial descent is derived from Jean de Meun, but his interpretation of the second amplifies the twelfth-century concept of poetic artifice, especially that of Alanus. Genius, poet-philosopher and priest of Venus, represents the regenerative agent of the virtuous descent into artifice. Gower's Genius actually bears little resemblance to the twelfth-century personifications of Bernardus and Alanus: the differences between them are more striking than the similarities.

CONCLUSIONS

In his commentary on the *Aeneid* and in *De Mundi,* Bernardus' syncretistic talents provided a wealth of *genii* from which other writers could select—"natural concupiscence," the god of human nature (Euridice), and also the astrological scribe of individual form, planetary ruler, aerial sprite, governor of Physis' garden, the agents of reproduction. The cosmic *genii* or *oyarses* generate all things; they also transmit communications to the lower spheres, where the *angeli* and *genii* then convey them to man. The latter spirits also affect or are affected by man's moral life. The *genii* of the cosmos guide the natural descent of the soul at birth, which marks man with natural concupiscence, the individual *genius*.

Alanus' Genius is a priest of Natura, i.e., an agent of generation (both generic and special) for mankind, and a governor of moral life. Venus functions as the agent of Genius, concupiscence: she represents man's appetite for good (temporal or spiritual), and his attitude toward the genial organs, ideally used only for procreation and the initiation of the natural descent. Antigenius / Antigamus and Jocus act antithetically to Genius, Hymen, and Cupid: they typify the sterility implied by sexual perversion and by vice and sin. Finally, Alanus' Genius, a poet-philosopher like Orpheus, was influenced by the astral artist, Pantomorph: he is an *artifex* who creates both men and the *figurae* of art.

Jean amalgamates the ideas of Bernardus and Alanus in his conception of the cosmic priest of Nature and the earthly bishop of God. In the chapel of forms he directs generation; on earth he counsels man to use his "genii" of reproduction. As a bishop, guide to spiritual life and good, to which man's judgment or concupiscence should adhere, he aligns himself with Christ, the Bon Pasteur, and condemns Deduit, the diversion of temporal life and good. He is not, however, a proponent of artifice: he disparages the poet Orpheus and the falsity of the *figurae* adorning Deduit's walls, as Nature, whose artistry is superior to Art's, denigrates demonic fantasies and visions.

Gower's priest of Venus, confessor of Amans, instructor in the seven deadly sins and the remedial virtues, leads the lover from the underworld of "Deduit" (artificial fantasies) to the "Bon Pasteur" (regeneration). These concepts are expressed by the two Venuses of the poem, the first who represents courtly love or lust, the second, *caritas* (she appropriately ascends to the heavens at the end of the poem). Genius is also a poet-philosopher (clerk) or Arion-Orpheus who relates classical tales: he represents the Word, or the Saviour, of the individual, Amans, and of society.

As the roles and meanings of Genius change in emphasis from work to work, so the major symbols associated with the figure also change. The pen of the scribal Pantomorph in *De Mundi* very clearly epitomizes the influence of the stars upon human nature at birth. In the *De Planctu,* the pen and parchment are symbols for the origin of soul and body, or the natural descent; an explanation for the human potential to choose good or evil; and the tools of the artist. They reappear in the *Roman* as symbols of the genitals. They are not actually depicted in the *Confessio,* although Genius, narrating classical tales, fills a scribal or clerical role.

Mirrors, gardens, and fountains also play important symbolic parts in these works. Urania's Mirror of Providence in *De Mundi* becomes the true Mirror of God in the *Roman,* associated with the fountain in the Beau Parc and contrasted with the false (narcissistic) mirror of the fountain of Deduit and demonic man-made mirrors and glasses. In the *Confessio,* Amans, suffering the misery induced by introversion and narcissism, confronts the reality of Venus' true mirror and is eventually healed. This mirror also reflects Eternal Idea: Urania's mirror depicts the exemplary forms of all things, and is a mnemonic aid for the generation of "images." The garden of Physis, whose Genius represents a vegetation god, was also used as a generative symbol and as a type of Eden: in Granusion man's body was originally created from the elements. The gardens of Jean de Meun, the Beau Parc and the Garden of Deduit, signify, first, the consequences of obedience or disobedience to natural law in using plow and field; second, they signify respectively the virtuous mode of life leading to the eternal truth of Paradise, and the vicious mode leading to the mutable and false underworld of the body or of earth. Such obedience results in crops (offspring, racial immortality, multiplication of virtues) and grants the individual admission to the eternal Beau Parc, where plowing is not necessary to ensure "growth." The Garden of Diversion, in contrast, belongs to those men who refuse to use their plows and fields and who suffer spiritual sterility. These symbols—in addition to the roles of Genius—are derived, in part, from the classical associations of the Genius. The snake, the cornucopia of seeds, the altar, plants, and chaplets present prototypes for the phallic symbol of the pen or plow, the Genius' role as priest, bishop, or clerk, and the symbol of the garden.

The pattern of the four descents organized many of the classical concepts of Genius. The relationship between human nature and Genius in the four works typifies one or more of the descents—the natural descent in the *De Mundi,* the vicious and virtuous descents in the *De Planctu,* the combination of the vicious-artificial and the virtuous-natural in Jean's *Roman,* and finally, the artificial descent in the *Confessio.* The other descents appear in some form in all of these works. In *De Mundi,* Natura complains to Noys about the lack of form and order in primordial matter. Noys rectifies the situation, and creation results: the great chain of being, mirrored in the microcosm, who is created with the help of Urania and Physis, and their genial aides. The *De Planctu* brings Natura to the dreamer complaining about man's sexual perversions and vices; Genius excommunicates these unnatural sinners from creation. Jean's *Roman* offers a similar complaint of Nature in the form of her confession to Genius. The excommunication in this work is two-fold: depicted by the image of castration, it severs the sexually and morally perverse man from natural and supernal grace. Perverse men are unnatural, i.e., artificial, untrue, like hallucinations, fantasies, and the figures of art. Of the four works, the *Confessio* is the most original in its approach to the descents. Amans, not Natura, complains to Venus about his love-melancholy and alienation from natural creation. Genius must regenerate Amans: he is the agent, not of generation or of excommunication, but of artificial renewal, the restoration of the soul to the body. The emphases in the four works change markedly—from creation to the excommunication of creation to re-creation. Gower's poem offers the most optimistic view of the problem of sin and its solution. The viewpoint has also shifted in these works— from a cosmic and generic one to a microcosmic (individual) and societal one in Gower. The pattern of the descents, then, unifies and organizes the major medieval works (or selected portions thereof) in which a Genius appears, and also the various classical *genii.*

As agent of the natural descent, Genius originated as the begetting spirit of the paterfamilias, corresponding to the Juno of the mother. The concept was transferred to other father figures—the founder of the city, the father of the state, the paternal figures of the gods. The gods blended into one ultimate father-figure—Jupiter, the World Soul. The cosmic Genius of Jove represented his "seed power," aided by the cosmic Juno. Eventually the components of the World Soul—the stars, planets, and luminaries—were ascribed *genii*. The Greek messenger demon filled in the gap between moon and man. This fertile universe is described in *De Mundi,* whose cosmic *genii* are controlled by Urania and Physis, sisters of Natura. In *De Planctu,* the sisters are replaced by Genius, the other self and lover of Natura, and the original begetting *genius* and *iuno,* Bernardus' twin *genii* of the reproductive organs, are replaced by Venus. In the *Roman,* Genius' role as generative priest of Nature includes the responsibility for man's use of his genial organs, of which he reminds Venus and Love. Venus and Genius alone remain (without Nature) in the *Confessio,* for Genius no longer represents a generative force, but the regenerative agent of *caritas.*

Genius is also a product of the natural descent—natural concupiscence. When the begetting spirit of the paterfamilias came to mean the virility or life of his son or of any individual, the emphasis shifted from the active, begetting principle to the passive, begotten principle. Soon each man had his own god of birth, born with him and living until his death. In one sense it stood for individual fortune, good or ill; in another, it represented the temperament and personality of each man. With the introduction of the Greek rational soul or *daemon* into Roman culture, that which was born with each man split into two parts. The idea took several forms— man had a good and evil *daemon* or *genius* or *manes;* or a good Genius and evil fleshly desires; or a *daemon* and a *genius;* or a soul and the soul-joined-to-body. Secondly, conflict between good and evil was staged either within man, or without him. Gradually the differences were formalized: within man there were two components, of good and evil, and without him, two forces of good and evil. The latter became, in the patristic sense, angels and demons. This divergence explains the complicated portions of the allegorization of the Orpheus-Euridice myth. Orpheus signifies the rational soul; Euridice, or *genius,* signifies the concupiscence of the flesh which can choose either good or evil. Her flight from Aristeus (virtue) exemplifies a flight from the good *genius,* angel, or *daemon;* her seduction by the snake suggests the gratification of the flesh, of the evil *genius* or *daemon.* In *De Mundi,* the good and depraved angels are cosmic messengers, but interpreted in the light of

Christianity; the two parts of man, soul and body, created by Urania and Physis are reminiscent of their classical analogues—*daemon* (rational soul) and *genius* ("life," virility, born with each man). The Orphic poet-priest Genius in Alanus' work is the good *daemon* or angel contrasted with the Euridice-figure, Venus, who as concupiscence chooses either good (marriage to Hymen) or evil (fornication with Antigenius, the evil *daemon*). In Jean de Meun's *Roman,* Genius is a priest of Nature and bishop of God, his two roles suggesting his responsibility toward the two components of human nature, the body and the soul, and the proper relationship between them. If man thinks, he will control his appetites, and choose natural good (reproduction of kind) and spiritual good (multiplication of virtues), constituting entry into the proper home of the soul, the Paradise of the Beau Parc. If he does not, his appetites control his reason, and he remains in the *infernum* of Deduit. Genius' allegiance to Nature and to her mirror, God and his Eternal Truth, underscores his relationship with man's rational soul, for he condemns the perilous mirror of the narcissistic garden, allied with false mirrors and glasses, demonic visitations, dreams, and fantasies. In the *Confessio,* the seven deadly sins (evil demons) are didactically presented by the priest Genius, Orphic figure and conscience of Amans.

The demonic intermediary of the artificial descent is an even later phenomenon, developing from two sources. The Genius, fickle god of birth, governed the fortune of each man; his analogue was the Greek messenger *daemon* who conveyed messages from the gods to man and from man to the gods. The fortunate aspect of the spirit was amplified by the magic art of astrology, which identified the *genius* with the Greek *daemon,* and which was condemned by the Church fathers and apologists. Knowledge of the future, or of the underworld ("summus Manium," inhabited by Di Manes), was the province of the Devil. The demon, however, often consorted with man through dreams and visions; the shadowy phantoms who appeared in dreams were eventually associated with the poetic figures, personifications, and artifice of literature, and the dream vision, which disguised truths under *involucra,* was incorporated into literary works which described a descent into an "underworld." The *De Planctu,* the *Roman,* and the *Confessio* are all dream visions or pseudo-dream visions. Genius in Alanus' work also represents the archetypal poet, Orpheus, source of the creativity of artifice, which conceals secret truths inside a false *cortex* or integument. Jean de Meun's Nature and Genius, however, condemn artifice—the false poet and pederast Orpheus, dreams, phantoms, and the "ugly figures" inscribed on the wall of Deduit's garden. Nature associates such falsity with the artificial aerial disturbances provoked by demons, but Genius associates it with the vicious and artificial behavior and illusions of man. Gower finds internal fantasies disruptive of the harmony of body and soul, dividing man and alienating him from nature. However, the poet's art, which may conceal truth beneath the integument of the false gods and figures of classical tales, serves to calm the soul, reconcile it to the body, and thereby regenerate man—as the art of Genius reunites Amans with himself, as the art of Arion unites the three estates, and as the art of Gower links the microcosm (in the eight books) with the macrocosm (in the Prologue).

This brief summary of the evolution of the Genius recapitulates the relationship between the classical and medieval figures, particularly in relation to the four descents. The medieval Genius did not completely disappear at the end of the Middle Ages: Spenser, for example, used the personification at several points in the *Faerie Queene,* and Shakespeare referred to the spirit throughout his plays.[29] It came to mean "inventive ability," "inspired talent" in later centuries, retaining little of its medieval significance, and rarely, if ever, accorded allegorical treatment. However, in the late nineteenth and twentieth centuries, the concepts of the shadow and the double, characterizing the split and divided self and analogous to the classical tutelary *genius* born with each man and the medieval demon afflicting and possessing man's mind, pervade literature and psychology.[30] These demonic expressions of the conflicts warring within the disturbed individual inhabit the dark underworld of the subconscious mind. In one sense, the Horatian god of human nature, moralized and allegorized during the Middle Ages, resurfaces in these later centuries, but reinterpreted within a psychological, rather than philosophical and religious, context. Man's need to understand himself, obviously not restricted to any one period, suggests that his projection of internal conflicts into external spirits, deities, personifications, or figures remains a universal phenomenon, a demonstration of the existence of Jung's collective unconscious.

Notes

INTRODUCTION

1. William Allan Neilson, *The Origins and Sources of the Court of Love* (1899; rpt. New York, 1967), p. 141.

2. C. S. Lewis, *The Allegory of Love* (London, 1936), p. 362. See also George D. Economou, "The Character Genius in Alan de Lille, Jean de Meun, and John Gower," *Chaucer Review*, 4 (1970), 203–10, who declares that the figure was "appropriated from the Roman god of generation by Christian poets interested in the purpose, meaning, and morality of sexual love in the world," p. 203, and therefore intimately associated with Nature in the *De Planctu* and *Roman*, but with Venus in the *Confessio*. Economou ignores the Genius of *De Mundi* discussed by Lewis.

3. C. S. Lewis, *Studies in Medieval and Renaissance Literature*, collected by Walter Hooper (Cambridge, 1966), p. 169.

4. *Ibid.*; E. C. Knowlton, "The Genii of Spenser," *Studies in Philology*, 25 (1928), 439. He also speaks of the Genius as a divine second self: see Knowlton, "Genius as an Allegorical Figure," *Modern Language Notes*, 39 (1924), 89.

5. On the Genius primarily as a spiritual double, see, for example, William Smith, ed. *Dictionary of Greek and Roman Biography and Myth* (London, 1850), II, 241–42; Th. Birt, "Genius," in *Ausführliches Lexikon der griechischen und römischen Mythologie*, ed. W. H. Roscher (Leipzig, 1886–90), I.2, 1615–17; and Georg Wissowa, *Religion und Kultus der Römer*, in *Handbuch der klassischen Altertumswissenschaft*, Vol. 5, pt. 4, 2nd ed. (Munich, 1912), pp. 175–76.

6. On the Genius primarily as the reproductive luck of the male or of the family, consult W. Warde Fowler, *The Roman Festivals of the Period of the Republic* (London, 1899), pp. 142–44; and H. J. Rose, "On the Original Significance of the Genius," *Classical Quarterly*, 17 (1923), 57–60.

7. For Genius as both double and reproductive principle, cf. L. Preller, *Römische Mythologie* (Berlin, 1858), I, 66–77 and 566–72; Walter F. Otto, "Genius," in *Paulys Real-Encyclopädie der classischen Altertumswissenschaft*, ed. Georg Wissowa and Wilhelm Kroll, VII.1 (Stuttgart, 1910), 1155–63; and W. Warde Fowler, *The Religious Experience of the Roman People* (London, 1911), p. 75, and *Roman Ideas of Deity* (London, 1914), pp. 17 ff.; et al.

CHAPTER ONE: THE EARLY CLASSICAL GENIUS: POPULAR RELIGIOUS BELIEFS

1. There are excellent chapters on early Italian household worship in Cyril Bailey, *Phases in the Religion of Ancient Rome* (Berkeley, 1932); Gordon J. Laing, *Survivals of Roman Religion* (New York, 1931); W. Warde Fowler, *The Religious Experience of the Roman People* (London, 1911) and *Roman Ideas of Deity* (London, 1914); and also William Reginald Halliday, *Lectures on the History of Roman Religion* (Liverpool, 1922). For specific spirits, consult in addition *Paulys Real-Encyclopädie der classischen Altertumswissenschaft* (Stuttgart, 1893–1967), s.v., and Georg Wissowa, *Religion und Kultus der Römer,* in *Handbuch der klassischen Altertumswissenshaft,* Vol. 5, pt. 4, 2nd ed. (Munich, 1912), s.v.

2. Carl Darling Buck, *A Dictionary of Selected Synonyms in the Principal Indo-European Languages* (Chicago, 1949), p. 280. See also p. 1503 on the Latin *genius.* For a fuller treatment of Indo-European synonyms for "genius" and words derived from the **gen* root, see A. Ernout and A. Meillet, *Dictionnaire étymologique de la langue latine,* 4th ed. (Paris, 1959), I, 272. For an examination of derivatives and classical *loci,* see E. Forcellini, *Totius Latinitatis Lexicon,* III (Prato, 1865), 198–99, and *Thesaurus Linguae Latinae,* VI.2 (Leipzig, 1925–34), 1826–42.

3. See Laing, p. 3, and Bailey, pp. 40 ff. In the simplest form of animism, according to Bailey, a spirit (or spirits) inhabits a specific spot.

4. E. C. Knowlton, "The Genii of Spenser," *Studies in Philology,* 25 (1928), 439. See Laing, p. 3; Bailey, pp. 40–45. Knowlton (p. 439) describes the modern sense of the *genius loci* as the mood or atmosphere of a scene.

5. Halliday, p. 26. See also H. J. Rose, *Primitive Culture in Italy* (London, 1926), pp. 151–53.

6. Franz Altheim, *A History of Roman Religion,* trans. Harold Mattingly (London, 1938), p. 59. See also Altheim's *Griechische Götter im alten Rom* (Giessen, 1930), especially pp. 47–71. He bases much of this theory on Walter F. Otto, *Die Manen; oder, Von den Urformen des Totenglaubens* (Berlin, 1923). Otto declares, p. 61, that "Der Geniusbegriff ist gewissermassen ein Gleichnis für den menschlichen Samen, der vom Vater den Sohn erzeugt, und vom Sohn weiterzeugend das Geschlecht fortpflanzt."

7. See Richard Broxton Onians, *The Origins of European Thought about the Body, the Mind, the Soul, the World, Time, and Fate,* 2nd ed. (Cambridge, 1954), p. 240; and also Attilio de Marchi, *Il culto privato di Roma antica,* I (Milan, 1896), 53–54.

8. The bearded snake represents the Genius and is accompanied by a female snake (the Juno), both signifying the "deified powers of reproduction of the family or clan," according to Rose, *Primitive Culture in Italy,* p. 151. For discussions of art involving the Genius as a serpent being offered fruit, consult de Marchi, I, 77–78, 98–102. Laing, p. 25, describes several different depictions, some disclosing an altar with entwined snake, some with snakes crawling toward the votive offerings placed on top of the altar, and some with a male and female snake moving toward it from either side. George Howe and G. A. Harrer, eds., *A Handbook of Classical Myth* (New York, 1929), p. 106, label the serpent with fruit a *genius loci.* Th. Birt in W. H. Roscher's *Ausführliches Lexikon der griechischen und*

römischen Mythologie (Leipzig, 1886–90), I.2, 1623–25, discusses the snake as a *Genius domus* whose offering of fruit represents "Fruchtbarkeit."

9. See Altheim, *A History of Roman Religion,* p. 169, and *Griechische Götter im alten Rom,* pp. 47–71. He distinguishes the beliefs of the two cultures, however: Etruria was obsessed with death, the shades, and the underworld; the ancient Italians were more concerned with life. Thus the Italians did not adopt a literal phallic form, but a symbolic one, for their Genius. The Etruscan association of **titus* (phallus) with the grave monument indicates, however, an equivalent desire to conquer death through the immortality of the family.

10. Ammianus Marcellinus, *Rerum Gestarum Libri Qui Supersunt,* ed. and trans. John C. Rolfe, Loeb Classical Library (London and Cambridge, Mass., 1935–39), II, 486 (25.2.3). Subsequent references to all primary sources, after an initial citation in a note, will be indicated by the appropriate book, chapter (or poem), and line numbers within the text. Whenever available, the Loeb Classical Library edition of a classical work has been used. Translations of passages within the text are my own, unless otherwise acknowledged.

11. T. *Livi Ab Urbe Condita XXVI–XXVII,* ed. and trans. Frank Gardner Moore, *Livy,* Vol. 7, Loeb Classical Library (London and Cambridge, Mass., 1943), pp. 72, 74 (26.19.7).

12. Suetonius, *De Vita Caesarum* 2.94.4, in *Suetonius,* ed. and trans. J. C. Rolfe, Loeb Classical Library, I (1914; rev., rpt. Cambridge, Mass., and London, 1928), 264.

13. Aulus Gellius, *Noctium Atticarum,* ed. and trans. John C. Rolfe, Loeb Classical Library, II (London and Cambridge, Mass., 1927), 2 (6.1.3).

14. Weston La Barre, *They Shall Take up Serpents: Psychology of the Southern Snake-Handling Cult* (Minneapolis, 1962), pp. 65–109, analyzes classical Near Eastern cults, and the religious and psychological implications of snake symbolism. La Barre includes an excellent bibliography on the snake, pp. 191–92. For the phallic and sacred snake, see William H. Desmonde, *Magic, Myth, and Money: The Origin of Money in Religious Ritual* (New York, 1962), p. 38; for its associations with deities and heroes (Bona Dea, Juno Sospita, Isis, Hermes, Satan, etc.), consult Laing, pp. 26–28, and La Barre, pp. 67–71; 85 ff.; for modern analogues in primitive cultures, see Rose, *Primitive Culture in Italy,* p. 151; Frank Byron Jevons, *An Introduction to the History of Religion,* 5th ed. (London, 1911), pp. 186–87.

15. Virgil, *Aeneid* 5.95, in *Virgil,* ed. and trans. H. Rushton Fairclough, I (1916; rev. Cambridge, Mass., and London, 1935), 452.

16. The paterfamilias embodied the Genius, according to Fowler, *Roman Ideas of Deity,* p. 17; H. J. Rose, "On the Original Significance of the Genius," *Classical Quarterly,* 17 (1923), 57–60. For artistic evidence of this identification, see Howe and Harrer, p. 106; Bailey, pp. 81–82; de Marchi, I, 76, 98 ff., and 92, plate 6.

17. The father on his deathbed breathed the reproductive soul of the family into his heir; his death, unlike that of other family members, necessitated great mourning. See Rose, *Primitive Culture,* p. 152. The father as priest of the family is discussed by Bailey, p. 80; Desmonde, pp. 51–52, 68; De Marchi, I, 76. That the family swore by the Genius of the paterfamilias is supported by Fowler, *Roman Ideas of Deity,* p. 18.

18. Catullus, *Veronensis Liber* 64.47–48, ed. and trans. F. W. Cornish, in *Catullus, Tibullus, and Pervigilium Veneris,* Loeb Classical Library (1912; rpt. London and New York, 1914), p. 100. For comments on the *genialis lectus,* see especially L. Preller, *Römische*

Mythologie (Berlin, 1858), I, 69; Walter Otto, "Iuno. Beiträge zum Verständnisse der ältesten und wichtigsten Thatsachen ihres Kultes," *Philologus,* 64 (N. S. 18) (1905), 179 f.; Wissowa, p. 176.

19. Juvenal, *Satura* 6.22, in *Juvenal and Persius,* ed. and trans. G. G. Ramsay, Loeb Classical Library (London and New York, 1918) p. 84, and see p. 85 n. Subsequent references to the works of both Juvenal and Persius will be indicated by parentheses and appropriate satire and line number(s) within the text.

20. "GENIALIBVS veluti genealibus: nam geniales proprie sunt qui sternuntur puellis nubentibus, dicti a generandis liberis." The quotation repeated almost verbatim by Isidore, Paulus Diaconus, and Rabanus Maurus (to be discussed in more detail in the third chapter) is found in *Servii Grammatici in Vergilii Aeneidos Commentarii* 6.603, ed. Georg Thilo and Hermann Hagen, in *In Vergilii Carmina Commentarii* (1881–87; rpt. Hildesheim, 1961), II, 84. There may at one time have been some confusion between the Genius and the Italic counterpart of Dionysus, Liber Pater. This god was celebrated (with obscene rites) during the Liberalia; it has been conjectured that his name, Liber, relates to the freeing of seed. See Lily R. Taylor, *The Divinity of the Roman Emperor* (Middletown, Connecticut, 1931), p. 49; W. Warde Fowler, *The Roman Festivals of the Period of the Republic* (London, 1899), p. 55.

21. The most extensive discussion of the Juno is that of Otto, "Iuno," pp. 160–223; see Wissowa, pp. 176, 181 ff. Richmond Lattimore, *Themes in Greek and Latin Epitaphs* (Urbana, 1962), p. 105, interprets the Juno as "femininity"; however, most scholars agree she is a correlative spirit to the masculine Genius, and a *tutela pariendi.* See Fowler, *Roman Festivals,* p. 143; Bailey, p. 70; Frank Byron Jevons, ed. *Plutarch's Romane Questions,* trans. 1683 by Philemon Holland (London, 1892), pp. liv–lv; and Th. Zielinski, "Marginalien," *Philologus,* 64 (N.S. 18) (1905), 20. De Marchi discusses a statuette of the Juno, "della padrona di casa," found near an altar, I, 77: ". . . vestita di chitone e mantello, è sdraiata su una cline col gomito sinistro appoggiato al cuscino e stende nella destra protesa una patera umbelicata; colla mano sinistra teneva forse qualcosa oggi mancante."

22. Wissowa, pp. 181–82, believes the word "iuno" may be related to "iuvenis," stemming from *iun-* in the same way *iunix* is linked with *iuvencus;* the name to him means "mannbares Weib, junge Frau." But Otto, *Die Manen,* p. 60, understands the term as "mein Mädchen," "meine Jungfer," with the same complexity of usage as the word *puella.*

23. For the relationship of the Juno to the goddess of childbirth, Lucina, see Birt, cols. 1614–15, and Bailey, p. 70.

24. Arnobius, *Adversus Nationes Libri VII,* ed. C. Marchesi, 2nd ed. (Turin, 1953), p. 145 (2.67). De Marchi, I, ix, n.1, speaks of the importance of the Genius in marriage. Although Arnobius alludes to the Genii of husbands, by the second century A.D. the two spirits of the familial household (the Genius and the Juno) were no longer distinguishable: Censorinus, in his *De Die Natali Liber,* ed. Otto Jahn (Berlin, 1845), a compilation of ancient and contemporary beliefs and philosophical systems, confused the two household spirits with the *lares,* and called them both *genii,* p. 7 (3.2–3).

25. Laing, p. 162; Bailey, p. 77, declares that the sacrifice of food at the family meal in an agricultural society represents the *pecunia* (wealth) of the family.

26. W. Warde Fowler, "Roman Religion," *Encyclopaedia of Religion and Ethics,* ed. James Hastings, X (New York, 1919), 845.

27. De Marchi, I, 76. Artistic representations of the Genius support the interpretation of this expression and underscore the power of the *genius* as life, "vita." See also p. 72, n. 7: the snake appearing with fruit in ancient art is indulged appropriately; he is offered what he represents.

28. See Onians, pp. 224–28. For example, Apuleius in *De Magia Liber* 4, in *Opera Omnia,* ed. G. F. Hildebrand (1842; rpt. Hildesheim, 1968), II, 448, laments the fact that learned labor has dried him up ("omnem gratiam corpore deterget, habitudinem tenuat, *sucum exsorbet,* colorem oblitterat, vigorem debilitat," my emphasis).

29. "Genialis" means "zeugungskräftig" literally, according to Wissowa, pp. 175–76, and Onians, p. 225; by metonymy, it came to mean "full of life, energy, vigor," indeed, "die ganze Persönlichkeit des Mannes," in the words of Wissowa. See also Preller, I, 69–70; Otto, *Die Manen,* p. 62.

30. Plautus, *Persa* 108, in *Plautus,* ed. and trans. Paul Nixon, 5 vols., Loeb Classical Library (London, New York, and Cambridge, Mass., 1916–38), III, 432.

31. Terence, *Phormio* 43–44, in *Terence,* ed. and trans. John Sargeaunt, Loeb Classical Library (Cambridge, Mass., and London, 1912), II, 10.

32. Plautus, *Truculentus* 182.

33. Martial, *Epigrams,* ed. and trans. Walter C. A. Ker, Loeb Classical Library (London and New York, 1919–20), I, 476 (7. 78. 4).

34. *Nonii Marcelli De Conpendiosa Doctrina,* ed. Wallace M. Lindsay (Leipzig, 1903), I, 169 (117.24–28). Apparently Nonius has misunderstood Lucilius' Epicurean notion of the helpful friend: see Lucilius, *The Twelve Tables* 692–93, in *Remains of Old Latin,* ed. and trans. E. H. Warmington, Loeb Classical Library, III (London and Cambridge, Mass., 1938), 222, and see p. 223 n. Food and money, according to Desmonde, p. 22, intimately influence the internal organs: man's monetary relations with others condition his drive and emotional state, just as blood sugar, blood pressure, and the digestive system influence his mood, energy, and attitudes.

35. Persius, *Satura* 4.27. The gods on the left and the left side of the gods ("dii laevi a laeva") were of ill omen: see Arnobius, *Adversus Nationes* 4.5.

36. Seneca, *Epistle* 95.41, in *Ad Lucilium Epistulae Morales,* ed. and trans. Richard M. Gummere, 3 vols., Loeb Classical Library (London and New York, 1917–25), III, 84.

37. See Servius, *In Vergilii Georgica Commentarii* 1.302. This matter will be discussed more completely in Chapter Three of this work.

38. The influence of Greek polytheism on Roman religion has been discussed by Jevons, ed. *Plutarch's Romane Questions,* p. xlvi and following pp.; and Bailey, pp. 109–12. For the Greek philosophical influence, see Bailey, pp. 214 ff.; and Fowler, *The Religious Experience of the Roman People,* pp. 358 ff.

39. This plenitude of *genii* is briefly discussed by Fowler, *Roman Ideas of Deity,* pp. 20–21.

40. See Taylor, pp. 9–18 and 47–48; and Desmonde, p. 59. Taylor traces the origins of this idea to Greece. The founder of a city (e.g., Timoleon of Syracuse) was honored on his birthday through his *agathos daemon;* thus the natal spirits of man and city-father were identical. For discussions of the *genius urbis,* see Wissowa, pp. 178 f., and Birt, cols. 1620 ff.

41. Fowler, *The Religious Experience of the Roman People,* p. 317. His explanation of the statement, p. 332 n., links Hercules with Genius (since both represent the male principle of life), and Juventas with Liber (*tirones* were sacrificed to her during the Liberalia, and Liber was another form of Genius).

42. Fowler, *Roman Ideas of Deity,* p. 21; see also Birt, col. 1621.

43. Discussions of the *genii* of the gods and the *genius Iovis* can be found in Preller, I, 74–76; Otto, "Genius," *Paulys Real-Encyclopädie,* cols. 1164–65; Fowler, *Roman Ideas of Deity,* pp. 20–21; and Birt, cols. 1619, 1622.

44. For the Etruscan background of the *genius Iovis* discussed in this paragraph, see Altheim, *Griechische Götter im alten Rom,* and his *History of Roman Religion,* pp. 59–61.

45. Birt, col. 1619.

46. Petronius, *Satyricon* 21, in *Petronius; Seneca: Apocolocyntosis,* ed. and trans. Michael Heseltine, Loeb Classical Library (1913; rev., rpt. London and Cambridge, Mass., 1930), p. 30.

47. Minucius Felix, *Octavius* 29.5, in *Tertullian: Apology, De Spectaculis; Minucius Felix,* ed. and trans. Gerald H. Rendall and T. R. Glover, Loeb Classical Library (London and New York, 1931), p. 404.

48. The change from an agricultural to an urban society is discussed by Bailey, p. 109, and Fowler, *The Religious Experience of the Roman People,* p. 358. The influence of foreign tutelary spirits on Italian religion and on the concept of the *genius* is analyzed by Taylor, pp. 9–10 ff., and 251 ff.; also, T. R. Glover, *The Conflict of Religions in the Early Roman Empire* (London, 1909), p. 15. For Augustus' motives and actions in the establishment of the state cult, see Taylor, passim, and Bailey, pp. 173–74.

49. The deification of the imperial Genius was encouraged by several factors—the Eastern ruler cult, the need for a paterfamilias substitute for the state "family," and the need for a state-ordained worship in order to hold the state together. See Jesse B. Carter, "Ancestor Worship (Roman)," in *Encyclopaedia of Religion and Ethics,* I, 465 f.; Fowler, *Roman Ideas of Deity,* pp. 83–105; Halliday, p. 176 f.; Bailey, p. 173; and especially, Taylor, pp. 67, 246, and passim. The information in this paragraph concerning the Genius of the emperor was garnered primarily from Taylor, pp. 151 ff.

50. Ovid, *Fasti* 5.145–46, ed. and trans. Sir James George Frazer, Loeb Classical Library (London and New York, 1931), p. 270. See also Taylor, p. 185.

51. The libation is discussed by Taylor, p. 151; the coin, p. 152. The coin, minted before 27 B.C., portrays Octavian on one side, and an "ithyphallic terminal figure" on the other— suggestive of a totemistic Genius.

52. Suetonius, *De Vita Caesarum* 4.27.3. See also Taylor, p. 152. Swearing by the Genius of the emperor was a custom current even in the third century: Tertullian, *Apologeticus* 32.2, declares, "Sed et iuramus, sicut non per genios Caesarum, ita per salutem eorum, quae est augustior omnibus geniis."

53. On the municipal cults and the state priests, see Taylor, esp. pp. 215, 221; on the sacrifice of victims, *ibid.*, p. 194; on the temples of Augustus, *ibid.*, pp. 193, 202, 216–17. Suetonius, *De Vita Caesarum* 2.60, tells us that Augustus' friends wanted to help finish the proposed temple of Jupiter Olympius, which had been dedicated to the imperial Genius.

54. See Taylor, p. 193. The protective nature of the Genius of Caesar is noted by Ammianus, *Rerum Gestarum* 24.2.21: a peace was made between the commander of an enemy garrison and Caesar; it was so generous that the people shouted, "salutarem genium affulsisse sibi clamitans Caesarem, magnum et lenem."

55. Minucius Felix, *Octavius* 29.5. Tertullian, *Apologeticus* 28.3, also complains of the irreligious worship of a living man: "Citius denique apud vos per omnes deos quam per unum genium Caesaris peieratur." In 32.2, he says, "Nescitis genios daemonas dici et inde diminutiva voce daemonia? Nos iudicium dei suspicimus in imperatoribus, qui gentibus illos praefecit."

56. Lines 611–17, in *Claudian*, ed. and trans. Maurice Platnauer, Loeb Classical Library (London and New York, 1922), II, 118.

57. Horace, *Epistles* 2.2.187–89, in *Satires, Epistles, and Ars Poetica*, ed. and trans. H. Rushton Fairclough, Loeb Classical Library (London and New York, 1926), p. 438.

58. L. Apuleius Madaurensis, *De Deo Socratis* 15.151, in *De Philosophia Libri*, ed. Paul Thomas, *Opera Quae Supersunt*, Vol. 3 (Stuttgart, 1970), p. 23.

59. *De Nuptiis Philologiae et Mercurii* 2.152, in *Martianus Capella*, ed. Adolf Dick (Stuttgart, 1969), p. 65.

60. *Remigii Autissiodorensis Commentum in Martianum Capellam Libri I–II*, ed. Cora E. Lutz (Leiden, 1962), pp. 184 and 118 (2.65.8 and 1.28.12); *Iohannis Scotti Annotationes in Marcianum*, ed. Cora E. Lutz (Cambridge, Mass., 1939), p. 68 (65.16).

61. Both repeat portions of Horace's definition. See Édouard Jeauneau, "L'Usage de la notion d'*integumentum* à travers les gloses de Guillaume de Conches," *Archives d'Histoire Doctrinale et Littéraire du Moyen Âge*, 32 (1957), 46; *Commentum Bernardi Silvestris super Sex Libros Eneidos Virgilii*, ed. Wilhelm Riedel (Greifswald, 1924), p. 54.

62. Gaius Plinius Secundus, *Naturalis Historia* 2.5.16, ed. and trans. H. Rackham, *Pliny: Natural History*, Vol. 1, Loeb Classical Library (Cambridge, Mass., and London, 1938), p. 180.

63. De Marchi, I, 209. See also Preller, I, 78; Birt, col. 1617; Wissowa, p. 177. However, some scholars think "Natalis" was a separate personification, not another name for the Genius: Otto, "Genius," cols. 1158–59, and *Die Manen*, pp. 60–61; Wilhelm Schmidt, *Geburtstag im Altertum* (Giessen, 1908), pp. 1, 22–23.

64. *Codex Theodosianus* 16.10.12, in *Codices Gregorianus, Hermogenianus, Theodosianus*, ed. Gustav Haenel (Leipzig and Bonn, 1837–42), fols. 1617–19. From the Emperors Theodosius, Arcadius, and Honorius Augustus to Rufinus, Praetorian Prefect: "Nullus omnino, exquolibet genere, ordine hominum, dignitatum, vel in potestate positus vel honore perfunctus, sive potens sorte nascendi seu humilis genere, conditione, fortuna, in nullo penitus loco, in nulla urbe sensu carentibus simulacris vel insontem victimam caedat, vel, secretiore piaculo, larem igne, mero genium, penates odore veneratus, accendat lumina, imponat tura, serta suspendat."

65. Ovid, *Tristia* 3.13.15, in *Tristia; Ex Ponto,* ed. and trans. Arthur Leslie Wheeler, Loeb Classical Library (London and Cambridge, Mass., 1924), p. 150. See also 5.5.13. Horace's description of a birthday celebration is very similar: in the *Odes* 4.11.1–8, in *Horace, The Odes and Epodes,* ed. and trans. C. E. Bennett, Loeb Classical Library (1914; rev., rpt. Cambridge, Mass., and London, 1927), p. 326, he mentions a jar of Alban wine, parsley for garlands, ivy for Phyllis' hair, silver vessels, dancing flames, and "ara castis / vincta verbenis." For a discussion of Roman birthday celebrations, see Schmidt, p. 25.

66. Albius Tibullus, 1.7.49–54, ed. and trans. J. P. Postgate, in *Catullus, Tibullus, and Pervigilium Veneris,* pp. 230, 232. Fire is mentioned in another passage (2.2.3–4).

67. See Fowler, *The Religious Experience of the Roman People,* p. 184; the food communion rituals in family ancestor worship constituted a form of communication and renewal of strength for the family. See Desmonde, pp. 24–25, 37, 54, 139.

68. Horace, *Ars Poetica* 209–11. In the *Odes* 3.17.14–16, he says, "Cras genium mero / Curabis, et porco bimestri / Cum famulis operum solutis." The pig is probably intended for some other spirit.

69. Petronius, *Satyricon* 34; Ovid, *Fasti* 3.523. See Onians, pp. 227 ff.: wine was "life-fluid itself and did not merely, like most food, contain life-fluid among other elements." Fowler, *Roman Ideas of Deity,* p. 18, speaks of the wine offered to the Genius and its "mystic connexion with blood"; see also de Marchi, I, 53–54.

70. Censorinus, *De Die Natali* 2.2–3. Schmidt, p. 26, comments on this passage; on p. 27, he declares that victims were offered only to the imperial Genius.

71. See John Edwin Sandys, *A History of Classical Scholarship* (1903; rpt. New York, 1958), Vol. I, s.v. index for citations of authors in the long section on the availability and influence of the classics in the Middle Ages. See also Chapter Three of this work.

CHAPTER TWO: THE LATE CLASSICAL GENIUS: PHILOSOPHICAL AND COSMOLOGICAL CONCEPTIONS

1. The astrological nature of the classical *genius* has been very briefly discussed by Attilio de Marchi, *Il culto privato di Roma antica,* I (Milan, 1896), 70–73; Edward B. Tylor, *Primitive Culture* (London, 1913), II, 201; and Richard Broxton Onians, *The Origins of European Thought about the Body, the Mind, the Soul, the World, Time, and Fate,* 2nd ed. (Cambridge, 1954), pp. 162–64.

2. Juvenal, *Satura* 6.562, in *Juvenal and Persius,* ed. and trans. G. G. Ramsay, Loeb Classical Library (London and New York, 1918), p. 128. Subsequent references to primary works, after an initial reference in a note, will be indicated by book, chapter, and line number(s) within the text. The Loeb Classical Library editions have been used whenever available. Translations of passages within the text are my own, unless otherwise acknowledged.

3. Persius, *Satura* 6.18–19, in *Juvenal and Persius,* p. 394.

4. *Iulii Firmici Materni Matheseos Libri VIII,* ed. W. Kroll and F. Skutsch (Stuttgart, 1968), I, 64–65 (2.19.12–13).

5. *Ambrosii Theodosii Macrobii Saturnalia* 1.19.16–18, in *Macrobius,* ed. James Willis (Leipzig, 1963), I, 111. But note that Charisius (c. A.D. 365) identifies the *genius* as the individual *tyche* or fortune: "hic genius ἡ τύχη ἑκάστου." See *Flavii Sosipatri Charisii Artis Grammaticae Libri V,* ed. Charles Barwick (Leipzig, 1964), p. 33 (1.11).

6. Prudentius, *Contra Orationem Symmachi* 2.71–74, in *Prudentius,* ed. and trans. H. J. Thomson, Loeb Classical Library (London and Cambridge, Mass., 1953), II, 12.

7. Soon, he says, every wall will arise "sub astro" and be assigned its own fortune and fate (2.450–53). The Christian apologists delighted in scoffing at the intricate system of *genii.* For example, Arnobius, *Adversus Nationes Libri VII,* ed. C. Marchesi, 2nd ed. (Turin, 1953), pp. 208–9, belittles the concept of Lateranus as a *genius* of the hearth (which was constructed from unbaked *laterculi*), and wonders whether a fireplace of *burned* clay still has a *genius* (4.6).

8. For analysis of and commentary upon the Stoic concept of the Generative Reason, see E. Zeller, *The Stoics, Epicureans, and Sceptics,* trans. Oswald J. Reichel (London, 1870), pp. 162 ff. and passim; also E. Vernon Arnold, *Roman Stoicism* (Cambridge, 1911), p. 161 and passim. For a brief but broad summary of microcosmic theories in Stoicism, see George Perrigo Conger, *Theories of Macrocosms and Microcosms in the History of Philosophy* (New York, 1922), pp. 13 ff.

9. Arnold, p. 161.

10. Virgil, *Aeneid* 6.724–29, in *Aeneid,* ed. and trans. H. Rushton Fairclough, 2 vols., Loeb Classical Library (1916–18; rev. Cambridge, Mass., 1934–35), I, 556. Fairclough's translation has been used throughout this chapter.

11. *S. Aurelii Augustini De Civitate Dei contra Paganos Libri,* ed. and trans. William M. Green, Loeb Classical Library, II (London and Cambridge, Mass., 1963), 396 (7.6). Green's translations are used throughout this chapter. *"Anima"* and *"animus"* appear to be used interchangeably in this passage. God is both the soul or life of the universe, and its mind or ruling principle.

12. Arnold, p. 230.

13. Onians, p. 125. An ancient Italian word for the concept of the Genius, Cerus or Kerus, associated with "creo" and "Ceres," stemmed from the Sanskrit *kri-kar* and meant "begetting spirit." See Ludwig Preller, *Römische Mythologie* (Berlin, 1858), I, 70–71; for the Genius-Ceres relationship, see Th. Birt, "Genius," in *Ausführliches Lexikon der griechischen und römischen Mythologie,* ed. W. H. Roscher (Leipzig, 1886–90), 1.2, col. 1615; and Onians, pp. 125–26, 148, 150. Martianus Capella, listing the inhabitants of the sixteen regions of heaven invited to the marriage of Mercury and Philology, links Ceres with a Genius: these two, plus Tellurus and Vulcan, arrived from the fifth region. See *De Nuptiis Philologiae et Mercurii* 1.49, in *Martianus Capella,* ed. Adolf Dick (Stuttgart, 1969), p. 28.

14. *Pauli Excerpta ex Libris Pompeii Festi de Significatione Verborum* 95, in *Sexti Pompeii Festi De Verborum Significatu Quae Supersunt cum Pauli Epitome,* ed. Wallace M. Lindsay (1913; rpt. Hildesheim, 1965), p. 84.

15. *Macrobii Commentarii in Somnium Scipionis* 1.6.36–40, in *Macrobius,* II, 25. See also Macrobius, *Commentary on the Dream of Scipio,* trans. William Harris Stahl (1952; rpt.

New York and London, 1966), p. 107. Stahl's translation has been used throughout this chapter.

16. Arnobius, *Adversus Nationes* 3.40. See also Preller, I, 76.

17. Macrobius, *Commentary,* trans. Stahl, p. 145 (1.14.16). The World Soul, he says, was begotten by the numbers seven and eight (1.6.3). The origin of the World Soul proceeded in seven steps; there are seven planetary spheres beneath the fixed sphere of the stars (1.6.47). It is relatively easy to understand how these spheres and their planets came to be regarded as part of the World Soul.

18. Calcidius, *Commentarius* 188, in *Timaeus: A Calcidio Translatus Commentarioque Instructus,* ed. J. H. Waszink (London and Leiden, 1962), pp. 212–13. J. A. W. Bennett, *The Parlement of Foules: An Interpretation* (Oxford, 1957), p. 195, declares that the three powers, Nature, Fortune, and Chance, are subordinated to the Trinity in this passage, but it is unlikely that Calcidius is discussing the Trinity per se. His Neo-Platonic concept slightly resembles that of Plotinus, who posits a system including a One, a Nous as a first emanation or divine mind, and a double World Soul, part of which contemplates the ideas of Nous, and part of which (called Nature) transforms them into matter. See George D. Economou, *The Goddess Natura in Medieval Literature* (Cambridge, Mass., 1972), pp. 14–16. Calcidius is discussed on pp. 20–24. The World Soul is identified with the Spiritus Sanctus in the twelfth century: see, for example, the commentary on the *Timaeus* (38.6–11) by Guillaume de Conches, in "Les Gloses de Guillaume de Conches," ed. J. M. Parent, in *La Doctrine de la création dans l'école de Chartres, étude et textes* (Paris and Ottawa, 1938), p. 166.

19. Plato, *Timaeus* 89E–90A, ed. and trans. R. G. Bury, *Plato,* Vol. 7, Loeb Classical Library (London and New York, 1929), pp. 244, 246.

20. Arnold, p. 246. Zeller, p. 332, explains the relationship between the *daemon* and reason: ". . . since reason alone protects man from evil, and conducts him to happiness—this, too, was the popular belief—reason may be described as the guardian spirit, or demon, in man."

21. Apuleius, *De Deo Socratis* 15.150–51, in *De Philosophia Libri,* ed. Paul Thomas, *Opera Quae Supersunt,* Vol. 3 (Stuttgart, 1970), p. 23.

22. Ammianus Marcellinus, *Rerum Gestarum Libri Qui Supersunt,* ed. and trans. John C. Rolfe, Loeb Classical Library (London and Cambridge, Mass., 1937), II, 166, 168 (21.14.2–4).

23. "Genium et genua" in Thomas, ed. *De Philosophia Libri.* But "Genium et Geniam" in *De Deo Socratis* 15.152, in *Opera Omnia,* ed. G. F. Hildebrand (1842; rpt. Hildesheim, 1968), II, 145. Although the first variant is perhaps preferable, the second also makes sense: if Apuleius were unaware of the existence of the Juno as a female counterpart to the masculine Genius, he might have regarded the Genia so. Both spirits, while lodged within the body, symbolize in two words (Genius and Genia) the union of soul (the spirits) and body. He later says that the *genius* becomes a *manes* after death. Thus the word *genius* itself implies "soul-within-the-body." See also Hildebrand's similar explanation of the Genia, bolstered by other references to the Juno, on pp. 145–146 n.

24. Servius, *In Vergilii Aeneidos Commentarii* 9.182, in *In Vergilii Carmina Commentarii,* ed. Georg Thilo and Hermann Hagen, 3 vols. (1881–87; rpt. Hildesheim, 1961), II, 325.

An elucidation of the Neo-Platonic background of the passage is provided by Edith Owen Wallace, *The Notes on Philosophy in the Commentary of Servius on the Eclogues, the Georgics, and the Aeneid of Vergil* (New York, 1938), pp. 150–56.

25. 1.302, in *In Vergilii Georgica Commentarii.*

26. For the influence of the Di Manes upon the *genius* and the "immortality of the soul," see Birt, cols. 1617–18; Georg Wissowa, *Religion und Kultus der Römer,* in *Handbuch der klassischen Altertumswissenschaft,* Vol. 5, pt. 4, 2nd ed. (Munich, 1912), p. 176; Walter F. Otto, *Die Manen; oder, Von den Urformen des Totenglaubens* (Berlin, 1923), p. 62; W. Warde Fowler, *Roman Ideas of Deity* (London, 1914), pp. 19, 23, and *The Religious Experience of the Roman People* (London, 1911), p. 75; William Reginald Halliday, *Lectures on the History of Roman Religion* (Liverpool, 1922), pp. 38–40; and especially Jesse Benedict Carter, "Ancestor Worship (Roman)," *Encyclopaedia of Religion and Ethics,* ed. James Hastings, I (New York, 1913), 465.

27. This classification of *daèmones* is provided by Arnold, p. 232.

28. For a short resumé of this little book on *daemones,* see C. S. Lewis, *The Discarded Image* (Cambridge, 1964), pp. 40–44. He also notes the importance of Apuleius for the Middle Ages.

29. Apuleius places it in a middle position; Calcidius, *Commentarius* 232, finds it "in medio positum"; and Martianus labels the Greek *daemon* (and the "angel") as "medioximus" in *De Nuptiis* 2.154.

30. See Augustine, *De Civitate Dei* 8.14–15; Calcidius, *Commentarius* 131, 135.

31. 2.150–68; the discussion presents a hierarchy of spirits that Bernardus Silvestris uses extensively in the second book of *De Mundi Universitate.* For a full examination of such spirits and their hierarchies, see Lynn Thorndike, *A History of Magic and Experimental Science,* Vols. I and II (New York, 1923–29).

32. Plato, *Symposium* 202E–203A, in *Great Dialogues of Plato,* trans. Eric H. Warmington and Philip G. Rouse (New York, 1956), p. 98.

33. *Apology* 31C–D, ed. and trans. Harold North Fowler, *Plato,* Vol. 1, Loeb Classical Library (1914; rpt. Cambridge, Mass., and London, 1947), p. 114. This was repeated by Calcidius, *Commentarius* 168, and summarized in *Quinti Septimi Florentis Tertulliani De Anima Liber,* ed. J. H. Waszink (Amsterdam, 1947), p. 56 (39.3).

34. Plutarch, *De Genio Socratis* 24, in *Plutarchi Scripta Moralia,* ed. Frederick Dübner, I (Paris, 1856), 716.

35. Tertullian, *De Anima* 39.3; he equates the *daemon* with the *genius* in *Apologeticus* 32.2–3, in *Tertullian: Apology, De Spectaculis; Minucius Felix,* ed. and trans. T. R. Glover and Gerald H. Rendall, Loeb Classical Library (London and New York, 1931), p. 156: "Ceterum daemonas, id est genios" (32.3).

36. *L. Annaei Flori Epitomae de Tito Livio Bellorum Omnium Annorum DCC* 2.17.8, in *Lucius Annaeus Florus: Epitome of Roman History; Cornelius Nepos,* ed. and trans. Edward Seymour Forster, Loeb Classical Library (London and New York, 1929), p. 308.

37. Tylor, II, 204, associates "the rites of the classic natal genius and the mediaeval natal saint," but Gordon J. Laing, *Survivals of Roman Religion* (New York, 1931), p. 8, believes the doctrine of veneration of the saint developed from that of the polytheistic deity.

38. *L. Caeli Firmiani Lactanti Divinae Institutiones* 2.14.1–4, in *Opera Omnia*, ed. Samuel Brandt and Georg Laubmann (Prague and Leipzig, 1890), pp. 162–63. Cf. Firmianus Lactantius, *Epitome Institutionum Divinarum*, ed. and trans. E. H. Blakenay (London, 1950), pp. 76–77 (28); and for additional commentary, Emil Schneweis, *Angels and Demons According to Lactantius* (Washington, 1944), pp. 92 and 140–42.

39. The medieval association of demons with magic and astrology is widely acknowledged and needs no extended proof. But see Augustine's *De Divinatione Daemonum*, an excellent early example; also Thorndike, Vols. I and II; and Theodore Otto Wedel, *The Mediaeval Attitude toward Astrology* (New Haven, London, and Oxford, 1920), esp. pp. 16, 23, 64, 69–70, 122. Also, it is interesting to note that *laruatus* (from *larva*) means "bewitched, enchanted," and is used as part of a doctor's diagnosis of madness as early as Plautus' *Menaechmi* (5.4.1).

40. And later, of course: see, e.g., Sigmund Freud, "A Neurosis of Demoniacal Possession in the Seventeenth Century," *On Creativity and the Unconscious*, sel. Benjamin Nelson (New York, 1958), pp. 264–300. See also this work, Chapter Six, n. 30.

CHAPTER THREE: THE CLASSICAL GENIUS IN THE MIDDLE AGES

1. Other pagan gods were similarly moralized. See Friedrich von Bezold, *Das Fortleben der antiken Götter im mittelalterlichen Humanismus* (Bonn and Leipzig, 1922); Hans Liebeschütz, ed. *Fulgentius Metaforalis: Ein Beitrag zur Geschichte der antiken Mythologie im Mittelalter* (Berlin and Leipzig, 1926); Ernest H. Wilkins, "Descriptions of Pagan Divinities from Petrarch to Chaucer," *Speculum*, 32 (1957), 511–22; Richard Hamilton Green, "Classical Fable and English Poetry in the Fourteenth Century," *Critical Approaches to Medieval Literature*, ed. Dorothy Bethurum (New York, 1960), pp. 110–34; Douglas Bush, *Mythology and the Renaissance Tradition in English Poetry* (Minneapolis, 1932), especially Chap. One; Jean Seznec, *The Survival of the Pagan Gods*, trans. Barbara F. Sessions (New York, 1953); Erwin Panofsky, *Studies in Iconology* (New York, 1939); John Block Friedman, *Orpheus in the Middle Ages* (Cambridge, Mass., 1970); George D. Economou, *The Goddess Natura in Medieval Literature* (Cambridge, Mass., 1972); and Winthrop Wetherbee, *Platonism and Poetry in the Twelfth Century* (Princeton, 1972).

2. John Edwin Sandys, *A History of Classical Scholarship* (1903; rpt. New York, 1958), Vol. I, details the extant manuscripts and popularity of various classical authors in the Middle Ages. See also James Stuart Beddie, "The Ancient Classics in the Mediaeval Libraries," *Speculum*, 5 (1930), 3–20; Henry Osborn Taylor, *The Classical Heritage of the Middle Ages*, 3rd ed. (New York, 1911), especially the first four chapters; and also Charles Homer Haskins, *The Renaissance of the Twelfth Century* (1927; rpt. Cleveland and New York, 1957), especially Chap. Four, "The Revival of the Latin Classics" (it examines the popularity of various authors in manuscripts, grammars, *florilegia*, glossaries, anthologies, etc.).

For the Greek heritage in the Middle Ages, particularly the Platonic tradition, consult Raymond Klibansky, *The Continuity of the Platonic Tradition during the Middle Ages* (London, 1950), and Paul Shorey, *Platonism: Ancient and Modern* (Berkeley, 1938), Chap. Four, "Platonism in the Middle Ages."

3. For causes and consequences of these renaissances, see Haskins; and Beddie, pp. 3–20.

4. The most important studies of the transmission of classical authors via *scholia, florilegia,* collections of *scholia, libri manuales,* and commentaries during the Middle Ages are Charles Homer Haskins, ''A List of Text-books from the Close of the Twelfth Century,'' *Harvard Studies in Classical Philology,* 20 (1909), 75–94; Edward Kennard Rand, ''The Classics in the Thirteenth Century,'' *Speculum,* 4 (1929), 249–69; and Eva Matthews Sanford, ''The Use of Classical Latin Authors in the *Libri Manuales,''* *Transactions of the American Philological Association,* 55 (1924), 190–248.

5. Bernardus Silvestris, *Commentum Bernardi Silvestris super Sex Libros Eneidos Virgilii,* ed. Wilhelm Riedel (Greifswald, 1924), p. 29. Subsequent references to all primary works, after the initial citation in a note, will then be incorporated into the text. All translations are my own, unless otherwise acknowledged. For studies of the commentary, see especially Wetherbee, pp. 105–11, and J. Reginald O'Donnell, ''The Sources and Meaning of Bernard Silvester's Commentary on the *Aeneid,''* *Mediaeval Studies,* 24 (1962), 233–49.

6. *Macrobii Commentarii in Somnium Scipionis* 1.11.5–6, in *Macrobius,* ed. James Willis (Leipzig, 1963), II, 46. See also William H. Stahl's translation of *Commentary on the Dream of Scipio* (1952; rpt. New York and London, 1966), p. 131.

7. Bernardus: ''Descensus autem ad inferos quadrifarius est: est autem unus naturae, alius virtutis, tertius vitii, quartus artificii,'' p. 30. Bernardus' commentary on the six books of the *Aeneid* is structured according to the six ages of man—*infantia, pueritia, adulescentia, juventus, virilitas,* and the descent into the underworld. For brief discussions of the four descents, see Daniel Carl Meerson, ''The Ground and Nature of Literary Theory in Bernard Silvester's Twelfth-Century Commentary on the *Aeneid,''* Diss. Chicago 1967; Green, pp. 110–34; and Friedman, pp. 142–43.

8. The passage on the four descents in Guillaume's gloss on *De Consolatione* is reprinted in Édouard Jeauneau, ''L'Usage de la notion d'*integumentum* à travers les gloses de Guillaume de Conches,'' *Archives d'Histoire Doctrinale et Littéraire du Moyen Âge,* 32 (1957), 42.

9. *S. Aurelii Augustini De Civitate Dei contra Paganos Libri,* ed. and trans. Willam M. Green, Loeb Classical Library, II (London and Cambridge, Mass., 1963), p. 422 (7.13; his trans.).

10. *Isidori Hispalensis Episcopi Etymologiarum sive Originum Libri XX,* ed. W. M. Lindsay (Oxford, 1911), Vol. I (8.11.88); *Pauli Excerpta ex Libris Pompeii Festi de Significatione Verborum,* in *Sexti Pompeii Festi De Verborum Significatu Quae Supersung cum Pauli Epitome,* ed. W. M. Lindsay (1913; rpt. Hildesheim, 1965), p. 84: ''Genium appellabant deum, qui vim optineret rerum omnium gerendarum''; Rabanus Maurus, *De Universo* 15, in *Patrologiae Cursus Completus: Series Latina,* ed. J. P. Migne, 111 (Paris, 1852), 433B: ''Genium autem dicunt quod quasi vim habeat omnium rerum gignendarum, seu a gignendis liberis.''

11. Martianus Capella, *De Nuptiis Philologiae et Mercurii* 2.152, in *Martianus Capella,* ed. Adolf Dick (Stuttgart, 1969), p. 65: ''. . . quem etiam Praestitem, quod praesit gerundis [or *gerendis*] omnibus''; *Remigii Autissiodorensis Commentum in Martianum Capellam Libri I–II,* ed. Cora E. Lutz (Leiden, 1962), pp. 118, 184: ''ET GENIUS . . . qui omnium rerum generationibus praeest,'' 1.28.12, and ''. . . eo quod praesit omnibus gerendis,'' 2.65.8; Mythographus Tertius, *De Diis Gentium et Illorum Allegoriis* 6.19, in *Scriptores*

Rerum Mythicarum Latini Tres Romae Nuper Reperti, ed. Georg Heinrich Bode (Celle, 1834), p. 185, cites Remigius' first definition.

12. In codices Parisinus 7959 saeculi X and Hamburgensis 52 saec. XI. *Servii in Vergilii Georgica Commentarii* 1.302, in *In Vergilii Carmina Commentarii,* ed. Georg Thilo and Hermann Hagen (1881–87; rpt. Hildesheim, 1961), III, 198 n.; *Remigii Commentum in Martianum* 1.28.12 and 2.65.8; Mythographus Tertius, *De Diis Gentium* 6.19; and "Hierarchia Alani," in *Alain de Lille: Textes inédits,* ed. Marie-Thérèse d'Alverny (Paris, 1965), p. 228.

13. P. 46. Guillaume cites Horace, *Epistle* 2.2.188–89, on Genius. D. W. Robertson, Jr., *A Preface to Chaucer* (Princeton, 1962), p. 199, n. 101, uses this passage to identify *genius* as natural inclination, but he ignores *genius* as Euridice; Friedman, pp. 106–9, translates and discusses Guillaume's gloss on the Orpheus-Euridice myth but, rather curiously, omits the passage (and any comment thereupon) mentioning *genius* as concupiscence.

14. Friedman, p. 109, sees it as a Platonic conflict between *nous,* or mind, and *thumose-pithumia,* or passion and desire. See also Wetherbee, p. 97.

15. See Giovanni Boccaccio, *Genealogie Deorum Gentilium Libri* 5.12, ed. Vincenzo Romano, 2 vols., *Opere,* Vols. 10–11 (Bari, 1951), II, 244–47. Friedman, Chap. Four, traces the evolution of Euridice as natural concupiscence from Boethius, Remigius on Boethius, Guillaume, Arnulf of Orléans, John of Garland, Mythographus Tertius (Albericus), the *Ovide Moralisé,* to Pierre Bersuire, Nicholas of Trivet, Boccaccio, and Colucio Salutati. Except for a few comments on Bernardus' theory of the four descents, pp. 142–43, and on his view of Orpheus, p. 112, he ignores his moralization of the myth entirely.

16. See this work, Chap. One, pp. 15–16, for a full description of lines and texts.

17. Such differences in the authors' views of Euridice, although slight, may have been influenced by the two major medieval approaches to the myth. Friedman, Chap. Four, distinguishes the Fulgentian approach (Euridice as "profound judgment"), later repeated and developed by John the Scot, Remigius on Martianus, and Thomas of Walsingham, from the Boethian approach (Euridice as "natural concupiscence"), which was much more popular during the Middle Ages. Bernardus' more sympathetic treatment of Euridice may have been colored by the Fulgentian tradition.

18. Apuleius, *De Deo Socratis* 15, in *De Philosophia Libri,* ed. Paul Thomas, in *Opera Quae Supersunt,* Vol. 3 (Stuttgart, 1970), pp. 23–24.

19. Cf. *Servii in Vergilii Aeneidos Commentarii* 9.182; and Mythographus Tertius, *De Diis Gentium* 6.19, in Bode, p. 185. This passage from Mythographus Tertius illustrates, through the italicized lines, his debt to Servius: *"Apud Plotinum philosophum* tamen et *alios* non paucos diu quaesitum est, *utrum per se mentis nostrae acies,* an potius *alicujus numinis impulsu ad cupiditates et consilia moveatur. Et primi,* qui *mentes humanas sponte sua moveri dixerunt, deprehenderunt tamen, ad omnia honesta Genio et numine quodam familiari nos impelli, quod nobis nascentibus datur; prava vero nostra mente cupere nos et desiderare. Nec enim,* inquiunt, *fieri potest, ut prava numinum voluntate cupiamus, quibus nihil malum placere constat.* Unde alibi Virgilius:

—Dîne hunc ardorem mentibus addunt,
Euryale? an sua cuique deus fit dira cupido?

ac si diceret: *O Euryale, diine nostris mentibus cupiditates ingerunt* [sic—"iniciunt"] *et desideria? an deus fit ipsa mentis cupiditas?"*

20. *Remigii Commentum in Martianum* 2.65.8. C. S. Lewis comments upon the original passage of Martianus in *Studies in Medieval and Renaissance Literature,* collected by Walter Hooper (Cambridge, 1966), p. 170, but he does not explain the apparent contradiction in Remigius between "generalis" (general, universal) and "specialis" (special, particular).

21. Virgil, *Aeneid* 6.119–20, in *Virgil,* ed. and trans. H. Rushton Fairclough, 2 vols., Loeb Classical Library (1916–18; rev. London and Cambridge, Mass., 1934–35), I, 514 (his trans.).

22. *Anicii Manlii Severini Boethii Philosophiae Consolatio,* ed. Ludwig Bieler, in *Opera,* Part 1 (Turnhout, 1957), p. 64 (3.12.55–58). See also Friedman's comment on Boethius' use of the myth, pp. 91–96.

23. *Remigii Commentum in Martianum* 2.65.15: "Sciendum vero quia duo sunt genii, unus bonus qui animam ad virtutes impellit, alter malus qui ad vitia stimulat." See also 1.29.11: ". . . CULTORES MENTIUM quos Genios appellant, qui mentes hortantur ad bonum et ad virtutis exercitium."

24. Mythographus Tertius, *De Diis Gentium* 6.18, in Bode, p. 184: "Quod autem addit Virgilius: *'Quisque suos patimur manes,'* sive *supplicia* varia relinquit intelligi, *quae sunt apud manes* (*ut si quis dicat: 'judicium patimur,'* id est *ea quae in judicio continentur*), sive *aliud* quid juxta Servium *verius est. Nam quum,* inquit, *nascimur, duos Genios sortimur; unus est, qui ad bona hortatur, alter, qui depravat ad mala.* Nec incongrue dicuntur Genii, quia quum quis hominum genitus fuerit,* ei statim observatores deputantur; *quibus assistentibus, post mortem aut asserimur in vitam meliorem, aut condemnamur in deteriorem; per quos aut vagationem,* id est ascensionem ad superna, *aut reditum mereamur in corpora. Ergo manes Genios dicit, quos cum vita sortimur.''* (*This line is from *De Nuptiis* 2.152: "ideoque dicitur Genius, quoniam cum quis hominum genitus fuerit.")

25. Cf. *Servii in Vergilii Aeneidos Commentarii* 6.603; Isidore, *Etymologiarum* 8.11.88; *Rabani Mauri De Universo,* col. 433B: "Genium autem dicunt, quod quasi vim habeat omnium rerum gignendarum, seu a gignendis liberis. Unde et geniales lecti dicebantur a gentibus, qui novo marito sternebantur," taken verbatim from Isidore; and *Pauli Excerpta* 94: "*Genialis lectus,* qui nuptiis sternitur in honore genii, unde et appellatus."

26. *Servii in Vergilii Georgica Commentarii* 1.302; Mythographus Tertius, *De Diis Gentium* 6.19, in Bode, p. 185, omits "*Genialis Hiems* voluptuosa, convivalis," but the remainder is basically the same: "Genio autem indulgere dicimus, quotiens voluptati operam damus. Unde e contrario habemus in Terentio: *Sive defraudans Genium.*"

27. See Mythographus Tertius 6.19, in Bode, p. 185. For the Servian transcription (9.182), see n. 19 above. After citing Remigius on Genius as a natural god controlling all generation, and Servius on *indulgere genio* (see n. 26 above), he then mentions Aeneas' uncertainty concerning the snake discovered crawling from Anchises' tomb: he did not know whether it was the *genius loci* or the Genius of his father. The passage concludes: "Aut certe a Pythagorae assertione excogitatum est, qui primus de medulla, quae in spina hominis est, anguem creari deprehendit. Quod et Ovidius in XV metamorphoseon inter Pythagorae dicta commemorat. Anguinam autem Genio plerumque dari speciem novimus. Ut Persius: *Pinge*

duos angues." The two snakes would be the early Genius and Juno of the household, although Mythographus Tertius may not have realized this. The development of the snake (Genius) from the "marrow" of the spine (spinal cord) can be explained by Bernardus' *De Mundi Universitate,* ed. Carl Sigmund Barach and Johann Wrobel (Innsbruck, 1876), pp. 70–71 (2.14.159 ff.). Two *genii* (the testicles?) control the reproduction of the species: during intercourse, blood from the brain passes to the loins, where it becomes sperm bearing the likeness of ancestors. We infer, then, that it is transmitted via the serpentine spinal cord.

28. For discussions of the virtuous descent by means of the *trivium* and *quadrivium* see especially Meerson's introduction; O'Donnell, pp. 233–49; and Wetherbee, pp. 107–11.

29. Guillaume de Conches in Jeauneau, p. 46. Cf. *Commentum Bernardi Silvestris,* pp. 53–54. Friedman, Chap. Four, establishes this interpretation of Orpheus as basically Boethian and traces its development through the Middle Ages.

30. The myth is treated as a dramatic conflict between reason and passion by Guillaume, Bernardus, the anonymous *Ovide Moralisé,* Nicholas Trivet, et al. See Friedman, Chap. Four.

31. The virtuous descent is frequently applied to the fables of heroes like Orpheus, Theseus, Amphiaraus, Aeneas, and Hercules, according to Green, p. 127. Martianus, *De Nuptiis* 2.156–59, labels as *semones* (*sermones*) or *semidei* (*semithei*) Hercules, Amphiaraus, Hammon, Dionysus, Isis, Osiris, and others. (According to Martianus, these demi-gods inhabit the upper atmosphere between the moon and earth, and the *heroes* and *manes,* the mid-air to the mountain-tops, 2.152–66). Hercules, in particular, was closely affiliated with the classical *genius* (the knot in the bride's girdle was called *nodus herculaneus*): see, for an examination of the related cults, W. Warde Fowler, *The Roman Festivals of the Period of the Republic* (London, 1899), pp. 142–44; and Frank Byron Jevons, ed. *Plutarch's Romane Questions,* trans. 1683 by Philemon Holland (London, 1892), p. l.

32. See Mythographus Tertius 11.12, in Bode, pp. 235–36.

33. *Horoscopica,* used to study the constellations, is the tool of *genethliaci,* who provide horoscopes for men: "Horoscopi etiam ab horoscopica, id est *horarum* fata *inspicientes,* nuncupati sunt. De hujusmodi Juvenalis: *Nemo mathematicus genium indemnatus habebit,"* Mythographus Tertius 11.13, in Bode, p. 236.

34. *Ioannis Saresberiensis Episcopi Carnotensis Policratici sive De Nugis Curialium et Vestigiis Philosophorum Libri VIII,* ed. Clemens C. J. Webb (London, 1909), p. 49: "Eos autem qui nocentiora praestigia artesque magicas et uarias species mathematicae reprobatae exercent, iam pridem sancti patres ab aula iusserunt, eo quod omnia haec artificia uel potius maleficia ex pestifera quadam familiaritate demonum et hominum nouerint profluxisse, uerumque persaepe proferunt sola intentione fallendi, a quibus animam fidelem Dominus arcens ait: Si dixerint uobis, et ita euenerit, ne credatis eis" (1.9). He also says, 1.12, p. 51, in speaking of sacrifices to raise the dead in necromancy, "Ea namque ludificantium demonum et humanae perfidiae illudentium fallacia est."

35. The Persius passage (*Satura* 6.18–19) concludes a discussion of *mathematici* and frequently inaccurate interpretations of the stars: "Quorum genelliaci, qui geneses id est natalitias horas attendunt, imitantur errorem; unde satiricus: 'Nota mathematicis genesis tua.' Idem uero horoscopi nominantur; unde rursus: 'Geminos, horoscope, uaro / producis genio,' " 1.12, p. 53.

36. Cf. the analyses of dreams in *Macrobii Commentarii* 1.1–4, esp. 1.2–3, and *Ioannis Policraticus* 2.15, pp. 88–94. Stahl's translation of Macrobius indicates the Greek sources for Macrobius' comments on dreams in the footnotes for those chapters.

37. Geoffrey of Monmouth and Laȝamon, among others, also refer, in almost identical passages, to the demonic *incubus*, which pressed upon men during sleep, swived women, and fathered Merlin; see Geoffrey of Monmouth, *Historia Regum Britanniae*, ed. Jacob Hammer (Cambridge, Mass., 1951), p. 121 (6.11.289 ff.); Laȝamon, *Brut*, ed. G. L. Brook and R. F. Leslie, *Early English Text Society*, No. 250 (London and New York, 1963), I, 409 (Otho MS., lines 7870–82); 408 (Caligula MS., lines 7872–81).

38. *Ioannis Policraticus* 2.15, pp. 92–93: ". . . superstitiosae religionis homines fictis numinibus, immo potius ueris demonibus et execrabilibus sacris eorum non debitam reuerentiam, quae nulla est, sed turpissimum exhibent famulatum. Quod latius ex gentilium libris colligitur. Eneas oraculorum indicio promissam et quaesitam inuenit Italiam, et in ea non tam numinum quam demonum nutu sedem statuit et sementem Romani generis in orto qui eis complacuerat seminauit." Also see Liebeschütz, pp. 3 and 14, in which he discusses the medieval patristic interpretation of the gods as demons.

39. *Macrobii Commentarii* 1.2.17. See also Wetherbee, p. 37; cf. Brian Stock, *Myth and Science in the Twelfth Century: A Study of Bernard Silvester* (Princeton, 1972), pp. 37–54.

40. 1.2.11. Macrobius' discussion of fabulous narrative and allegory (as well as dreams) had great influence during the Middle Ages; see Green, "Classical Fable and English Poetry," pp. 110–28, and "Alan of Lille's *De Planctu Naturae*," *Speculum*, 31 (1956), 652–59. Much of the following discussion assumes familiarity with the very incisive and full analyses of kinds of *integumentum* and of the relationship between Platonism and poetic theory in the twelfth century presented in Wetherbee, *Platonism and Poetry*, passim, and "Introduction," in his trans. of *The Cosmographia of Bernardus Silvestris* (New York and London, 1973), esp. pp. 13–19; Stock, esp. pp. 31–62 on "Twelfth-Century Approaches to Myth"; and Hennig Brinkmann, "Verhüllung ('integumentum') als literarische Darstellungsform im Mittelalter," in *Miscellanea Mediaevalia*, 8 (Berlin and New York, 1971), pp. 314–39. None of these, however, links the enigmatic *somnium*, the artificial descent, and the demonic art of *praestigia* with those twelfth-century theories.

41. Friedman, Chap. Four. Friedman does not relate the Fulgentian tradition to the artificial descent or to the theories of poetry developed in the twelfth century.

42. "Sicque serpentis ictu moritur, quia nimiae subtilitatis suae intercepta secretis, velut ad inferos transmigrat," 8.20, in Bode, p. 212. Friedman, p. 134, translates the dependent clause as "because when her exceedingly subtle secrets had been [discovered]," a rendering which reduces the impact of the snake's action.

43. *Remigii Autissiodorensis Commentum in Martianum Capellam Libri III–IX*, ed. Cora E. Lutz (Leiden, 1965), p. 310 (9.480.18–19).

44. For fuller discussions of the grove and the temple, and Bernardus' theory of education and eloquence, see especially Wetherbee, *Platonism and Poetry*, pp. 107–8; O'Donnell, pp. 243–47; and Meerson, esp. the fourth chapter of the introduction.

45. The *Cebetis Tabula* describes a tablet which depicts a multitude gathered around a gate leading into a circle called Life; the Daemon stands by the gate and shows these souls how to enter, warns them against vice and Fortuna, and advocates the journey to the inner circle

of True Knowledge and Virtue. See *Cebetis Tabula* 4, in *Theophrasti Characteres; Marci Antonini Commentarii; Epicteti Dissertationes ab Arriano Literis Mandatae, Fragmenta et Enchiridion cum Commentario Simplicii Cebetis Tabula; Maximi Tyrii Dissertationes (Graece et Latine)*, ed. Frederick Dübner (Paris, 1842), p. 2 of *Cebetis*. The Neo-Pythagorean bias and the mystic secrets of the work are elucidated by Robert Joly, "Le Tableau de Cébès et la philosophie religieuse," *Collection Latomus*, 61 (1963), 1–86. This short work utilizes all four "descents"—the descent of the soul into nature, the descent into vice (and fortune), and after the ascent to the circle of Knowledge and Virtue, a descent back into Life. The implicit descent into artifice occurs in the explanation (by a *senex*) of the tablet's meaning to the visitors to the temple.

CHAPTER FOUR: THE FERTILE UNIVERSE: GENIUS AND THE NATURAL DESCENT IN THE *DE MUNDI UNIVERSITATE* OF BERNARDUS SILVESTRIS

1. Brief discussions of the themes and subjects of *De Mundi* and its place within the twelfth-century School of Chartres are presented in B. Hauréau, *Histoire de la philosophie scolastique*, Part 1 (Paris, 1872), I, 407–19; Reginald L. Poole, "The Masters of the Schools at Paris and Chartres in John of Salisbury's Time," *English Historical Review*, 35 (1920), 321–42; and F. J. E. Raby, *A History of Secular Latin Poetry in the Middle Ages*, 2nd ed. (Oxford, 1957), II, 5–12. Raby also pinpoints the basic sources of *De Mundi;* for more detailed analyses of sources and *Weltanschauung*, see A. Clerval, *Les Écoles de Chartres au moyen-âge (du Ve au XVIe siècle)* (Paris, 1895), pp. 259–61; and J. M. Parent, *La Doctrine de la création dans l'école de Chartres, étude et textes* (Ottawa and Paris, 1938), pp. 17 ff.

2. Early studies of the philosophy and cosmogony of the work were generated by a controversy concerning its pagan/Christian, pluralistic/monistic bias. For the dualistic (but primarily pagan) view, consult Étienne Gilson, "La Cosmogonie de Bernardus Silvestris," *Archives d'Histoire Doctrinale et Littéraire du Moyen Âge*, 3 (1928), 5–24. For the monistic–Christian view (the pantheistic paganism of the work explained as a device of the fabulous narrative), see Theodore Silverstein, "The Fabulous Cosmogony of Bernardus Silvestris," *Modern Philology*, 46 (1948–49), 92–116. Recent studies have extended Silverstein's perceptions: see Winthrop Wetherbee, *Platonism and Poetry in the Twelfth Century* (Princeton, 1972), pp. 158–86; and Brian Stock, *Myth and Science in the Twelfth Century: A Study of Bernard Silvester* (Princeton, 1972).

3. "Mentem de caelo, corpus trahet ex elementis, / Ut terras habitet corpore, mente polum." *Bernardi Silvestris De Mundi Universitate Libri Duo sive Megacosmus et Microcosmus*, ed. Carl Sigmund Barach and Johann Wrobel (Innsbruck, 1876), p. 55 (2.10.15–16). Cf. *The Cosmographia of Bernardus Silvestris*, trans. Winthrop Wetherbee (New York and London, 1973). Subsequent references to all primary texts, after an initial bibliographical entry, will be indicated by book, chapter, and line number(s) within the text. All translations are my own unless otherwise noted.

4. *Commentum Bernardi Silvestris super Sex Libros Eneidos Virgilii*, ed. Wilhelm Riedel (Greifswald, 1924), p. 30. The relationship between Bernardus' concept of the natural descent in the commentary and in *De Mundi* has not been fully recognized, although Wetherbee, *Platonism and Poetry*, p. 177, describes Book Two as a type of *Aeneid*, in that Na-

tura's descent resembles Aeneas'; and Stock, p. 179, suggests that the descent of Natura and Urania constitutes a Macrobian "allegory of the descent of the soul from the One" (cf. pp. 163–64).

5. In a footnote Ernst Robert Curtius briefly discusses three Silvestran genii (Pantomorph, vegetation god of Granusion, tutelary spirit) without seeing any relationship among them, in European Literature and the Latin Middle Ages, trans. Willard R. Trask (New York, 1953), p. 118, n. 30. Wetherbee perceives Pantomorph to be a divine analogue of the twin genii of generation, in Platonism and Poetry, pp. 182–84; in the Introduction to his translation, Cosmographia, p. 44, he concludes that three of them—Pantomorph, the tutelary spirit, and the twin genii—represent the "guiding principles of natural virtue and procreation" for man.

6. Calcidius divides the universe into twelve parts: "Uolucris uero currus imperatoris dei aplanes intellegenda est, quia et prima est ordine et agilior ceteris omnibus motibus, sicut ostensum est, undecim uero partes exercitus dinumerat hactenus: primam aplanem, deinde septem, planetum, nonam aetheris sedem, quam incolunt aetherei daemones, decimam aeream, undecimam humectae substantiae, duodecimam terram, quae immobilis ex conuersione mundi manet." Calcidii Commentarius 178, in Timaeus: A Calcidio Translatus Commentarioque Instructus, ed. J. H. Waszink, Plato Latinus, Vol. 4 (London and Leiden, 1962), p. 207.

7. C. S. Lewis analyzes this Genius in Studies in Medieval and Renaissance Literature, collected by Walter Hooper (Cambridge, 1966), p. 170. See also The Allegory of Love (London, 1936), p. 362; cf. E. C. Knowlton, "The Allegorical Figure Genius," Classical Philology, 15 (1920), 381–82.

8. "The tutelary spirits of marriage" for Silverstein, p. 109, n. 118; "the masculine and feminine aspects of creativity latent in matter," or else the testicles, for Stock, pp. 218–19.

9. Stock, p. 176.

10. Stock, pp. 190, 203, 220; genius is also "that which has spiritual or heavenly quality" for Robert B. Woolsey, "Bernard Silvester and the Hermetic Asclepius," Traditio, 6 (1948), 343.

11. Curtius, p. 110, n. 15, and pp. 110–11, calls the immutable circle, composed of the fifth element, pantomorphos, the Aplanon ("not wandering," "fixed"); Macrobius uses the word to refer to the fixed sphere of stars and the fixed sphere of earth. See Macrobii Commentarii in Somnium Scipionis 1.11.6 and 8, in Macrobius, ed. James Willis, 2 vols. (Leipzig, 1963), II, 46. The Macrobian definition explains Bernardus' discussion of the two parts of the world, the superior and inferior aplanes, in Commentum, p. 30. The fixed sphere of stars ruled by Pantomorph is apparently the superior Aplanon from which souls descend into the underworld or inferior Aplanon, earth. On Bernardus' Aplanon, see also Stock, pp. 167–69.

12. Woolsey, pp. 341–43; see also the Latin Asclepius 3.19b, in Hermetica, ed. and trans. Walter Scott, 4 vols. (1924–36; rpt. London, 1968), I, 322, 324. The astrological implications of Bernardus' use of his source (ignored by Woolsey) are explored by Stock, pp. 167–79.

13. Woolsey, p. 342; Latin Asclepius 3.19b, in Scott, I, 322, 324. Ousiarch (Bernardus' oyarses) or usiarch, from ousia or usia (hyle, silva, matter or being), means "ruler of ousia" and represents a Stoic emanation of the one Deity. See Scott, III, 113–16; Lewis,

The Allegory of Love, p. 362, Friedrich von Bezold, *Das Fortleben der antiken Götter im mittelalterlichen Humanismus* (Bonn and Leipzig, 1922), pp. 78–79. Von Bezold specifically equates the usiarchs with the planetary gods.

14. Scott, III, 109, 119–20. See Latin *Asclepius* 3.19b, in Scott, I, 324. For more detail concerning the thirty-six Decani, see Excerptum 6 of *Stobaei Hermetica* in Scott, I, 410-19, and the notes in III, 363–86.

15. Scott, III, 119–20.

16. Lynn Thorndike, *A History of Magic and Experimental Science,* Vol. II (New York, 1929), devotes an entire chapter to "Bernard Silvester; Astrology and Geomancy," including a review of the two lesser known works. See also Wetherbee, *Platonism and Poetry,* pp. 153–58, on the *Mathematicus.*

17. Discussions of the astrological sources and aspects of *De Mundi* appear in Thorndike, Vol. II, Chapter 39; Theodore Otto Wedel, *The Mediaeval Attitude toward Astrology* (New Haven, London, and Oxford, 1920), esp. pp. 33–35; Charles Homer Haskins, *Studies in the History of Mediaeval Science* (New York, 1924), Chap. Two ("Adelard of Bath"), and Chap. Five ("Some Twelfth-Century Writers on Astronomy"). A brief examination of Hermetic and astrological influences and analogues is provided by Theodore Silverstein, ed. *Liber Hermetis Mercurii Triplicis De VI Rerum Principiis,* in *Archives d'Histoire Doctrinale et Littéraire du Moyen Âge,* 30 (1955), 217–45; and "The Fabulous Cosmogony," pp. 95–98. The fullest treatment is Stock's, passim.

18. Here the astrological and Neo-Platonic concepts are linked. Macrobius in *Commentarii* 1.12.1–2 explains the stages by which a soul descends into the underworld, beginning with its entry from the Milky Way into the portal of Cancer (belonging to men); it returns to the heavens through the portal of Capricorn (belonging to the gods). They are also called "portals of the sun" because the solstices force the sun to remain within the zodiacal bounds of its path. Cf. *Die Quaestiones Naturales des Adelardus von Bath,* ed. Martin Müller, in *Beiträge zur Geschichte der Philosophie und Theologie des Mittelalters: Texte und Untersüchungen,* Vol. 31, pt. 2 (Münster, 1934), p. 63.

19. Bernardus must have seen Horace's full definition of "the companion from birth who rules the star" (*Epistle* 2.2.187–89). Guillaume de Conche's transcription, in Édouard Jeauneau, "L'Usage de la notion d' *integumentum* à travers les gloses de Guillaume de Conches," *Archives d'Histoire Doctrinale et Littéraire du Moyen Âge,* 32 (1957), 46, defines the *genius* as "deus albus et ater mortalis in unumquodque caput"; Bernardus, *Commentum,* p. 54, cites a different line from the Horatian passage: *genius* is "naturae deus humanae mortalis in unum- / quodque caput."

20. Mythographus Tertius, *De Diis Gentium et Illorum Allegoriis* 11.13, in *Scriptores Rerum Mythicarum Latini Tres Romae Nuper Reperti,* ed. Georg Heinrich Bode (Celle, 1834), p. 236. The line in question is from Juvenal's *Satura* 6.562.

21. John says, "Quorum genelliaci [*genethliaci*], qui geneses id est natalitias horas attendunt, imitantur errorem; unde satiricus: 'Nota mathematicis genesis tua.' Idem uero horoscopi nominantur; unde rursus: 'Geminos, horoscope, uaro producis genio.' " In *Ioannis Saresberiensis Episcopi Carnotensis Policratici sive De Nugis Curialum et Vestigiis Philosophorum Libri VIII,* ed. Clemens C. J. Webb (London, 1909), I, 53 (1.12). The second quoted line is from Persius, *Satura* 6.18–19; the first, from Juvenal, *Satura* 14.248.

22. *Cebetis Tabula*, p. 2 (4), in *Theophrasti Characteres; Marci Antonini Commentarii; Epicteti Dissertationes ab Arriano Literis Mandatae, Fragmenta et Enchiridion cum Commentario Simplicii Cebetis Tabula; Maximi Tyrii Dissertationes (Graece et Latine)*, ed. Frederick Dübner (Paris, 1842). This Greek work was translated by Odaxius in the tenth century; modern editions of the Greek original, with introductions and commentary, include C. S. Jerram, ed. *Cebetis Tabula* (Oxford, 1878), and Richard Parsons, ed. *Cebes' Tablet* (Boston, 1887). There is some dispute concerning the author of the work; most probably he lived in the first century A.D. He is mentioned by Calcidius in his commentary on the *Timaeus* as a Platonic philosopher; however, Robert Joly, "Le Tableau de Cébès et la philosophie religieuse," *Collection Latomus*, 61 (1963), 1–86, views him as a Neo-Pythagorean using Stoic and Cynic ideas to veil the revelation involved.

23. Claudius Claudianus, "De Consulatu Stilichonis" 2.424–76, in *Claudian*, ed. and trans. Maurice Platnauer, 2 vols. (New York and London, 1922), II, 32, 34, 36. Cf. Macrobius' *Saturnalia* 1.19.16–18, I, 111: the caduceus with its entwined serpents, male and female, joined in a knot at one end, and in a kiss at the other, represents human generation, over which preside four gods—the sun (*daemon*), moon (*tyche*), Eros, and Necessitas. Claudian's *senex*, like Bernardus' Pantomorph, however, seems to preside over the whole process of human generation (or of time and necessity). Boccaccio later glosses this *integumentum* of Claudian; the region represents Eternity; the cave, finite time; the snake, one year. The *senex* is God. Souls must be drawn from Eternity into finite time (*natura naturata*); the process by which they are drawn is *natura naturans*. See *Genealogie Deorum Gentilium*, ed. Vincenzo Romano, *Opere*, Vols. 10–11, 2 vols. (Bari, 1951), I, 16–17.

24. *Architrenius* 8, in *The Anglo-Latin Satirical Poets and Epigrammatists of the Twelfth Century*, ed. Thomas Wright, 2 vols. (London, 1872), I, 369 f.

25. See Curtius' short section on the Book of Nature *topos*, pp. 319–26, esp. p. 320 on Bernardus.

26. According to Paulus, who rephrases the Augustinian definition of Genius: "*Genium* appellabant deum, qui vim optineret rerum omnium gerendarum [genendarum]. Aufustius: 'Genius,' inquit, 'est deorum filius, et parens hominum, ex quo homines gignuntur. Et propterea Genius meus nominatur, quia me genuit.' " *Pauli Excerpta ex Libris Pompeii Festi de Significatione Verborum*, 94–95, in *Sexti Pompeii Festi De Verborum Significatu Quae Supersunt cum Pauli Epitome*, ed. Wallace M. Lindsay (1913; rpt. Hildesheim, 1965), p. 84.

27. See Gilson, pp. 12 ff.; recent commentators have argued against such a complete identification of the fabulous Noys with Logos, e.g., Wetherbee, "Introduction," *The Cosmographia*, p. 39, and George D. Economou, *The Goddess Natura in Medieval Literature* (Cambridge, Mass., 1972), p. 63. The two are parallel figures, as Endelechia, the World Soul, is parallel to, but not the same as, the Holy Spirit (Wetherbee, "Introduction," p. 40; Economou, pp. 62, 65).

28. See 1.4.125 for Natura as *artifex*. Such artistry is, however, also attributed to God, Noys, and Physis at various points in the text. According to Stock, p. 78, n. 27, Bernardus favors the metaphor of the "fashioning" of either world or man for or by an *artifex*.

29. For Martianus' conception of Genius as the mind or *nous* of Jove (derived from the Stoic notion of the World Soul), see *De Nuptiis Philologiae et Mercurii Libri VIIII* in *Martianus Capella*, ed. Adolf Dick (Stuttgart, 1969), p. 39 (1.92). The distinction between the

natural Genius and the supernatural Nous, which Bernardus amplifies, was made in a gloss on *De Nuptiis:* see *Iohannis Scotti Annotationes in Marcianum,* ed. Cora E. Lutz (Cambridge, Mass., 1939), p. 52 (39.14–15).

30. *De Nuptiis* 2.125.

31. The seven spheres, each of which is governed by an usiarch, are ruled as a group by Heimarmene in the Latin *Asclepius* 3.19b, in Scott, I, 324. See also III, 110, 121–22.

32. "Huius spectaculi praefigurabat imagine, quam pestilens, quam contrarius immineret humanae soboli mox futurae veneno sui sideris et pernecabili qualitate," 2.5.64–66. Erwin Panofsky, *Studies in Iconology* (New York, 1939), pp. 73 ff., admits that planetary identification transformed the mythological Saturn into a malefic power (Chap. Three, pp. 69–94, presents an excellent overview of Saturn's history). Bernardus' portrait of Saturn (and also of Jupiter) is viewed as topical allegory by Stock, pp. 180–84 (Saturn, Bernard of Clairvaux; Jupiter, Pope Eugenius III).

33. "Saturnumque gravem nostro Iove frangimus una," *Satura* 5.50, in *Juvenal and Persius,* ed. and trans. G. G. Ramsay, Loeb Classical Library (London and New York, 1918), p. 372. The passage in which the line appears, but with the line itself omitted, was cited by John of Salisbury in the *Policraticus,* I, 52–3 (1.12), in a discussion of *mathematici.*

34. *Iulii Firmici Materni Matheseos Libri VIII,* ed. W. Kroll and F. Skutsch (Stuttgart, 1968), I, 64–65 (2.19.12–13). See also Batman's translation of the thirteenth-century Bartholomaeus Anglicus: *Batman uppon Bartholome his book De Proprietatibus Rerum* (London, 1582), p. 171a (11.3.20). Maternus, he says, seeks out the *genius* by the planets, but "Other seeke for the good *Genius,* from the 11. house, which therefore they call *Bonus Demon,* & require the naughtie *Genius* from the 6. house, which they call *Malus Demon.*" Here the sixth house, not the twelfth, is the *malus daemon* (i.e., saturnine). Cf. Scott, II, 280, n. 3: the early *agathos daemon* (bonus genius) of one of the twelve divisions of the zodiac, whose planet was called *agathos daemoniarch,* was diametrically opposite to the *agathē̄ tyche* (*bona fortuna*).

35. *Commentarii* 1.19.19–20. Cf. *De Mundi* 2.1.45–49; 2.5.101–14; and Geoffrey Chaucer, *A Treatise on the Astrolabe* 2.4, in *The Works of Geoffrey Chaucer,* ed. F. N. Robinson, 2nd ed. (Boston, 1957), p. 551.

36. *Commentarii* 1.12.14. See also Stock, pp. 179–80, who believes that the *ratiocinatio* and *intelligentia* from Saturn represent the theoretical sciences, and the *vis agendi* from Jupiter, the practical sciences.

37. Saturn's hatred of fertility, explicable perhaps given his castration, implies *prudentia* and *sapientia:* see Mythographus Tertius, *De Diis Gentium* 1.4–6, in Bode, pp. 153–55; and Joannes Ridevallus, *Fulgentius Metaforalis,* ed. Hans Liebeschütz (Leipzig and Berlin, 1926), pp. 74 ff.

38. *Saturnalia* 1.19.17. For the sun as regulator of planets and astrological signs, and the *daemon* as transmitter of this information, see 1.23.5–7. For the influence of sun and moon on the descent of the soul, see *Commentarii* 1.19.23; 1.12.14. Firmicus Maternus, *Matheseos* 4.18.1, reveals how to determine one's *daemon* (ascendant sign of the zodiac): count from sun to moon if born during the day, from moon to sun if born at night. See also the sixth excerpt of *Stobaei Hermetica* in Scott, I, 414 ff., for a discussion of the good and evil *daemones* influencing the planets through the rule of the thirty-six Decani.

39. Wetherbee, trans. *The Cosmographia,* p. 106, n. 45.

40. Cf. *Calcidii Commentarius* 132; *Martiani Capellae De Nuptiis* 2.153.

41. "Cum igitur homo condictante quidem providentia novum figmentum, nova fuerit creatura, de clementissimo et secundario spirituum ordine deligendus est genius in eius custodiam deputatus. Cuius tam ingenita, tam refixa benignitas, ut ex odio malitiae displicentis pollutae fugiat conversantem," 2.7.67–72.

42. "Ex istorum quoque numero secundus est genius, qui de nascendi principiis homini copulatus vitanda illi discrimina vel mentis praesagio vel soporis imagine vel prodigioso rerum spectaculo configurat," 2.7.81–85. Cf. *De Nuptiis* 2.151–52.

43. Cf. *De Mundi* 2.7.100–5; *Calcidii Commentarius* 135; and *L. Caeli Firmiani Lactanti Divinae Institutiones,* ed. Samuel Brandt, in *Opera Omnia,* ed. Samuel Brandt and Georg Laubmann (Prague and Leipzig, 1890), pp. 162–65 (2.14). See also this work, Chap. Two, pp. 38–40.

44. Cf. *De Mundi* 2.7.110–15 and *De Nuptiis* 2.167, although Martianus includes additional spirits in this general aerial region— *semones, semidei, heroes, fauni, fones,* and *satyri,* among others.

45. In the *Commentum Bernardi Silvestris,* p. 5, Aeolus signifies the birth of a child; his name, from *eon olus,* "destruction of eternity," suggests his function, in that, at birth, "eternity" or life of the soul ends. This "death" occurs when the soul descends from Paradise into the lustful (and inferior) body—the underworld. In addition, Aeolus is associated with winds and storms because birth, under the effects of various constellations (or stars in their ascendency), releases the storms of vice.

46. *Calcidii Commentarius* 129: "Summum enim esse locum ait ignis sereni, huic proximum aethereum, cuius corpus esse ignem aeque, sed aliquanto crassiorem quam est altior ille caelestis, dehinc aeris, post humectae substantiae, quam Graeci hygran usian appellant, quae humecta substantia aer est crassior, ut sit aer iste quem homines spirant, imus uero atque ultimus locus terrae." C. S. Lewis explains that Bernardus knew no Greek and therefore read the words "hygran usian" as one—"Granusion." See *The Discarded Image* (Cambridge, 1964), pp. 59–60; also Stock, pp. 192–93, for other probable sources and analogues.

47. Wrobel's edition reads "genio," but Wetherbee's translation, based on other editions and manuscripts of the work, substitutes "gremio": "The earth, through that fecundity which it had received out of the womb of Nature, suddenly teemed with life," p. 111. Cf. Tullio Gregory, *Anima mundi: La filosofia di Guglielmo di Conches e la scuola di Chartres* (Florence, 1955), p. 187, n. 5. I prefer "genio," given its linear context and Bernardus' consistency in ascribing *genii* to every other region of the universe.

48. "Terrae vero et mari dominatur Iuppiter Plutonius; et hic nutritor est animantium mortalium et fructiferarum ⟨ar⟩borum omnium, ⟨cuius⟩ viribus fructus [arbusta et] terra⟨e⟩ vegetantur," *Asclepius* 3.19b, in Scott, I, 324 (Scott's trans.).

49. See Macrobius' *Commentarii* 1.14.13.

50. In the *Commentarii* 1.12.14, the soul is said to receive *phytikon,* or *natura plantandi et augendi corpora,* from the lunar sphere. The resemblance between the functions of the moon, Physis, and the Genius of Granusion is striking.

51. "Praedicti sibi fontis aquam, sibi floris amicat / Blanditias, genii virgo, studentis opus," from *Ars Versificatoria* 1.3.111, in Edmond Faral, *Les Arts poétiques du XIIe et du XIIIe siècle: Recherches et documents sur la technique littéraire du moyen âge* (Paris, 1924), p. 149. See Wetherbee on this passage and on Matthieu's works in general, in *Platonism and Poetry*, pp. 146–51. He translates the lines thus: "The virgin [Natura] makes the water of the fountain and the alluring beauty of the flowers, the work of a zealous genius, favor her" (p. 150, n. 48).

52. In 2.3, p. 152:

> "Hic Genius studet in melius, ver gramine pictum
> Eximio terrae gremio praesentat amictum.
> Pullulat herbula, nuntiat aurula veris honorem;
> Flosculus emicat et rosa praedicat orta teporem.
> Fons vitreus, fons nectareus nova gramina florum
> Vivificat, fovet, amplificat spiramen odorum.
> Non spoliat, non depretiat rigor hostis iniquus
> Temperiem, retinet speciem flos veris amicus."

53. Bernardus' strange explanation of physiological changes during intercourse may shed light on a similar passage in Mythographus Tertius. After discussing the Genius as a natural god of generation and also the capacity for pleasure (*indulgere genio*), he mentions the *genius loci* and the Genius of the paterfamilias, both of which assume the form of a snake. This snake is supposedly created from the "marrow" of the human spine, perhaps the spinal cord: "Aut certe a Pythagorae assertione excogitatum est, qui primus de medulla, quae in spina hominis est, anguem creari deprehendit." Does, then, blood from the brain course down the spinal cord to become sperm? Is this "descent" controlled by the *genius*? See *De Diis Gentium* 6.19, in Bode, p. 185.

54. "Eundem esse genium et larem multi veteres memoriae prodiderunt, in quis etiam Granius Flaccus in libro quem ad Caesarem de indigitamentis scriptum reliquit. Hunc in nos maximam quin immo omnem habere potestatem creditum est. Nonnulli binos genios in his duntaxat domibus quae essent maritae collendos putaverunt." In *Censorini De Die Natali Liber* 3.2–3, ed. Otto Jahn (Berlin, 1845), p. 7. (Boccaccio in *Genealogie Deorum* 12.65 cites the passage verbatim in a chapter entitled "De Laribus Mercurii filiis.") The two *genii* (of Censorinus or of Bernardus) may have come from Apuleius, who mentions a Genius and a Genia (perhaps a scribal error for *genua*, which occurs in other manuscripts) in *De Deo Socratis* 15.152, *Opera Omnia*, ed. G. F. Hildebrand, 2 vols. (1842; rpt. Hildesheim, 1968), II, 145.

55. The line appears after the discussion of the two *genii:* "Euclides autem Socraticus duplicem omnibus omnino nobis genium dicit adpositum, quam rem apud Lucilium in libro satirarum XVI licet cognoscere," 3.3.

56. Excerptum 22, in Scott, I, 454–55.

57. *De Die Natali* discusses the following topics sequentially: *genius,* born with man; theories of generation; nature and source of semen; formation of the infant during pregnancy; lengths of gestation and the number seven; the zodiac and stars; technical nature of music; Pythagorean systems and the embryonic development of man; finite and infinite time; the monthly divisions of the calendar year. See also *Macrobii Commentarii* 1.6.62 on the

number seven: "hic denique est numerus qui hominem concipi, formari, edi, vivere, ali ac per omnes aetatum gradus tradi senectae atque omnino constare facit."

CHAPTER FIVE: THE MORAL UNIVERSE: GENIUS AND THE FOUR DESCENTS IN THE *DE PLANCTU NATURAE* OF ALANUS DE INSULIS

1. C. S. Lewis believes that he is a "patron ↙f generation" in the poem, and points to his pen and parchment to establish a link with the Pantomorph of *De Mundi Universitate,* in *Studies in Medieval and Renaissance Literature,* collected by Walter Hooper (Cambridge, 1966), pp. 170–71. Cf. Ernst Robert Curtius, *European Literature and the Latin Middle Ages,* trans. Willard R. Trask (New York, 1953), p. 118. Winthrop Wetherbee, *Platonism and Poetry in the Twelfth Century* (Princeton, 1972), p. 210, views Alanus' Genius in part as a personification embodying both Pantomorph and the sexual *genii* of *De Mundi.*

2. E. C. Knowlton defines Genius as the "experienced morality" of Natura, her "firmness of disposition; he is her seemingly older, harmonious, other self," in "The Allegorical Figure Genius," *Classical Philology,* 15 (1920), 382. See also "The Goddess Nature in Early Periods," *Journal of English and Germanic Philology,* 19 (1920), 245. Knowlton bases his argument upon the priestly role of Genius; this role also allows F. J. E. Raby to acknowledge him as Natura's representative on earth, in *A History of Secular Latin Poetry in the Middle Ages,* 2nd ed. (Oxford, 1957), II, 21.

3. Edwin Greenlaw, "Some Old Religious Cults in Spenser," *Studies in Philology,* 20 (1923), 226, 231–34. Greenlaw analyzes the whole of the *De Planctu Naturae* in terms of the ancient Magna Mater cult, basing his interpretation of Alanus' work—and of Spenser's—upon Grant Showerman, *The Great Mother of the Gods* (Madison, 1901), pp. 220 ff.

4. G. Raynaud de Lage, *Alain de Lille, poète du XIIe siècle* (Montreal and Paris, 1951), pp. 90–92. The conclusions of his excellent chapter on Alanus' Genius are summarized in "*Natura* et *Genius,* chez Jean de Meung et chez Jean Lemaire de Belges," *Le Moyen Âge,* 58 (1952), 125–28. These two functions of Genius are also discussed by Wetherbee, p. 207. Hennig Brinkmann attributes the dual role of Genius to the influence of Martianus Capella: he is the "generalis omnium praesul" found beneath the *numina* between the sun and the moon, and a tutelary for each man from birth. See "Verhüllung ('integumentum') als literarische Darstellungsform im Mittelalter," in *Miscellanea Mediaevalia,* 8 (Berlin and New York, 1971), p. 333.

5. Raynaud de Lage, *Alain de Lille,* p. 92. See also Wetherbee, p. 198, who extends Raynaud de Lage's interpretation: Natura functions as a type of the Church, and Genius as her priest, who must excommunicate fallen men. Even sexual reproduction is endowed with "quasi-sacramental significance."

6. Richard Hamilton Green, "Alan of Lille's *De Planctu Naturae*," *Speculum,* 31 (1956), 672. The relationship between man and nature or between the microcosm and the macrocosm was a favorite subject for the twelfth-century writer. Bernardus Silvestris' *De Mundi Universitate,* as we have seen, was divided into two books, *Megacosmus* and *Microcosmus;* other works also attended to the subject, e.g., Gilbert de la Porrée's *Liber de Sex Principiis,* William of St. Thierry's *De Natura Corporis et Animae,* and Godfrey of St. Victor's

Microcosmus. M.-D. Chenu states that the theme of "man as microcosm" was widely disseminated in the first decades of the twelfth century, in *Nature, Man, and Society in the Twelfth Century,* sel., ed., trans. Jerome Taylor and Lester K. Little (Chicago and London, 1968), pp. 28–29. He also says, echoing Green's statement, that "Man, then, who exists within Nature, is himself a nature . . . . The moral life of men is a particular instance of life as found in the universe; the universe of human liberty presupposes the universe of Nature, and it fulfills the promise of that universe of Nature," pp. 26–27.

7. C. S. Lewis, *The Allegory of Love* (London, 1936), p. 362.

8. *Alani de Insulis Liber de Planctu Naturae* in *Patrologiae Cursus Completus: Series Latina,* ed. J. P. Migne, 210 (Paris, 1855), 439C. I have also consulted the edition by Thomas Wright, in *The Anglo-Latin Satirical Poets and Epigrammatists of the Twelfth Century,* 2 vols. (London, 1872), Vol. II, and the translation of *The Complaint of Nature* by Douglas M. Moffat (New York, 1908). Subsequent references to this work will be indicated in parentheses by editors' initials and column or page number(s). All translations are my own, unless otherwise explicitly acknowledged. The best studies of the work are those of Raynaud de Lage, *Alain de Lille,* which investigates the philosophical and poetic aspects of the work; Green, pp. 649–74, which treats it as fabulous narrative; and Wetherbee, pp. 188–210, which examines the roles of Natura and grace in terms of poetic theory. For the most extensive treatment of Alanus' philosophy and its historical place, see Matthias Baumgartner, *Die Philosophie des Alanus de Insulis, im Zusammenhange mit den Anschauungen des XII Jahrhunderts Dargestellt,* in *Beiträge zur Geschichte der Philosophie des Mittelalters: Texte und Untersuchungen,* Vol. 2, pt. 4 (Münster, 1896).

9. "Restringitur etiam circa substantialem differentiam et specificam quae adveniens generi facit speciem, ut hoc universale rationabile, unde Boetius: *Natura est reformans specificam differentiam.*" *Venerabilis Alani Liber in Distinctionibus Dictionum Theologicalium, PL,* 210, col. 871. Subsequent references to the *Distinctiones* will be noted in parentheses by abbreviated title (*"Dist."*) and column number. This cataloguing and differentiation of the species is very similar to the function of Natura (as seen in the Tabula Fati) of *Bernardi Silvestris De Mundi Universitate Libri Duo sive Megacosmus et Microcosmus,* ed. Carl Sigmund Barach and Johann Wrobel (Innsbruck, 1876), pp. 57–58 (2.11). See also Baumgartner, pp. 76–84. He says, "Die Natur hat alle Dinge erzeugt, sie bringt deren Formen oder Species hervor," p. 82. The differences of the abundant species constitute the hierarchy of the plenitude of nature. See Arthur O. Lovejoy, *The Great Chain of Being* (Cambridge, 1936). The universal reason providing special differences is the moral aspect of Nature as distinguished from the cosmological: see Raynaud de Lage, *Alain de Lille,* Chapter Two, "Nature—le contexte philosophique"; Chapter Three, "Nature—son aspect cosmologique"; and Chapter Four, "Nature—son aspect moral." Cf. D. S. Brewer on Alanus' Natura in his edition of Chaucer's *Parlement of Foulys* (London and Edinburgh, 1960), pp. 26-30; and George D. Economou, *The Goddess Natura in Medieval Literature* (Cambridge, Mass., 1972), esp. pp. 72–96 on Natura in the *De Planctu,* but also for her poetic and philosophical context in the Middle Ages.

10. *De Planctu,* M—453D-54A, W—469-70: "Imperantis igitur imperio ego obtemperans, operando quasi varia rerum sigillans cognata ad exemplaris rei imaginem exempli exemplans effigiem, ex conformibus conformando conformia, singularum rerum reddidi vultus sigillatos."

11. See M.-Th. d'Alverny, "Le Cosmos symbolique du XIIe siècle," *Archives d'Histoire Doctrinale et Littéraire du Moyen Âge*, 28 (1953), 35 ff., on "l'univers visible et l'univers archetype."

12. For Natura as the *anima mundi*, see Tullio Gregory, *Anima mundi: La filosofia di Guglielmo di Conches e la scuola di Chartres* (Florence, 1955), p. 188, but also Chap. Four, "L'idea di natura"; M.-D. Chenu, "Découverte de la nature et philosophie de l'homme à l'école de Chartres au XIIe siècle," *Cahiers d'Histoire Mondiale*, 2 (1954), 321 ff. Also see Chenu, *Nature, Man, and Society*, Chap. One, and pp. 20–21. He notes the medieval equation of the world soul with the idea of nature on p. 21, n. 43, and says that the theory of the world soul was "adduced to subserve the lofty conception of Nature, for the universe too has its animating principle, its 'entelechy,' " pp. 20–21.

13. *Pauli Excerpta ex Libris Pompeii Festi de Significatione Verborum* 94, in *Sexti Pompeii Festi De Verborum Significatu Quae Supersunt cum Pauli Epitome*, ed. Wallace M. Lindsay (1913; rpt. Hildesheim, 1965), p. 84.

14. Lewis, *The Allegory of Love*, pp. 361–62; *Studies in Medieval and Renaissance Literature*, pp. 170–71. E. C. Knowlton had discovered the same relationship in "The Allegorical Figure Genius," pp. 380–81.

15. "Quod ⟨superius est⟩ graeco nomine paradisus dicitur latine vero ortus, quia ab eo res oriuntur." *Commentum Bernardi Silvestris super Sex Libros Eneidos Virgilii*, ed. Wilhelm Riedel (Greifswald, 1924), p. 29. Subsequent references will be noted by page number(s) within the text.

16. "Hierarchia Alani," in *Alain de Lille: Textes inédits*, ed. Marie-Thérèse d'Alverny (Paris, 1965), p. 228. For very brief discussions of Alanus' substantifying *genii*, see Wetherbee, pp. 207–8, and Brinkmann, p. 333.

17. *De Planctu*, M—479C, W—517; however, Migne's edition omits purple. Raynaud de Lage relates the four colors of his vestments to the colors of the Tabernacle described in Exodus 26:1 and the colors of the priest's garb in Exodus 28:5–6 on p. 92.

18. "Sermo de Sphaera Intelligibili," in *Textes inédits*, ed. d'Alverny, pp. 297–8. Subsequent references to the sermon will be indicated by page number(s) within the text. Mlle. d'Alverny includes an excellent commentary upon the work on pp. 163–80. Wetherbee, p. 206, briefly discusses Genius' role in relation to the doctrine of secondary forms espoused by Alanus and Gilbert de la Porrée.

19. D'Alverny, ed., *Textes inédits*, pp. 169–70. She discusses the association of the figure of Natura with the three mirrors in the *Anticlaudianus*, explaining them as symbolic representations of the four spheres (pp. 168–9). Although she offers many analogues and sources for the concept of the four spheres, she does not mention the three gifts of Noys in Bernardus' *De Mundi*, which seem to me to highlight the transfusion of eternal Idea. Urania is given a mirror of Providence which reflects eternal forms, Natura, a table of Fate which lists the classes of species, and Physis, the brief *liber recordationis*, a textbook of natural causes and natural philosophy (her daughters are Theory and Practice) explaining the differences among animals within the sensible world.

20. She becomes the efficient cause of the universe in *Dist.* 871; see also Knowlton, "The Goddess Nature in Early Periods," pp. 224–53.

21. "In prima [sensible sphere] regnant ychones, id est, subiecta suarum formarum, pur-puramentis ornata, que dicuntur ychones, id est, ymagines, quia ad similitud⟨inem⟩ eter-norum exemplarium que ab eterno fuerunt in mente diuina, in veritatem essendi sunt pro-ducta," p. 300.

22. See Howard R. Patch, *The Goddess Fortuna in Mediaeval Literature* (1927; rpt. New York, 1967), pp. 45, 116. She is described as bald with a long lock of hair at the front. Wetherbee, p. 203, interprets Falsitas as the "failure of human art" and ascribes it to the corruption of man.

23. The *topos* of the *puer senex* developed from late pagan antiquity and represented the human ideal, the combination of physical virility and wise maturity which was frequently prefigured in religious saviors, and which is regarded as an archetype of the collective un-conscious by Curtius, pp. 98–101.

24. Mythographus Secundus 90: "Isis autem est Genius Aegypti, qui per sistri motum, quod gerit in dextra, Nili accessus recessusque significat; per fistulam [Servius: "situlam"], quam sinistra retinet, omnifluentiam lacrimarum [S: "lacunarum"]. Isis autem lingua Aegyptiorum est *terra,* quam Isin volunt esse." See *Scriptores Rerum Mythicarum Latini Tres Romae Nuper Reperti,* ed. Georg Heinrich Bode (Celle, 1834), p. 106; cf. *Servii Grammatici in Vergilii Aeneidos Commentarii* 8.696, in *In Vergilii Carmina Commentarii,* ed. Georg Thilo and Hermann Hagen, 3 vols. (1881–87; rpt. Hildesheim, 1961), II, 302.

25. *Apulei Liber de Deo Socratis* 15.153, in *De Philosophia Libri,* ed. Paul Thomas, *Opera Quae Supersunt,* Vol. 3 (Stuttgart, 1970), p. 24; *Martiani Capellae De Nuptiis Philologiae et Mercurii* 2.162–64, in *Martianus Capella,* ed. Adolf Dick (Stuttgart, 1965), p. 68.

26. Green indicates his preference for "Antigenius" instead of "Antigamus," noting that Wright's manuscripts read "Antigenius" (see Wright, pp. 480–81). See "Alan of Lille's *De Planctu Naturae,*" p. 671, n. 48. Curtius, p. 118, prefers "Antigamus" (Enemy of Marriage).

27. For a full discussion of the two Venuses see Green, pp. 660 ff. He defines the mon-strous Venus as vice in general and sexual aberration in particular; the heavenly Venus rep-resents her antithesis. But note that Green also declares, "In a sense he [Genius] too is that *Venus caelestis* in human nature which has been rejected," p. 672. Alanus' personifications cannot be rigidly categorized or differentiated; their functions and meanings frequently overlap.

28. She admits "Genium vero qui mihi in sacerdotali ancillatur officio, decens est suscitari, qui eos a naturalium rerum catalogo, a meae jurisdictionis confinio, meae judiciariae potes-tatis assistente praesentia, vestrae assensionis conveniente gratia, pastorali virga excommu-nicationis eliminet" (M—476A, W—510).

29. Simon de Tournai, "Sententiae," in *Textes inédits,* ed. d'Alverny, p. 307. Cf. "La Somme 'Quoniam Homines' d'Alain de Lille," ed. P. Glorieux, in *Archives d'Histoire Doctrinale et Littéraire du Moyen Âge,* 28 (1953), 282 (2.144). Apparently Simon copied the passage from Alanus.

30. "La Somme 'Quoniam Homines,' " pp. 281, 283–85 (2.143–45).

31. "*Theophania* dicitur Dominica apparitio, id est quam habent angeli et sancti de Deo in patria; unde et Joannes Scotus ait quod Deus in futuro videbitur per quasdam theophanias;

NOTES: THE MORAL UNIVERSE

quia, sicut sol videtur in aere mediante radio aeri commisto, sic divina natura per quamdam illuminationem qua mens hominis illuminabitur. Dicitur etiam illa Spiritus sancti Patris apparitio per vocem, per columbae speciem facta super Christum baptizandum," *Dist.* 971.

32. "Ait Johannes Scotus quod theophania, id est scientia angelorum de Deo sit ex consequentibus signis non ex substantificis geniis, id est ex substantialibus naturis. . . ." "La Somme 'Quoniam Homines,' " p. 138 (1.8). See also pp. 281–82; "Expositio Prosae de Angelis," in *Textes inédits,* p. 205; and "Hierarchia Alani," p. 228. On theophany see d'Alverny, "Le Cosmos symbolique du XII siècle," pp. 40–48.

33. "Hierarchia Alani," *Textes inédits,* p. 228.

34. Bernardus' Noys is said to be parallel to, but not identical with, the Verbum Dei, and Natura, to the Spiritus Sanctus, in Economou, pp. 63, 65. Wetherbee, p. 207, points to Genius as a "type of the divine wisdom, the Word, through whom man expresses the likeness of the godhead within himself"; also, he hints at the analogy between "deus nature" Genius and the Logos, implied by the relationship between "genius" and the "informing presence discerned by inspired, 'theophanic' vision," p. 208.

35. "Infernum vocaverunt philosophi hanc sublunarem regionem quia inferior pars mundi est et plena miserie et doloris." See Édouard Jeauneau, "L'Usage de la notion d'*integumentum* à travers les gloses de Guillaume de Conches," *Archives d'Histoire Doctrinale et Littéraire du Moyen Âge,* 32 (1957), 42.

36. Guillaume, in Jeauneau, p. 46, declares that Orpheus ". . . dicitur quasi Oreaphone, id est optima vox." In Bernardus' commentary, Calliope is described as "optima vox," Orpheus as "orea phone," "bona vox," p. 54. The relationship between the Muse Calliope and her musician-poet son, Orpheus, suggests there is a bond between the heavenly music of the spheres and earthly music, the gift of genius: first, Orpheus, despite his skill, cannot be a musician unless he understands the profound and eternal secrets of art (Mythographus Tertius, *De Diis Gentium* 8.20, in Bode, p. 212); second, the section on the Muses in Mythographus Tertius immediately precedes that on Orpheus; third, in the late classical period, the Muses were connected with the music of the spheres, and in the ninth century became explicitly linked with the art of music, not poetry; finally, they supposedly conferred immortality on their servants (gifted with genius?)—poets, musicians, scholars or thinkers (see Curtius, pp. 228–46). Early Christian poetry rejected the Muses, choosing to see Christ as a cosmic musician and Orpheus figure (Curtius, p. 235); see also John Block Friedman, *Orpheus in the Middle Ages* (Cambridge, Mass., 1970), Chap. Three ("Orpheus-Christus in the Art of Late Antiquity").

37. See *Commentum Bernardi,* the sixth book; Curtius, pp. 481–82; and Daniel Carl Meerson, "The Ground and Nature of Literary Theory in Bernard Silvester's Twelfth-Century Commentary on the *Aeneid,*" Diss. Chicago 1967, pp. 55 ff.

38. A portion of the poem appears in *Textes inédits,* pp. 37–38.

39. See the short excursus, "Grammatical and Rhetorical Technical Terms as Metaphors," in Curtius, pp. 414–16. Alanus, says Curtius, p. 414, is using such terms—metaplasm, anastrophe, tmesis—as metaphors to bolster his "philosophical criticism of contemporary culture."

40. ". . . Sed potius se grammaticis constructionibus destruens, dialecticis conversionibus invertens, rhetoricis coloribus decoloratis suam artem in figuram, figuramque in vitium transfert," M—459C–D, W—480.

41. See "Jest and Earnest in Medieval Literature," Curtius, pp. 417–35. The *iocus* was a rhetorical trick or device; Ausonius' *ioci* offered a mixture of jest and earnest as a stylistic ideal. Alanus' Jocus differs somewhat: he epitomizes *extreme* mannerism, but wholly associated with sterile mirth or laughter, not earnest—i.e., Genius' seriousness and later grief over man's fall.

42. "Dicitur etiam luxuria, unde in Evangelio: *Hoc genus daemonii non ejicitur nisi in oratione et jejunio*," *Dist*. 759.

43. Curtius, p. 313.

44. Orpheus "habet citharam, orationem rhetoricam, in qua diversi colores quasi diversi numeri resonant," *Commentum Bernardi*, p. 54.

45. "Scribit enim in quantum est philosophus humanae vitae naturam. Modus vero agendi talis est: sub integumento describit quid agat vel quid patiatur humanus spiritus in humano corpore temporaliter positus. Atque in hoc scribendo . . . utrumque narrationis ordinem observat, artificialem poeta, naturalem philosophus," *Commentum Bernardi*, p. 3.

CHAPTER SIX: THE LATER MEDIEVAL GENIUS: IMPLICATIONS AND CONCLUSIONS

1. *The Allegory of Love* (London, 1936), p. 362.

2. Rosemond Tuve says, "Irony is Jean's chief instrument to indicate (as he constantly does) what is fallacious or absurdly inadequate about positions taken by the *personae*, or exactly where he himself stands on a question . . . ." See *Allegorical Imagery* (Princeton, 1966), p. 327; also pp. 268–330, in "Imposed Allegory." For an example of her iconographical treatment of Genius (from the figures accompanying the text), see pp. 327–28. She admits that such figures greatly help the reader to understand Jean's intentions when a problem is not explained in the text. Charles Dahlberg thinks most critics wrong who imagine that Friend, Old Woman, and Genius "express the poets' opinions." He sees the *Roman* as a mirror of the Lover's quest for *pudendum;* we must understand the characters in terms of his "con-game." *The Romance of the Rose by Guillaume de Lorris and Jean de Meun,* trans. Dahlberg (Princeton, 1971), pp. 5, 9–10, 13, 19. For his treatment of Genius see p. 408 n.: he says, for example, that the rose motif in the head of Genius' crosier in one illustration indicates his allegiance to Venus—he is only a "pretender to priestly status."

3. John V. Fleming, *The Roman de la Rose: A Study in Allegory and Iconography* (Princeton, 1969), p. 197, see also pp. 192 ff., 209 ff.

4. See Gérard Paré, *Le Roman de la Rose et la scolastique courtoise* (Paris and Ottawa, 1941), Chap. Four; *Les Idées et les lettres au XIIIe siècle: Le Roman de la Rose* (Montreal, 1947), passim; Alan M. F. Gunn, *The Mirror of Love: A Reinterpretation of 'The Romance of the Rose'* (1950; rpt. Lubbock, Texas, 1952), passim.

5. See Gunn, pp. 244 f., 282–83, 396–97. Genius, as an instructor, helps youth to realize complete maturity—"in the language of Aristotle, . . . an 'entelechy'," p. 282. He also says, "The principle of plenitude with its corollaries, the principles of continuity and replenishment, results logically, therefore, in Jean de Meun's emphasis upon the process by which individuals mature and reach the point when—like the gold of the alchemist—they can bring forth others like themselves, and thus fulfill their duty to God and Nature.

"The theme of Jean de Meun's narrative completes, then, the development of the major theme of his poem as an exposition—the doctrine of replenishment," p. 282.

6. George D. Economou, *The Goddess Natura in Medieval Literature* (Cambridge, Mass., 1972), p. 123.

7. Ernest Langlois, ed. *Le Roman de la Rose par Guillaume de Lorris et Jean de Meun,* V (Paris, 1924), 99 n. See also Dahlberg, pp. 416–17 n.

8. See Jean de Meun, *Le Roman* 16272–76, in *Le Roman de la Rose,* ed. Langlois, 5 vols. (Paris, 1914–24), IV, 140. Subsequent references to the poem will be incorporated into the text. Translations consulted are those of Dahlberg and of Harry W. Robbins, *The Romance of the Rose by Guillaume de Lorris and Jean de Meun,* ed. Charles W. Dunn (New York, 1962). Translations are my own, unless otherwise acknowledged in the text.

9. Gunn, p. 129; cf. Paré, "Vision du monde extérieur," in *Le Roman,* pp. 52–86.

10. Tuve, pp. 269–70; Dahlberg, pp. 9–10, agrees.

11. See Gunn, passim. The mirror is a "symbol of the whole generative process" and a "symbol of love's birth in the mirror of the eye"; as a son is the "image" of his father, so God's creatures are his "images," p. 267. The carbuncle of the Trinity, he says, contains universal ideal forms, p. 268; he refers to the mirrors of the *Anticlaudianus,* and discusses the other mirrors of the *Roman* throughout his work.

12. This exhortation to fecundity has misled scholars into assuming reproduction is his *only* responsibility to man, Nature, and God; his advice—in their view—has no moral significance. Cf. Gunn, pp. 244–45, 253–55; Paré, *Le Roman,* p. 162; D. W. Robertson, Jr., *A Preface to Chaucer* (Princeton, 1962), pp. 199–202; Fleming, pp. 209, 219; Economou, pp. 122–23.

13. Gunn, pp. 253–67. He declares, p. 435, that man's primary responsibility, according to Nature and Genius, is to "glorify God by the perpetuation of his earthly image."

14. Ernst Robert Curtius, *European Literature and the Latin Middle Ages,* trans. Willard R. Trask (New York, 1953), pp. 313 f. The quill to Isidore is "symbol of the divine Word, the Logos, which is revealed in the duality of the Old and the New Testament." The plowshare was used as a metaphor for *stylus; arare* and *exarare* ("plow up") were used figuratively for writing. (In Jean de Meun's *Roman,* Genius cries, "Arez, Arez!" to Love's barons, meaning "Plow! Plow!" and referring primarily to the sexual act.)

15. Tuve declares that the tree is both "Christ and cross as is usual"; the three streams merging into one with the three-faceted gem "points to the Trinity," pp. 276–77. Cf. Dahlberg, pp. 419–20 n.; Paré, *Les Idées,* pp. 293–94.

16. It is the "Mind of God": see Gunn, p. 273. The paradisal garden is the source of Eternal Ideas (p. 259).

17. Langlois, V, 104 n.

18. Robertson, p. 95, states that the well is "that mirror in the mind where Cupid operates. It has been tainted by Cupid ever since the Fall, when cupidity gained ascendancy over the reason." The two crystals are "not the eyes of his beloved, as one romantic account of the poem would have it, but his own eyes. . . ." Cf. Paré, *Les Idées,* pp. 293–94. Gunn, p. 270, says the Mirror of Narcissus typifies the vision of man, which has gone astray: he sees only phantasms.

19. Dahlberg, pp. 417–18 n.; Langlois, V, 100 n.

20. Nature says,

> "Si dit l'en que ce font deables
> A leur cros e a leur chaables,
> A leur ongles, a leur havez,
> Mais teuz diz ne vaut deus navez. . . ."

(17905–8.)

21. Gunn, p. 269, explains the mirror-image, "generated or imitated by Art from Nature," as "an example of the way in which the generative processes of Nature are continued—even though with less success—by man in his capacity as artificer and as image-maker."

22.   "Qui mainte diverse figure
> Se font pareir en aus meïsmes
> Autrement que nous ne deïsmes
> Quant des miroers palions,
> Don si briement nous passions;
> E de tout ce leur semble lores
> Qu'il seit ainsinc pour veir defores."

(18350–56.)

23. Winthrop Wetherbee, *Platonism and Poetry in the Twelfth Century* (Princeton, 1972), p. 262.

24. Russell A. Peck, ed. *Confessio Amantis of John Gower* (New York and Chicago, 1968), p. xiii.

25. John Gower, *The English Works of John Gower*, ed. G. C. Macaulay, *Early English Text Society*, E. S. nos. 81–82, 2 vols. (1900; rpt. London, 1957), I, 39 (1.127–31). Subsequent references to book and line number(s) will be incorporated into the text.

26. George D. Economou, "The Character Genius in Alan de Lille, Jean de Meun, and John Gower," *Chaucer Review*, 4 (1970), 209, views Genius as having a dual role—Christián priest and priest of Venus. He is "the moral agent that bridges the worlds of true religion and the religion of love . . . ." Genius is also a priest in John Gower's *Vox Clamantis*, but a corrupt and lascivious one who "visits the ladies in their cloister under the guise of righteous authority, but when he comes to their bedchambers, he casts righteousness aside and wields his power over them"; see *Vox Clamantis*, trans. Eric W. Stockton (Seattle, 1962), p. 180. Gower also declares that neither Venus nor Genius instructs the cloisters to adhere to the laws concerning the flesh.

27. Donald G. Schueler, "Gower's Characterization of Genius in the *Confessio Amantis*," *Modern Language Quarterly*, 33 (1972), 253–54, points to the presence of Nature throughout the *Confessio*, and demonstrates the priest Genius' service to Venus as a representation of the *lex naturalis*. Therefore there is no real discrepancy between his role as priest and his role as clerk of Venus: he mediates "between man's natural self and the divine will," p. 245.

28. R. D. Laing, *The Divided Self* (1960; rpt. Middlesex, Eng., 1971), passim. Note his definition of "schizoid": "The term schizoid refers to an individual the totality of whose experience is split in two main ways: in the first place, there is a rent in his relation with his

world and, in the second, there is a disruption of his relation with himself," p. 17. Amans is alienated from Nature, the outside world, and from himself at the beginning of the poem. "The schizoid individual fears a real live dialectical relationship with real live people. He can relate himself only to depersonalized persons, *to phantoms of his own phantasies* (*imagos*), perhaps to things, perhaps to animals," p. 77 (my emphasis). We think of Amans at the beginning of the *Confessio,* and of the false garden of Deduit, Nature's discussion of dream phantoms and mirrors, and the Mirror of Narcissus in the *Roman* of Jean de Meun.

29. The two major appearances of Spenser's Genius occur in the *Faerie Queene,* 3.6 and 2.12. In the first instance, the tutelary Genius of the Garden of Adonis effects the natural descent (birth); in the second, the Genius in the Bower of Bliss is associated with the vicious and artificial descents. Brief but illuminating discussions of the *genii* of Spenser are provided by C. S. Lewis in *The Allegory of Love,* pp. 362–63; *Studies in Medieval and Renaissance Literature,* collected by Walter Hooper (Cambridge, 1966), pp. 171–74; and E. C. Knowlton, "The Genii of Spenser," *Studies in Philology,* 25 (1928), 439–56. Many Shakespearian plays allude to a *genius:* see Knowlton, p. 448 n.

30. For example, see Claire Rosenfield, "The Shadow Within: The Conscious and Unconscious Use of the Double," *Daedalus,* 92 (1963), 326–44; Sigmund Freud, "A Neurosis of Demoniacal Possession in the Seventeenth Century," *On Creativity and the Unconscious,* sel. Benjamin Nelson (New York, 1958), pp. 264–300; C. G. Jung, "Gnostic Symbols of the Self," in *Aion,* trans. R. F. C. Hull, *The Collected Works of C. G. Jung,* ed. Sir Herbert Read, Michael Fordham, and Gerhard Adler, Vol. 9, pt. 2 (New York, 1959), pp. 184–221; also *The Archetypes and the Collective Unconscious,* trans. R. F. C. Hull, *The Collected Works of C. G. Jung,* Vol. 9, pt. 1; Otto Rank, "The Double as Immortal Self," *Beyond Psychology* (New York, 1941), pp. 62–101; Stanley M. Coleman, "The Phantom Double. Its Psychological Significance," *British Journal of Medical Psychology,* 14 (1934), 254–73; and John Todd and Kenneth Dewhurst, "The Double: Its Psycho-Pathology and Psycho-Physiology," *Journal of Nervous and Mental Disease,* 122 (1955), 47–56.

Selected Bibliography

PRIMARY SOURCES

Adelardus of Bath. *De Eodem et Diverso*. Ed. H. Willner. *Beiträge zur Geschichte der Philosophie und Theologie des Mittelalters: Texte und Untersuchungen*, Vol. 4, pt. 1. Münster, 1903.

——. *Die Quaestiones Naturales des Adelardus von Bath*. Ed. Martin Müller. *Beiträge zur Geschichte der Philosophie und Theologie des Mittelalters: Texte und Untersuchungen*, Vol. 31, pt. 2. Münster, 1934.

Alanus de Insulis. *Alain de Lille: Textes inédits*. Ed. Marie-Thérèse d'Alverny. Études de Philosophie Médiévale, No. 52. Paris, 1965.

——. *The Anticlaudian of Alain de Lille: Prologue, Argument and Nine Books Translated, with an Introduction and Notes*. Trans. William Hafner Cornog. Philadelphia, 1935.

——. *The Complaint of Nature*. Trans. Douglas M. Moffat. Yale Studies in English, No. 36. New York, 1908.

——. *De Planctu Naturae*, in *The Anglo-Latin Satirical Poets and Epigrammatists of the Twelfth Century*. Ed. Thomas Wright. 2 vols. Rerum Britannicarum Medii Aevi Scriptores, No. 59. London, 1872.

——. *Alani de Insulis Liber de Planctu Naturae*, in *Patrologiae Cursus Completus: Series Latina*. Vol. 210. Ed. J. P. Migne. Paris, 1855.

——. *Venerabilis Alani Liber in Distinctionibus Dictionum Theologicalium*, in *Patrologiae Cursus Completus: Series Latina*. Vol. 210. Ed. J. P. Migne. Paris, 1855.

——. "La Somme 'Quoniam Homines' d'Alain de Lille," ed. P. Glorieux, *Archives d'Histoire Doctrinale et Littéraire du Moyen Âge*, 28 (1953), 113–364.

Ammianus Marcellinus. *Ammiani Marcellini Rerum Gestarum Libri Qui Supersunt*, in *Ammianus Marcellinus*. Ed. and trans. John C. Rolfe. 3 vols. Loeb Classical Library. London and Cambridge, Mass., 1935–39.

Anglo-Latin Satirical Poets and Epigrammatists of the Twelfth Century. See Alanus de Insulis.

Apuleius Madaurensis. *L. Apuleii Opera Omnia*. Ed. G. F. Hildebrand. Vol. 2. 1842; rpt. Hildesheim, 1968.

Apuleius Madaurensis. *De Philosophia Libri*. Ed. Paul Thomas. In *Opera Quae Supersunt*, Vol. 3. Bibliotheca Scriptorum Graecorum et Romanorum Teubneriana. Stuttgart, 1970.

Arnobius Afer. *Adversus Nationes Libri VII*. Ed. C. Marchesi. 2nd ed. Corpus Scriptorum Latinorum Paravianum. Turin, 1953.

——. *The Case Against the Pagans*. Trans. George E. McCracken. 2 vols. Ancient Christian Writers, No. 8. Westminster, Maryland, 1949.

Augustinus, Aurelius. *S. Aurelii Augustini De Civitate Dei contra Paganos Libri*. Ed. and trans. William M. Green. Vol. 2 of 7 vols. Loeb Classical Library. London and Cambridge, Mass., 1963.

Avianus, Flavius. *Aviani Fabulae*. Ed. Antonio Guaglianone. Turin, 1958.

Bartholomaeus, Anglicus. *Batman uppon Bartholome his book De Proprietatibus Rerum*. London, 1582.

Bernardus Silvestris. *Commentum Bernardi Silvestris super Sex Libros Eneidos Virgilii*. Ed. Wilhelm Riedel. Greifswald, 1924.

——. *The Cosmographia of Bernardus Silvestris*. Trans. Winthrop Wetherbee. New York and London, 1973.

——. *Bernardi Silvestris De Mundi Universitate Libri Duo sive Megacosmus et Microcosmus*. Ed. Carl Sigmund Barach and Johann Wrobel. Bibliotheca Philosophorum Mediae Aetatis, No. 1. Innsbruck, 1876.

Biblia sacra iuxta Vulgatam Clementinam. Ed. Alberto Colunga and Laurentio Turrado. 4th ed. Biblioteca de autores Cristianos. Madrid, 1965.

Boccaccio, Giovanni. *Genealogie Deorum Gentilium*. Ed. Vincenzo Romano. 2 vols. *Opere*, Vols. 10–11. Scrittori d'Italia, No. 200–1. Bari, 1951.

Boethius, Anicius Manlius Severinus. *Anicii Manlii Severini Boethii Philosophiae Consolatio*. Ed. Ludwig Bieler. In *Opera*, Part 1. Corpus Christianorum Series Latina, Vol. 94. Turnhout, 1957.

——. *The Consolation of Philosophy*. Trans. Richard H. Green. New York, Indianapolis, and Kansas City, 1962.

Calcidius. *Timaeus: A Calcidio Translatus Commentarioque Instructus*. Ed. J. H. Waszink. *Plato Latinus*, Vol. 4. Corpus Platonicum Medii Aevi. London and Leiden, 1962.

Catullus, Gaius Valerius. *Catullus, Tibullus, and Pervigilium Veneris*. Ed. and trans. F. W. Cornish, J. P. Postgate, and J. W. Mackail. Loeb Classical Library. 1912; rpt. London and New York, 1914.

Cebes. *Cebes' Tablet*. Ed. Richard Parsons. Boston, 1887.

——. *Cebetis Tabula*, in *Theophrasti Characteres; Marci Antonini Commentarii; Epicteti Dissertationes ab Arriano Literis Mandatae, Fragmenta et Enchiridion cum Commentario Simplicii Cebetis Tabula; Maximi Tyrii Dissertationes (Graece et Latine)*. Ed. Frederick Dübner. Paris, 1842.

Censorinus. *Celse, Vitruve, Censorin, Frontin*. Ed. and trans. into French by M. Nisard. Paris, 1842.

——. *De Die Natali Liber*. Ed. Otto Jahn. Berlin, 1845.

Charisius, Flavius Sosipater. *Flavii Sosipatri Charisii Artis Grammaticae Libri V*.

Ed. Charles Barwick. Bibliotheca Scriptorum Graecorum et Romanorum Teubneriana. Leipzig, 1925.

Chaucer, Geoffrey. *The Works of Geoffrey Chaucer*. Ed. F. N. Robinson. 2nd ed. Boston, 1957.

Cicero, Marcus Tullius. *De Senectute, De Amicitia, De Divinatione*. Ed. and trans. William Armistead Falconer. Loeb Classical Library. 1923; rpt. Cambridge, Mass. and London, 1946.

Claudianus, Claudius. *Claudian*. Ed. and trans. Maurice Platnauer. 2 vols. Loeb Classical Library. London and New York, 1922.

Codex Theodosianus. Codices Gregorianus, Hermogenianus, Theodosianus. Ed. Gustav Haenel. Corpus Iuris Romani Anteiustiniani, Fasc. 2–6. Leipzig and Bonn, 1837–42.

Dunchad (Martin of Laon). *Glossae in Martianum*. Ed. Cora E. Lutz. Philological Monographs, No. 12. Lancaster, Penn., 1944.

Firmicus Maternus, Julius. *Iulii Firmici Materni Matheseos Libri VIII*. Ed. W. Kroll and F. Skutsch. 2 vols. Bibliotheca Scriptorum Graecorum et Romanorum Teubneriana. Stuttgart, 1968.

Florus, Lucius Annaeus. *L. Annaei Flori Epitomae de Tito Livio Bellorum Omnium Annorum DCC Libri II*, in *Lucius Annaeus Florus: Epitome of Roman History; Cornelius Nepos*. Ed. and trans. Edward Seymour Forster. Loeb Classical Library. London and New York, 1929.

Fulgentius, Fabius Planciades. *Fabii Planciadis Fulgentii Mitologiae*, in *Opera*. Ed. Rudolph Helm. Leipzig, 1898.

——. *Fulgentius the Mythographer*. Trans. Leslie George Whitbread. Columbus, Ohio, 1971.

Gellius, Aulus. *A. Gellii Noctium Atticarum*. Ed. and trans. John C. Rolfe. Vol. 2 of 3 vols. Loeb Classical Library. London and Cambridge, Mass., 1927.

Geoffrey of Monmouth. *Historia Regum Britanniae: A Variant Version Edited from Manuscripts*. Ed. Jacob Hammer. Mediaeval Academy of America, Publication No. 57. Cambridge, Mass., 1951.

Gower, John. *Confessio Amantis*. Ed. Russell A. Peck. New York, Chicago, San Francisco, Atlanta, and Dallas, 1968.

——. *The English Works of John Gower*. Ed. G. C. Macaulay. 2 vols. *Early English Text Society*, E. S. 81–82. 1901; rpt. London, 1957.

——. *Vox Clamantis*. Trans. Eric W. Stockton. Seattle, 1962.

Guillaume de Conches. *Glosae super Platonem, texte critique avec introduction, notes et tables*. Ed. Édouard Jeauneau. Textes Philosophiques du Moyen Âge, Vol. 13. Paris, 1965.

Guillaume de Lorris and Jean de Meun. *Le Roman de la Rose par Guillaume de Lorris et Jean de Meun*. Ed. Ernest Langlois. 5 vols. Société des Anciens Textes Français, Vols. 117–21. Paris, 1914–24.

——. *The Romance of the Rose by Guillaume de Lorris and Jean de Meun*. Trans. Charles Dahlberg. Princeton, 1971.

——. *The Romance of the Rose by Guillaume de Lorris and Jean de Meun*.

Trans. Harry W. Robbins, Ed. Charles W. Dunn. New York, 1962.

Hermetica: The Ancient Greek and Latin Writings which contain Religious or Philosophical Teachings ascribed to Hermes Trismegistus. Ed. and trans. Walter Scott. 4 vols. 1924–36; rpt. London, 1968.

Horace Flaccus, Quintus. *Horace, The Odes and Epodes.* Ed. and trans. C. E. Bennett. Loeb Classical Library. 1914; rev. and rpt. Cambridge, Mass., and London, 1927.

——. *Satires, Epistles, and Ars Poetica.* Ed. and trans. H. Rushton Fairclough. Loeb Classical Library. London and New York, 1926.

Hugh of St. Victor. *The Didascalicon of Hugh of St. Victor: A Medieval Guide to the Arts.* Trans. Jerome Taylor. Records of Civilization Sources and Studies, No. 64. 1961; rpt. New York and London, 1968.

Isidorus, Bishop of Seville. *Isidori Hispalensis Episcopi Etymologiarum, sive Originum Libri XX.* Ed. W. M. Lindsay. 2 vols. Scriptorum Classicorum Bibliotheca Oxoniensis. Oxford, 1911.

Joannes Scotus. See John Scot.

John of Salisbury. *The Metalogicon of John of Salisbury: A Twelfth-Century Defense of the Verbal and Logical Arts of the Trivium.* Trans. Daniel D. McGarry. Berkeley and Los Angeles, 1962.

——. *Ioannis Saresberiensis Episcopi Carnotensis Policratici sive De Nugis Curialium et Vestigiis Philosophorum Libri VIII.* Ed. Clemens C. J. Webb. 2 vols. London, 1909.

John Scot. *Iohannis Scotti Annotationes in Marcianum.* Ed. Cora E. Lutz. Mediaeval Academy of America, Publication No. 34. Cambridge, Mass., 1939.

——. *Iohannis Scotti Eriugenae Periphyseon (De Divisione Naturae) Liber Primus.* Ed. I. P. Sheldon-Williams, w. collab. Ludwig Bieler. Scriptores Latini Hiberniae, Vol. 7. Dublin, 1968.

Juvenalis, Decimus Junius. *Juvenal and Persius.* Ed. and trans. George Gilbert Ramsay. Loeb Classical Library. London and New York, 1918.

Lactantius, Lucius Caecilius Firmianus. *Epitome Institutionum Divinarum.* Ed. and trans. E. H. Blakenay. London, 1950.

——. *L. Caeli Firmiani Lactanti Opera Omnia.* Ed. Samuel Brandt and Georg Laubmann. Corpus Scriptorum Ecclesiasticorum Latinorum, Vol. 19. Prague and Leipzig, 1890.

Laȝamon. *Brut.* Ed. G. L. Brook and R. F. Leslie. Vol. 1 (text). *Early English Text Society,* No. 250. London, New York, and Toronto, 1963.

Livius, Titus. *T. Livi Ab Urbe Condita XXI-XXII.* Ed. and trans. B. O. Foster. *Livy,* Vol. 5 of 13 vols. Loeb Classical Library. London and New York, 1929.

——. *T. Livi Ab Urbe Condita XXVI-XXVII.* Ed. and trans. Frank Gardner Moore. *Livy,* Vol. 7 of 13 vols. Loeb Classical Library. London and Cambridge, Mass., 1943.

Lucilius, Gaius. *The Twelve Tables,* in *Remains of Old Latin.* Ed. and trans. E. H. Warmington. Vol. 3. Loeb Classical Library. London and Cambridge, Mass., 1938.

Macrobius, Ambrosius Theodosius. *Commentary on the Dream of Scipio*. Trans. William Harris Stahl. 1952; rpt. New York and London, 1966.

——. *Macrobius*. Ed. James Willis. 2 vols. Bibliotheca Scriptorum Graecorum et Romanorum Teubneriana. Leipzig, 1963.

Martialis, Marcus Valerius. *Epigrams*. Ed. and trans. Walter C. A. Ker. 2 vols. Loeb Classical Library. London and New York, 1919–20.

Martianus Minneius Felix Capella. *De Nuptiis Philologiae et Mercurii Libri VIIII*. In *Martianus Capella*. Ed. Adolf Dick. Bibliotheca Scriptorum Graecorum et Romanorum Teubneriana. Stuttgart, 1969.

Minucius Felix, Marcus. See Tertullianus.

Mythographi Latini: C. Julius Hyginus, Fabularum Liber; Poeticon Astronomicon; Fabius Fulgentius, Mythologicon; Virgiliana Continentia; Placidus Lactantius, Narrationes Fabularum Quae in P. Ovidii Nasonis Libris XV Metamorphoseon Occurrunt; Albricus Philosophus, De Deorum Imaginibus. Amsterdam, 1681.

Nonius Marcellus. *Nonii Marcelli De Conpendiosa Doctrina*. Ed. Wallace M. Lindsay. 3 vols. Leipzig, 1903.

Ovidius Naso, Publius. *Fasti*. Ed. and trans. Sir James George Frazer. Loeb Classical Library. London and New York, 1931.

——. *Tristia; Ex Ponto*. Ed. and trans. Arthur Leslie Wheeler. Loeb Classical Library. London and Cambridge, Mass., 1924.

Paulus Diaconus. *Pauli Excerpta ex Libris Pompeii Festi de Significatione Verborum*, in *Sexti Pompeii Festi De Verborum Significatu Quae Supersunt cum Pauli Epitome*. Ed. Wallace M. Lindsay. Bibliotheca Scriptorum Graecorum et Romanorum Teubneriana. 1913; rpt. Hildesheim, 1965.

Persius Flaccus, Aulus. See Juvenalis.

Petrarcha, Francesco. *L'Africa*. Ed. Nicola Festa. *Edizione nazionale della opere di Francesco Petrarca*, Vol. 1. Florence, 1926.

Petronius Arbiter. *Satyricon*, in *Petronius; Seneca: Apocolocyntosis*. Ed. and trans. Michael Heseltine. Loeb Classical Library. 1913; rev. London and Cambridge, Mass., 1930.

Plato. *Apology*. Ed. and trans. Harold North Fowler. *Plato*, Vol. 1. Loeb Classical Library. London and New York, 1914.

——. *Symposium*, in *Great Dialogues of Plato*. Trans. Eric H. Warmington and Philip G. Rouse. New York, 1956.

——. *Timaeus*. Ed. and trans. R. G. Bury. *Plato*, Vol. 7. Loeb Classical Library. London and New York, 1929.

Plautus, Titus Maccius. *Plautus*. Ed. and trans. Paul Nixon. 5 vols. Loeb Classical Library. New York, London, and Cambridge, Mass., 1916–38.

Plinius Secundus, Gaius. *Natural History, Books I–II*. Ed. and trans. H. Rackham. *Pliny: Natural History*, Vol. 1 of 10 vols. Loeb Classical Library. Cambridge, Mass., and London, 1938.

Plutarchus. *De Genio Socratis*, in *Plutarchi Scripta Moralia*, Vol. 1. Ed. Frederick Dübner. Opera Graece et Latine, No. 3. Paris, 1856.

Prudentius Clemens, Aurelius. *Contra Orationem Symmachi,* in *Prudentius.* Ed. and trans. H. J. Thomson. Vol. 2 of 2 vols. Loeb Classical Library. London and Cambridge, Mass., 1953.

Rabanus Maurus. *B. Rabani Mauri De Universo,* in *Patrologiae Cursus Completus: Series Latina.* Vol. 111. Ed. J. P. Migne. Paris, 1852.

Remigius of Auxerre. *Remigii Autissiodorensis Commentum in Martianum Capellam Libri I–II.* Ed. Cora E. Lutz. Leiden, 1962.

———. *Remigii Autissiodorensis Commentum in Martianum Capellam Libri III–IX.* Ed. Cora E. Lutz. Leiden, 1965.

Salutati, Colucio. *Colucii Salutati De Laboribus Herculis.* Ed. B. L. Ullman. 2 vols. Zurich, 1951.

Scriptores Rerum Mythicarum Latini Tres Romae Nuper Reperti. Ed. Georg Heinrich Bode. 2 vols. Celle, 1834.

Seneca, Lucius Annaeus. *Ad Lucilium Epistulae Morales.* Ed. and trans. Richard M. Gummere. 3 vols. Loeb Classical Library. London and New York, 1917–25.

Servius, Marius Honoratus. *Servii Grammatici Qui Feruntur in Vergilii Carmina Commentarii.* Ed. Georg Thilo and Hermann Hagen. 3 vols. 1881–87; rpt. Hildesheim, 1961.

Spenser, Edmund. *The Poetical Works of Edmund Spenser.* Ed. J. C. Smith and E. De Selincourt. 1912; rpt. London, New York, and Toronto, 1965.

Suetonius Tranquillus, Gaius. *De Vita Caesarum,* in *Suetonius.* Ed. and trans. J. C. Rolfe. 2 vols. Loeb Classical Library. 1914; rev. Cambridge, Mass., and London, 1928.

Terentius Afer, Publius. *Terence.* Ed. and trans. John Sargeaunt. 2 vols. Loeb Classical Library. Cambridge, Mass., and London, 1912.

Tertullianus, Quintus Septimius Florens. *Apologeticus,* in *Tertullian: Apology, De Spectaculis; Minucius Felix.* Ed. and trans. T. R. Glover and Gerald H. Rendall. Loeb Classical Library. London and New York, 1931.

———. *Quinti Septimii Florentis Tertulliani De Anima.* Ed. J. H. Waszink. Amsterdam, 1947.

Tibullus, Albius. See Catullus.

Vergilius Maro, Publius. *Virgil.* Ed. and trans. H. Rushton Fairclough. 2 vols. Loeb Classical Library. 1916–18; rev. London and Cambridge, Mass., 1934–35.

SECONDARY SOURCES

Altheim, Franz. *Griechische Götter im alten Rom. Religionsgeschichtliche Versuche und Vorarbeiten,* Vol. 22, pt. 1. Giessen, 1930.

———. *A History of Roman Religion.* Trans. Harold Mattingly. London, 1938.

d'Alverny, Marie-Thérèse. "Le Cosmos symbolique du XIIᵉ siècle," *Archives d'Histoire Doctrinale et Littéraire du Moyen Âge,* 28 (1953), 31–81.

Arnold, E. Vernon. *Roman Stoicism: Being Lectures on the History of the Stoic Philosophy with Special Reference to its Development within the Roman Empire.* Cambridge, 1911.

Bailey, Cyril. *Phases in the Religion of Ancient Rome.* Sather Classical Lectures, Vol. 10. Berkeley, 1932.

Baumgartner, Matthias. *Die Philosophie des Alanus de Insulis, im Zusammenhange mit den Anschauungen des XII Jahrhunderts dargestellt. Beiträge zur Geschichte der Philosophie des Mittelalters: Texte und Untersuchungen,* Vol. 2, pt. 4. Münster, 1896.

Beddie, James Stuart. "The Ancient Classics in the Mediaeval Libraries," *Speculum,* 5 (1930), 3–20.

Bennett, J. A. W. *The Parlement of Foules: An Interpretation.* Oxford, 1957.

Bevan, Edwyn Robert. *Holy Images: An Inquiry into Idolatry and Image-Worship in Ancient Paganism and in Christianity.* London, 1940.

——. *Stoics and Sceptics.* Oxford, 1913.

Bezold, Friedrich von. *Das Fortleben der antiken Götter im mittelalterlichen Humanismus.* Bonn and Leipzig, 1922.

Birt, Th. "Genius," in *Ausführliches Lexikon der griechischen und römischen Mythologie.* Ed. W. H. Roscher. Vol. 1, pt. 2. Leipzig, 1886–90.

Brewer, D. S., ed. *The Parlement of Foulys of Geoffrey Chaucer.* London and Edinburgh, 1960.

Brinkmann, Hennig. "Verhüllung ('integumentum') als literarische Darstellungsform im Mittelalter," in *Miscellanea Mediaevalia,* 8. Berlin and New York, 1971.

Buck, Carl Darling. *A Dictionary of Selected Synonyms in the Principal Indo-European Languages: A Contribution to the History of Ideas.* Chicago, 1949.

Bush, Douglas. *Mythology and the Renaissance Tradition in English Poetry.* Minneapolis, 1932.

Carter, Jesse Benedict. "Ancestor Worship (Roman)," in *Encyclopaedia of Religion and Ethics.* Ed. James Hastings. Vol. 1. New York, 1913.

Chenu, Marie-Dominique. "Découverte de la nature et philosophie de l'homme à l'école de Chartres au XIIᵉ siècle," *Cahiers d'Histoire Mondiale,* 2 (1954), 313–25.

——. "L'Homme et la nature. Perspectives sur la renaissance du XIIᵉ siècle," *Archives d'Histoire Doctrinale et Littéraire du Moyen Âge,* 27 (1952), 39–66.

——. *Nature, Man, and Society in the Twelfth Century: Essays on New Theological Perspectives in the Latin West.* Sel., ed., trans. Jerome Taylor and Lester K. Little. Chicago and London, 1968.

Clerval, A. *Les Écoles de Chartres au moyen-âge (du Vᵉ au XVIᵉ siècle).* Paris, 1895.

Coleman, Stanley M. "The Phantom Double. Its Psychological Significance," *British Journal of Medical Psychology,* 14 (1934), 254–73.

Conger, George Perrigo. *Theories of Macrocosms and Microcosms in the History of Philosophy.* 1922; rpt. New York, 1967.

Cornford, Francis MacDonald. *Plato's Cosmology: The Timaeus of Plato*. London, 1937.

Curtius, Ernst Robert. *European Literature and the Latin Middles Ages*. Trans. Willard R. Trask. Bollingen Series 36. New York, 1953.

Desmonde, William H. *Magic, Myth, and Money: The Origin of Money in Religious Ritual*. New York, 1962.

Duff, J. Wight. *A Literary History of Rome: From the Origins to the Close of the Golden Age*. Ed. A. M. Duff. 3rd ed. 1953; rpt. London, 1960.

——. *A Literary History of Rome in the Silver Age: From Tiberius to Hadrian*. Ed. A. M. Duff. 2nd ed. New York, 1960.

Economou, George D. "The Character Genius in Alan de Lille, Jean de Meun, and John Gower," *Chaucer Review*, 4 (1970), 203–10.

——. *The Goddess Natura in Medieval Literature*. Cambridge, Mass., 1972.

Ellspermann, Gerard L. *The Attitude of the Early Christian Latin Writers toward Pagan Literature and Learning*. Catholic University of American Patrisitic Studies, No. 82. Washington, D.C., 1949.

Erhardt-Siebold, Erika von, and Rudolf von Erhardt. *The Astronomy of Johannes Scotus Erigena*. Baltimore, 1940.

Ernout, A., and A. Meillet. *Dictionnaire étymologique de la langue latine, histoire des mots*. 2 vols. 4th ed. Paris, 1959.

Faral, Edmond. *Les Arts poétiques du XIIe et du XIIIe siècle: Recherches et documents sur la technique littéraire du moyen âge*. Bibliothèque de l'École des Hautes Études: Sciences, Historiques et Philologiques, Fasc. 238. Paris, 1924.

——. "Le Manuscript 511 du 'Hunterian Museum' de Glasgow," *Studi medievali*, 9, N. S. (1936), 18–119.

Fisher, John H. *John Gower: Moral Philosopher and Friend of Chaucer*. New York, 1964.

Fleming, John V. *The Roman de la Rose: A Study in Allegory and Iconography*. Princeton, 1969.

Fowler, W. Warde. *The Religious Experience of the Roman People: From the Earliest Times to the Age of Augustus*. London, 1911.

——. *The Roman Festivals of the Period of the Republic: An Introduction to the Study of the Religion of the Romans*. London, 1899.

——. *Roman Ideas of Deity: In the Last Century before the Christian Era*. London, 1914.

——. "Roman Religion," *Encyclopaedia of Religion and Ethics*. Ed. James Hastings. Vol. 10. New York, 1919.

Franceschini, E. "Di un commento al VI dell'Eneide attributo a Nicola Trevet," *Studi e note di filologia latina medievale,* Pubblicazione della Università del Sacro Cuore, serie 4, 30 (1938), 129–40.

Freud, Sigmund. "A Neurosis of Demoniacal Possession in the Seventeenth Century," in *On Creativity and the Unconscious: Papers on the Psychology of Art, Literature, Love, and Religion*. Sel. Benjamin Nelson. New York, 1958.

Friedman, John Block. *Orpheus in the Middle Ages*. Cambridge, Mass., 1970.

Garin, Eugenio. *Medioevo e rinascimento: Studi e richerche.* Bibliotheca di cultura moderna, Fasc. 506. Bari, 1954.

Gilson, Étienne. "La Cosmogonie de Bernardus Silvestris," *Archives d'Histoire Doctrinale et Littéraire du Moyen Âge,* 3 (1928), 5–24.

Glover, T. R. *The Conflict of Religions in the Early Roman Empire.* London, 1909.

Green, Richard Hamilton. "Alan of Lille's *Anticlaudianus: Ascensus Mentis in Deum,*" *Annuale Medievale,* 8 (1967), 3–16.

——. "Alan of Lille's *De Planctu Naturae,*" *Speculum,* 31 (1956), 649–74.

——. "Classical Fable and English Poetry in the Fourteenth Century," *Critical Approaches to Medieval Literature: Selected Papers from the English Institute, 1958–59.* Ed. Dorothy Bethurum. New York, 1960.

Greenlaw, Edwin. "Some Old Religious Cults in Spenser," *Studies in Philology,* 20 (1923), 216–43.

Gregory, Tullio. *Anima mundi: La filosofia de Guglielmo di Conches e la scuola di Chartres.* Medioevo e rinascimento, No. 3. Florence, 1955.

Grellner, Sister Mary Alice. "John Gower's *Confessio Amantis:* A Critical Assessment of Themes and Structure." Diss. Wisconsin 1969.

Gunn, Alan M. F. *The Mirror of Love: A Reinterpretation of 'The Romance of the Rose'.* 1950; rpt. Lubbock, Texas, 1952.

Hadas, Moses. *A History of Latin Literature.* New York, 1952.

Halliday, William Reginald. *Lectures on the History of Roman Religion: From Numa to Augustus.* Liverpool and London, 1922.

Haskins, Charles Homer. "A List of Text-books from the Close of the Twelfth Century," *Harvard Studies in Classical Philology,* 20 (1909), 75–94.

——. *The Renaissance of the Twelfth Century.* 1927; rpt. Cleveland and New York, 1957.

——. *Studies in the History of Mediaeval Science.* New York, 1924.

Hauréau, B. *Histoire de la philosophie scolastique.* Pt. 1, vol. 1. Paris, 1872.

——. *Notices et extraits de quelques manuscrits latins de la Bibliothèque Nationale.* Vol. 1. Paris, 1890.

Henderson, Joseph L., and Maud Oakes. *The Wisdom of the Serpent: The Myths of Death, Rebirth, and Resurrection.* New York, 1963.

Jeauneau, Édouard. "L'Usage de la notion d'*integumentum* à travers les gloses de Guillaume de Conches," *Archives d'Histoire Doctrinale et Littéraire du Moyen Âge,* 32 (1957), 35–100.

Jevons, Frank Byron. *An Introduction to the History of Religion.* 5th ed. London, 1911.

——, ed. *Plutarch's Romane Questions.* Trans. 1683 by Philemon Holland. Bibliothèque de Carabas, Fasc. 7. London, 1892.

Joly, Robert. "Le Tableau de Cébès et la philosophie religieuse," *Collection Latomus,* 61 (1963), 1–86.

Jung, C. G. *Aion: Researches into the Phenomenology of the Self.* Trans. R. F. C. Hull. *The Collected Works of C. G. Jung.* Ed. Sir Herbert Read, Michael

Fordham, and Gerhard Adler. Vol. 9, pt. 2. Bollingen Series 20. New York, 1959.

——. *The Archetypes and the Collective Unconscious.* Trans. R. F. C. Hull. *The Collected Works of C. G. Jung.* Ed. Sir Herbert Read, Michael Fordham, and Gerhard Adler. Vol. 9, pt. 1. Bollingen Series 20. New York, 1959.

——. "On the Nature of the Psyche," in *The Structure and Dynamics of the Psyche.* Trans. R. F. C. Hull. *The Collected Works of C. G. Jung.* Ed. Sir Herbert Read, Michael Fordham, and Gerhard Adler. Vol. 8. Bollingen Series 20. New York, 1960.

——. *Psyche and Symbol: A Selection from the Writings of C. G. Jung.* Ed. Violet S. de Laszlo. Garden City, New York, 1958.

King, William. *An Historical Account of the Heathen Gods and Heroes: Necessary for the Understanding of the Ancient Poets.* Intro. Hugh Ross Williamson. Carbondale, Ill., 1965.

Klibansky, Raymond. *The Continuity of the Platonic Tradition during the Middles Ages: Outlines of a Corpus Platonicum Medii Aevi.* London, 1950.

Knowlton, E. C. "The Allegorical Figure Genius," *Classical Philology,* 15, (1920), 380–84.

——. "The Genii of Spenser," *Studies in Philology,* 25 (1928), 439–56.

——. "Genius as an Allegorical Figure," *Modern Language Notes,* 39 (1924), 89–95.

——. "The Goddess Nature in Early Periods," *Journal of English and Germanic Philology,* 19 (1920), 224–53.

——. "Nature in Earlier Italian," *Modern Language Notes,* 36 (1921), 329–34.

——. "Nature in Old French," *Modern Philology,* 20 (1923), 309–29.

——. "Notes on Early Allegory," *Journal of English and Germanic Philology,* 29 (1930), 159–81.

La Barre, Weston. *They Shall Take Up Serpents: Psychology of the Southern Snake-Handling Cult.* Minneapolis, 1962.

Laing, Gordon J. *Survivals of Roman Religion.* New York, 1931.

Laing, R. D. *The Divided Self: An Existential Study in Sanity and Madness.* 1960; rpt. Middlesex, England, and Baltimore, Maryland, 1971.

Langlois, Ernest. *Origines et sources du Roman de la Rose.* Bibliothèque des Écoles Françaises d'Athènes et de Rome, Fasc. 58. Paris, 1891.

Lattimore, Richmond. *Themes in Greek and Latin Epitaphs.* Urbana, 1962.

Leonhard, Zelma Bernice. "Classical Mythology in the *Confessio Amantis* of John Gower." Diss. Northwestern 1944.

Levi-Strauss, Claude. *Totemism.* Trans. Rodney Needham. Boston, 1963.

Lewis, C. S. *The Allegory of Love: A Study in Medieval Tradition.* London, 1936.

——. *The Discarded Image: An Introduction to Medieval and Renaissance Literature.* Cambridge, 1964.

——. *Studies in Medieval and Renaissance Literature.* Collected by Walter Hooper. Cambridge, 1966.

Liebeschütz, Hans, ed. *Fulgentius Metaforalis: Ein Beitrag zur Geschichte der antiken Mythologie im Mittelalter.* Studien der Bibliothek Warburg. Leipzig and Berlin, 1926.

Lotspeich, Henry Gibbon. *Classical Mythology in the Poetry of Edmund Spenser.* Princeton Studies in English, No. 9. 1932; rpt. Princeton, 1965.

Lovejoy, Arthur O. *The Great Chain of Being: The Study of the History of an Idea.* Cambridge, 1936.

Marchi, Attilio de. *Il culto privato di Roma antica.* 2 vols. Milan, 1896–1903.

Meerson, Daniel Carl. "The Ground and Nature of Literary Theory in Bernard Silvester's Twelfth-Century Commentary on the *Aeneid.*" Diss. Chicago 1967.

Muscatine, Charles. *Chaucer and the French Tradition: A Study in Style and Meaning.* Berkeley and Los Angeles, 1957.

Neilson, William Allan. *The Origins and Sources of the Court of Love.* Harvard Studies and Notes in Philology and Literature, No. 6. 1899; rpt. New York, 1967.

Nelson, William. *The Poetry of Edmund Spenser: A Study.* New York, 1963.

O'Donnell, J. Reginald. "The Sources and Meaning of Bernard Silvester's Commentary on the *Aeneid,*" *Mediaeval Studies,* 24 (1962), 233–49.

Onians, Richard Broxton. *The Origins of European Thought about the Body, the Mind, the Soul, the World, Time, and Fate: New Interpretations of Greek, Roman and Kindred Evidence, Also of Some Basic Jewish and Christian Beliefs.* 2nd ed. Cambridge, 1954.

Otto, Walter F. *Die Manen; oder, Von den Urformen des Totenglaubens: Eine Untersuchung zur Religion des Grieschen, Römer und Semiten und zum Volksglauben überhaupt.* Berlin, 1923.

——. "Genius," in *Paulys Real-Encyclopädie der classischen Altertumswissenschaft.* Ed. Georg Wissowa and Wilhelm Kroll. Vol. 7, pt. 1. Stuttgart, 1910.

——. "Iuno. Beiträge zum Verständnisse der ältesten und wichtigsten Thatsachen ihres Kultes," *Philologus,* 64 (N. S. 18), (1905), 160–223.

Panofsky, Erwin. *Studies in Iconology: Humanistic Themes in the Art of the Renaissance,* New York, 1939.

Paré, Gérard. *Les Idées et les lettres au XIIIe siècle: Le Roman de la Rose.* Montreal, 1947.

——. *Le Roman de la Rose et la scolastique courtoise.* Publications de l'Institut d'Études Médiévales d'Ottawa, 10. Ottawa and Paris, 1941.

Parent, J. M. *La Doctrine de la création dans l'école de Chartres, étude et textes.* Publications de l'Institut d'Études Médiévales d'Ottawa, 7. Ottawa and Paris, 1938.

Partridge, Eric. *Origins.* New York, 1958.

Patch, Howard R. *The Goddess Fortuna in Mediaeval Literature.* 1927; rpt. New York, 1967.

Piehler, Paul. *The Visionary Landscape: A Study in Medieval Allegory.* Montreal, 1971.

Poole, Reginald L. "The Masters of the Schools at Paris and Chartres in John of Salisbury's Time," *English Historical Review*, 35 (1920), 321–42.

Preller, Ludwig. *Römische Mythologie*. 2 vols. Berlin, 1858.

Raby, F. J. E. *A History of Secular Latin Poetry in the Middle Ages*. 2 vols. 2nd. ed. Oxford, 1957.

Rand, Edward Kennard. "The Classics in the Thirteenth Century," *Speculum*, 4 (1929), 249–69.

———. *The Founders of the Middle Ages*. 2nd. ed. Cambridge, Mass., 1941.

Rank, Otto. *Beyond Psychology*. New York, 1941.

Raynaud de Lage, G. *Alain de Lille, poète du XIIe siècle*. Université de Montréal Publications de l'Institut d'Études Médiévales, 12. Montreal, 1951.

———. *"Natura* et *Genius,* chez Jean de Meung et chez Jean Lemaire de Belges," *Le Moyen Age: Revue d'Histoire et de Philologie*, 58 (1952), 125–43.

Robertson, Jr., D. W. *A Preface to Chaucer: Studies in Medieval Perspectives*. Princeton, 1962.

Róheim, Géza. *Magic and Schizophrenia*. Post. ed. Warner Muensterberger and S. H. Polinksky. Bloomington, 1955.

Rose, H. J. "Ancient Italian Beliefs Concerning the Soul," *Classical Quarterly*, 24 (1930), 129–35.

———. "On the Original Significance of the Genius," *Classical Quarterly*, 17 (1923), 57–60.

———. *Primitive Culture in Italy*. London, 1926.

Rosenfield, Claire. "The Shadow Within: The Conscious and Unconscious Use of the Double," *Daedalus*, 92 (1963), 326–44.

Sandys, John Edwin. *A History of Classical Scholarship*, Vol. 1, *From the Sixth Century B.C. to the End of the Middle Ages*. 1903; rpt. New York, 1958.

Sanford, Eva Matthews. "The Use of Classical Latin Authors in the *Libri Manuales,*" *Transactions of the American Philological Association*, 55 (1924), 190–248.

Scaglione, Aldo. *Nature and Love in the Late Middle Ages*. Berkeley and Los Angeles, 1963.

Schmidt, Wilhelm. *Geburtstag im Altertum. Religionsgeschichtliche Versuche und Vorarbeiten*, Vol. 7, pt. 1. Giessen, 1908.

Schneweis, Emil. *Angels and Demons according to Lactantius*. Catholic University of America Studies in Christian Antiquity, No. 3. Washington, 1944.

Schueler, Donald G. "Gower's Characterization of Genius in the *Confessio Amantis,*" *Modern Language Quarterly*, 33 (1972), 240–56.

Seznec, Jean. *The Survival of the Pagan Gods: The Mythological Tradition and its Place in Renaissance Humanism and Art*. Trans. Barbara F. Sessions. New York, 1953.

Shorey, Paul. *Platonism: Ancient and Modern*. Sather Classical Lectures, Vol. 14. Berkeley, 1938.

Showerman, Grant. *The Great Mother of the Gods*. University of Wisconsin Bulletin, Philosophy and Literature Series, Vol. 1. Madison, 1901.

Silverstein, Theodore. "The Fabulous Cosmogony of Bernardus Silvestris," *Modern Philology*, 46 (1948–49), 92–116.

——, ed. *"Liber Hermetis Mercurii Triplicis de VI Rerum Principiis,"* Archives *d'Histoire Doctrinale et Littéraire du Moyen Âge*, 30 (1955), 217–302.

Smith, William, ed. *Dictionary of Greek and Roman Biography and Myth*. Vol. 2 of 3 vols. London, 1850.

Stahl, William Harris. "To a Better Understanding of Martianus Capella," *Speculum*, 40 (1965), 102–15.

Stahl, William Harris, Richard Johnson, E. L. Burge. *Martianus Capella and the Seven Liberal Arts*. Vol. 1. New York and London, 1971.

Stock, Brian. *Myth and Science in the Twelfth Century: A Study of Bernard Silvester*. Princeton, 1972.

Taylor, Henry Osborn. *The Classical Heritage of the Middle Ages*. 3rd ed. New York, 1911.

Taylor, Lily Ross. *The Divinity of the Roman Emperor*. Philological Monographs, No. 1. Middletown, Conn., 1931.

Thorndike, Lynn. *A History of Magic and Experimental Science*, Vols. 1 and 2, *During the First Thirteen Centuries of our Era*. New York, 1923–29.

Tillyard, E. M. W. *The Elizabethan World Picture*. New York, 1959.

Todd, John, and Kenneth Dewhurst. "The Double: Its Psycho-Pathology and Psycho-Physiology," *Journal of Nervous and Mental Disease*, 122 (1955), 47–56.

Tuve, Rosemond. *Allegorical Imagery: Some Mediaeval Books and their Posterity*. Princeton, 1966.

Tylor, Edward B. *Primitive Culture: Researches into the Development of Mythology, Philosophy, Religion, Language, Art, and Custom*. 2 vols. London, 1913.

Van Windem, J. C. M. *Calcidius on Matter, His Doctrine and Sources: A Chapter in the History of Platonism*. Philosophia Antiqua, Vol. 9. Leiden, 1959.

Wallace, Edith Owen. *The Notes on Philosophy in the Commentary of Servius on the Eclogues, the Georgics, and the Aeneid of Vergil*. New York, 1938.

Warton, Thomas. *Observations on the Fairy Queen of Spenser*. Vol. 1 of 2 vols. London, 1807.

Wedel, Theodore Otto. *The Mediaeval Attitude toward Astrology, Particularly in England*. Yale Studies in English, No. 60. New Haven, London, and Oxford, 1920.

Wetherbee, Winthrop. "The Function of Poetry in the 'De Planctu Naturae' of Alain de Lille," *Traditio*, 25 (1969), 87–125.

——. *Platonism and Poetry in the Twelfth Century: The Literary Influence of the School of Chartres*. Princeton, 1972.

Wilkins, Ernest H. "Descriptions of Pagan Divinities from Petrarch to Chaucer," *Speculum*, 32 (1957), 511–22.

Williams, Lynn Flickinger. "The Gods of Love in Ancient and Medieval Literature as Background of John Gower's *Confessio Amantis*." Diss. Columbia 1967.

Wissowa, Georg. *Religion und Kultus der Römer. Handbuch der klassischen Altertumswissenschaft,* Vol. 5, pt. 4. 2nd ed. Munich, 1912.

Woolsey, Robert B. "Bernard Silvester and the Hermetic *Asclepius,*" *Traditio,* 6 (1948), 340–44.

Zeller, E. *The Stoics, Epicureans, and Sceptics.* Trans. Oswald J. Reichel. London, 1870.

Zielinski, Th. "Marginalien," *Philologus,* 64 (N. S. 18), (1905), 1–26.

Zilsel, Edgar. *Die Entstehung des Geniebegriffes: Ein Beitrag zur Ideengeschichte der Antike und des Frühkapitalismus.* Tübingen, 1926.

Index

Achates (in Virgil), 61
Adam, 55, 66, 101
Adelard of Bath, 70
Adonis, Garden of, 169*n*29
Aeneas: and Genius-snake, 8-9, 151*n*27; descent of, 43, 44, 47, 54, 56, 61-62, 152*n*31; oracle of, 58, 153*n*38
Aenigma, 5, 57-58, 62, 112
Aeolus, 82, 83, 159*n*45
Aethericon, 77, 85; *see also Phytikon*
Agathe tyche, 158*n*34; *see also Tyche*
Agathos daemon, 37, 38, 76, 158*n*34; *see also Daemon; Genius*
Agathos daemoniarch, 158*n*34; *see also Daemoniarch*
Ages: four, 72, 121, 126-27; six, 149*n*7
Alanus de Insulis (Alain de Lille), 3, 18, 46, 63, 117, 131, 163*n*18, 164*n*29, 165*n*39
—— *Anticlaudianus*, 106, 118, 163*n*19, 167*n*11
—— *Distinctiones*, 91, 102, 103, 104, 111, 162*n*9, 163*n*20
—— *De Planctu Naturae*, 58, 60, 63, 65, 72, 88-114, 129, 132; general description of Genius' roles in, 2, 5, 88-90, 113-14, 115, 131, 137*n*2; Genius in, and Bernardus' *genii*, 2, 88, 91, 92, 93, 96, 115, 131; general description of descents in, 5, 62, 63, 88-90, 113-14, 115, 133; as type of dream vision, 62, 107-8, 135; Genius in, and Urania and Physis, 90, 91, 134; influence of, on Jean de Meun, 117-18, 122, 125; influence of, on Gower, 126, 127, 128, 130; classical *genii* in, summary, 135; *see also individual personifications*

—— *Quoniam Homines*, 104
—— "Rhythmus de Incarnatione et de Septem Artibus," 106
—— *Sermo de Sphaera Intelligibili*, 94-96, 118
Alexander (the Great), 8
All-Forms: *see* Pantomorph
Altheim, Franz, 139*n*9
d'Alverny, Marie-Thérèse, 163*n*19
Amans (in Gower), 1, 125-30 *passim*, 131, 132, 133, 135, 168*n*28
Ammianus Marcellinus, 8, 31-32, 36-37, 55, 143*n*54
Amomum, 84
Amor (in Jean de Meun), 116, 117, 119, 121, 134, 167*n*14
Amphiaraus, 152*n*31
Anangke: *see* Necessity
Anastrophe, 165*n*39
Angel, Christian (*angelus*): classical origins of, 4-5, 38, 134; fallen (renegade, deserter), 5, 39, 80; like cosmic *daemon*, 38-39, 41; in Lactantius, 39, 79-80; in Pseudo-Dionysius, 79-80, 103-4; and theophany, 103-5, 164*n*31, 165*n*32; as *calodaemon* in Alanus, 103, 104; as type of ypophany, 104; role of, in *oraculum*, 107
Angelus, classical: etymology of, 39; as *daemon*, 39; in Calcidius, 39, 79-80; *genius* as, 39, 80; as intermediary, "medioximis," 39, 147*n*29; in *De Mundi*, 67, 68, 79-82, 87, 104, 131
Anima, 23, 72
Animales virtutes, 58
Animalia, 79

50-55, 106; on natural descent, 44-50, 66, 90-91; on Orpheus and Euridice, 46-55, 103, 112, 129, 152*n*30, 165*n*36, 166*n*44; on *genius* as Euridice, 46-55 *passim*, 101, 131, 156*n*19; on artificial descent, 56; on integument and poet's role, 59, 113, 166*n*45; *genius* in, and Genius in *De Mundi*, 66, 81, 131; on superior Aplanon, and Beau Parc, 121; structure of, and descents, 149*n*7; on Aeolus, 159*n*45
—— *Experimentarius,* 70
—— *Mathematicus,* 70
—— *De Mundi Universitate* (or *Cosmographia*), 2, 18, 63, 65-87, 90, 92, 97, 104, 105, 118, 132, 134-35, 161*n*6, 162*n*9; general description of *genii* in, 2, 66-68, 86-87, 131; *genii* in, influence of on Alanus, 2, 88, 91, 93, 99, 115, 131, 134; Pantomorph in, and Alanus' Genius, 2, 92, 97, 115-16, 131; natural descent in, 5, 46, 63, 65-87, 91, 105, 133-34; sources of, 70; digression in, 79-82; influence of, on Matthieu de Vendôme, 84; influence of, on Jean de Meun, 84, 117, 118; influence of, on Spenser, 84; general description of classical *genii* in, 134-35; descent of sperm in, 152*n*27, 160*n*53; *see also individual personifications*
Bersuire, Pierre, 150*n*15
Birt, Th., 138*n*8
Boccaccio, Giovanni, 47, 60, 150*n*15, 157*n*23, 160*n*54
Boethius, 45, 46, 51, 52, 63, 91, 150*n*15, 150*n*17, 162*n*9
Bona fortuna, 158*n*34
Bon Pasteur, 121, 122, 123, 131
Bonus Demon, 158*n*34
Book of Memory (Liber Recordationis), 73, 74, 82, 118, 163*n*19
Bower of Bliss, 169*n*29
Brinkmann, Hennig, 161*n*4
Brutus, Marcus Junius, 36-37

Cacodaemon (cacos daemon), 37, 38, 76, 80, 102; *see also Daemon*
Caduceus, 28, 157*n*23
Caelum, 66, 70

Caesar: *see* Augustus
Calcidius, 43, 157*n*22; on parts of universe, 5, 67; on World Soul, 29, 146*n*18; on *daemones,* 35, 38-39, 147*n*29; on *angeli,* 39, 80; as source of *De Mundi,* 70; on *humecta substantia,* 82
Caligula, 14
Calliope, 54, 106, 165*n*36; *see also* Muses
Calodaemon, 103; *see also Daemon*
Cancer, portal of, 70, 72, 75, 105, 156*n*18; *see also* Capricorn
Caritas, 6, 129, 132, 134
Cassius Longinus, 36
Casus: *see* Chance
Cato, as Image, 98, 112
Catullus, Valerius, 9
Cebetis Tabula (Cebes' *Table*), 62, 72, 92, 153*n*45, 157*n*22
Censorinus, 16, 18, 86, 140*n*24, 160*n*57
Ceres, 27, 28, 34, 145*n*13
Cerinthus (in Tibullus), 18
Cerus, 145*n*13
Chain of Being, Great: in *De Mundi,* 65-66, 133; in *De Planctu,* of Natura, 91-92, 98; in *De Planctu,* of Genius, 97-98
Chance (Casus, personification in Calcidius), 29, 146*n*18
Chapel, of Nature: *see* Temple
Charisius, 145*n*5
Chastity (personification in Alanus), 89, 101
Chaucer, Geoffrey, 62, 63; *see also* Eagle
Chenu, M.-D., 161*n*6, 163*n*12
Cherubim (type of epiphany), 103
Christ, 102, 105, 131, 165*n*36, 167*n*15; *see also* Logos
Christianity, and classical Genius, 4-5, 18, 38-40
Cicero, 42-43; as Image, 98, 112
City-founder: *see Genius: urbis*
Claudian, 15, 72, 92, 94, 97, 157*n*23
Clotho, 74, 75, 119; *see also* Parcae
Codex Theodosianus, 3, 17, 143*n*64
Collective unconscious, 136, 164*n*23
Communion, Christian, 18
Concupiscence: as *genius,* 46-50, 63, 101, 117, 131, 134; as Euridice, 46-49, 101, 131, 134; and Venus, 101, 135; and Amans, 128

200 INDEX

Truth (Veritas, personification in Alanus), 89, 95, 96, 109, 113
Turnus, as Image, 98, 112
Tutela pariendi: see Juno
Tuve, Rosemond, 116, 118, 166*n*2, 167*n*15
Tyche, 23, 28, 40, 78, 145*n*5, 157*n*23, 158*n*34
Tylor, Edward B., 147*n*37

Ulysses, as Image, 98, 112
Underworld (*infernum*): four descents into, 3-6, 43-64, 81; as human body, 4, 44, 45, 67, 68, 83-85, 97, 99, 122-23, 128, 132, 159*n*45; as sublunar region, 4, 37. 45, 67, 68, 81, 86, 97, 105, 132, 165*n*35; Pluto, god of, 37, 53; descent of Aeneas into, 43, 44; as inferior Aplanon, 43-44, 45; as earthly pleasures, temporal good, 51-54, 122; and *manes,* 52-53; as aerial region, 55, 56; as poetic artifice, 59, 60, 109-14, 136; as "profound study," 61, 114; as earth and sea, 83; descent of soul into, and astrology, 99; of deadly sins, 102, 125; as sorrow, 105; as "cortex," 109, 113, 136; as postlapserian world, 121; as Deduit and his Garden, 122-23, 131; and spiritual death, 122-23; as Hell, 123; as artificial fantasies, 125, 131; as sexual perversion, vice, distortion, 125; as courtly love, 126; as classical tales, 128, 130; knowledge of, as province of Devil, 135; Etruria obsessed with, 139*n*9; descent into, and sixth age of man, 149*n*7; *see also* Descent(s); *Manes*
Universe: Calcidian, 5, 67, 155*n*6; Augustinian, 26; Paulus' concept of, 27-28, 29; Bernardus' concept of, 79-81
Urania (goddess), 66-86 *passim,* 90, 91, 118, 129, 132, 133, 134, 135, 163*n*19
Usia: *see* Ousia
Usiarch: *see* Ousiarch

Valerius Soranus, 25
Varro, 25-30 *passim,* 43; *see also* Augustine, Saint
Venus: as goddess, temple of, 1; as goddess, in Gower, 1, 6, 127, 129, 131-32, 133, 134, 136*n*2, 168*n*26, 168*n*27; as planet, influence of on soul, 29, 76-77, 98; as

intelligible god, 34; as goddess, in Jean de Meun, 117, 120, 134, 166*n*2; as goddess, and natural descent in Alanus, 81, 99-100; double, 101, 164*n*27; as goddess, and vicious descent in Alanus, 101-2, 107, 126; as *figura,* in Alanus, 108; as goddess, and artificial descent in Alanus, 109-11; as goddess, roles of in Alanus summarized, 114, 131, 134, 135; Alanus', influence of on Jean's Venus, 119, 125, 129
Verbum Dei: *see* Logos
Verrius Flaccus, 27
Vesta, 7, 34
Villainy (personification in Guillaume de Lorris), 123
Virgil, 42-43; *Aeneid* 5.95, on *genius loci* and Genius of the father as snake, 8-9, 54*n*27, 160*n*53; *Aeneid* 6.730-31, on World Soul, 24-25, 38; *Aeneid* 9.184-85, on the origin of desire, 31, 32-33, 48, 49, 150*n*19; *Aeneid* 6.743, on *manes,* 33, 38, 53, 55, 151*n*24; *Aeneid* 6.119-20, on Orpheus, 47, 51-52; *Aeneid* 6.897, on *manes* and *insomnium,* 57; figures from the *Aeneid,* associated with Alanus' Genius, 98, 112-13
Virtue(s): Aristeus as, in Orpheus-Euridice myth, 52, 53; personified, in *De Planctu,* 89, 101, 104, 105-6, 108; as type of ypophany, 104; personified, in *Cebetis Tabula,* 153*n*45
Visio, 58; *see also* Dream(s)
Visum (phantasma, apparition), 57; *see also* Dream(s)
Volteius (in Horace), 19
Vulcan, 34, 145*n*13

Wetherbee, Winthrop, 125*n*23, 154*n*4, 155*n*5, 159*n*47, 161*n*1, 161*n*5, 164*n*22, 165*n*34
William of St. Thierry, 161*n*6
Wissowa, Georg, 140*n*22, 141*n*29
Woolsey, Robert B., 155*n*10
Word (of God): *see* Logos
World Soul (*anima mundi*): Stoic, as Jupiter Progenitor and Genetrix, 4, 25-30, 66, 134, 145*n*11; and Genius or *genii,* 4, 5,